Class and Nation

Class and Nation

Historically and in the Current Crisis

by Samir Amin

Translated by Susan Kaplow

Monthly Review Press
New York and London

Originally published as *Classe et nation
dans l'histoire et la crise contemporaine*
by Les Éditions de Minuit, Paris, France
copyright © 1979 by Les Éditions de Minuit

Library of Congress Cataloging in Publication Data
Amin, Samir.
    Class and nation, historically and in the
current crisis.
    Translation of Classe et nation dans
l'histoire et la crise contemporaine.
    Includes bibliographical references.
    1. Capitalism.   2. Economic history.
3. Social classes.   4. Nationalism.
5. Historical materialism.   I. Title.
HB501.A58713   305.5   79-3022
ISBN 0-85345-522-8 (cl)
ISBN 0-85345-532-6 (pb)

Monthly Review Press
62 West 14th Street, New York, N.Y. 10011
47 Red Lion Street, London WC1R 4PF

Manufactured in the United States of America

10 9 8 7 6 5 4 3 2 1

Contents

Introduction

A reader once remarked that my works deal with three sets of problems: (a) concrete analyses of the situation of third world countries (Egypt, the Maghreb, West Africa, the Congo), (b) a theory of capitalist accumulation on a world scale, and (c) an interpretation of historical materialism. Indeed, this classification also corresponds to the sequence of my work. Doubtless, concrete analysis of a situation is never neutral; it always implicitly entails a theory. The first of my analyses (Nassarian Egypt, West Africa, the neocolonial Congo and Maghreb, and allegedly socialist attempts to break with imperialist domination) were in large part based on a theoretical interpretation of imperialism. This interpretation, formulated between 1954 and 1957, was questionable, due to the inadequacies of the Marxism which prevailed in the 1950s, inadequacies which marked my own intellectual and political formation.

The theory in question enabled me to criticize bourgeois theoretical explanations of underdevelopment but did not enjoin a practical political elaboration of substituting national liberation movements for bourgeois nationalist politics. I produced my first works, concerning the Arab and African countries indicated, between 1960 and 1967; they suffered from this limitation. This unsatisfactory state of affairs obliged me to reexamine the theory of imperialism, which in turn brought me to rewrite *(Unequal Development)* and to further explore *(Unequal Exchange and the Law of Value)* the theory of accumulation in the years 1968–1973.

This was also the time of the clear failure of revisionist Marxism and, with the cultural revolution in China, of the elaboration of a global alternative. These favorable conditions led me to reconsider the most basic questions of historical materialism. *Imperialism and Unequal Development, The Arab Nation, The Law of Value and Historical Materialism,* written, as was this work, between 1973 and 1978, contain my interpretations of historical materialism. They also reexamine, in light of these interpretations, the concrete situations which most interest me: those of the third world in general and of Africa and the Arab world in particular.

If I were to summarize what seems essential to me in this study, I would emphasize the following points.

From the beginning, there have been two competing interpretations of historical materialism. The first virtually reduces the method to a linear economic determinism: the development of the productive forces automatically brings about the necessary adjustment in the relations of production by means of social revolutions, the makers of which lay bare historical necessity. Then the political and ideological superstructure is transformed to meet the requirements of the reproduction of the relations of production. The other interpretation emphasizes the double dialectic of forces and relations of production on the one hand and of these latter and the superstructure on the other.

The first interpretation assimilates laws of social evolution to laws of nature. From Engels' attempt at a *Dialectics of Nature* to the positivist interpretation of Kautsky, from Bolshevism itself to the Soviet dia-mat (dialectical materialism), this interpretation pursues the philosophical work of the Enlightenment and constitutes the radical bourgeois interpretation of Marxism. The second interpretation contrasts the objective character of natural laws with the combined objective-subjective character of social laws.

The first interpretation either fails to deal with alienation or extends it to all of human history. Alienation thus becomes the product of a human nature which transcends the history of social systems; it has its roots in anthropology, that is, in the permanent relation between humanity and nature. History develops by "the force of circumstance." The idea which people (or classes) have that they make history is naive: the scope of their apparent freedom is narrow because the determinism of technical progress weighs so heavily. The second interpretation leads us to distinguish two levels of alienation: (1) that which results from the permanence of the humanity-nature relation, a relation which transcends social modes, defines human nature in its permanent dimension but does not have a direct role in the evolution of social history; i.e., anthropological alienation, and (2) that which comprises the ideological superstructure of societies, or social alienation.

Attempts to detail the successive contents of this social alienation led to the conclusion that all precapitalist social class systems had the same type of social alienation, which I consider to be alienation in nature. Its characteristics derive, on the one hand, from the transparency of the economic relations of exploitations and, on the other hand, from the limited degree of mastery over nature at the corresponding levels of development of the productive forces. This social alienation necessarily had an absolute, religious character, due to the dominant place of ideology in social reproduction. In contrast, social alienation under capitalism is produced in part by the growing opacity of economic relations due to the generalization of commodity relations and in part by the qualitatively higher degree of mastery over nature. Commodity alienation thus replaces nature, with the economy as the external force which determines social evolution. The struggle for the abolition of exploitation and of classes entails liberation from economic determinism. Communism must put an end to social alienation, although it cannot abolish anthropological alienation.

This interpretation reasserts the unity of universal history. This unity is not to be found in an overly detailed succession of modes of production. The classic line of development—slavery-feudalism-capitalism—is not only peculiar but is also largely mythical. The opposition between a European and a so-called Asian line belongs to a family of Eurocentric philosophies of history. Unity is recreated by the necessary succession of three families of modes of production: the family of communal modes, that of tributary modes, and the capitalist mode, the first to have universal characteristics. The unity of the family of tributary modes is expressed in the universal character of social alienation in nature, in contrast to the social commodity alienation of capitalism.

The peculiarity of Western history in this perspective resides exclusively in the incomplete character of its specific form of the tributary mode, the feudal mode, which was produced by its combination with communal modes.

My intention in developing these general reflections on history is to propose a number of conclusions of a general and theoretical nature concerning the relations among class struggles—classes being defined in the framework of the economic formations which control the major, successive social systems and within which the dialectic of class struggle operates. This framework seems to be defined primarily by the state, the reality of which may cross-cut other realities depending on circumstances, either those of the nation or those of the ethnic group.

Current political preoccupations furnish inspiration. Recent developments in our world everywhere underline the importance of the nation and of the state: the class struggle is the motive force of history but it occurs within a state-national framework which sets its scope, its modalities, and its outcomes.

This book first presents a system of theoretical concepts concerning these questions, then a series of accounts which follow the historical sequence of evolution. This is the reverse of the order in which I did research, as I began with reflections and observations about the contemporary world (imperialism, national liberation, socialist construction) and went back to the theoretical analysis of capitalism (and particularly of the dialectic between class struggle and economic laws in the capitalist mode) and then to the history of its gradual establishment (the mercantilist and then the pre-imperialist periods during which the laws of unequal development operated in the then forming state-national framework). The lessons derived from this twofold series of experiences (the transition to socialism and the transition to capitalism) have suggested certain theses which seem to throw new light on earlier periods, those of precapitalist societies and those of transitions to class societies. This second test of principles in the light of facts enables me to further elaborate them.

The first chapter presents the system of concepts and the relations among state, nation, and economy. The rest analyzes unequal development: Chapters 2 and 3 as it occurred in precapitalist formations, Chapters 4 and 5 as it took place in the bourgeois revolution and the capitalist centers, and Chapters 6, 7, and 8 as it takes place in the imperialist system and the socialist transition.

Chapter 1

Classes, Nations, and the State
in Historical Materialism

History is a weapon in the ideological battle between those who want to change society (a society in a given sense) and those who want to maintain its basic features. I do not believe the pronouncements of those who claim to be above the fray, because people make history, albeit within objectively determined conditions. In fact, social laws do not operate like natural laws. And I do not believe in a single cosmogony embracing nature and society—even when it goes under the name of a materialist dialectic.

On the contrary, those who want to change society necessarily have ideas of a higher quality than those who wish to keep it from changing. This is because society changes. Those who want to stop its motion must therefore ignore the evidence. To do this, they encumber thought with so much detail as to justify their refusal to abstract and generalize, although these are part of any scientific attitude. They rely instead on moral reflection—Platonic or Confucian. But those who want to change society are not gods living outside of it: there is a wide margin between the goals that they think they are adopting, those that they really (often implicitly) adopt, and the results obtained.

I will try here to make an inventory of what history teaches us. This will be provisional, modest, but dangerous in that it invites all manner of criticism. It is based on the presupposition that only the present gives meaning to the past. I share the viewpoint of those who want a classless society. Further, I contend that the struggle for social liberation from class exploitation is indissolubly linked to the national liberation struggle of the people of Asia and Africa.

The inventory can be presented in the form of seven theses, which will be elaborated in this book. The theses and their theoretical conclusions can be summarized as follows:

First thesis: universal history can be understood. The best narrative history, using an eclectic, empirical method, can offer only immediate explanations: it invokes multiple, direct, causal connections operating on different planes (a certain ideology accounts for a particular behavior, a given economic fact causes a certain development, etc.). It is possible to go beyond this level by basing an analysis on a universally applicable set of concepts, those of historical materialism. These concepts are not given *a priori* but are deduced from history itself. In the evolution of all human societies we can identify several major universal tendencies resulting from the same basic dialectic, namely, that between productive forces and relations of production.

Second thesis: universal history is always the history of unequal development. Unequal development is universal, although its character, sphere of operation, and form are not merely infinite rearrangements of a few simple laws. A periodization of history must be based on the dialectic between general tendencies and the unequal development expressing these tendencies.

Third thesis: history is, in the final analysis, the history of class struggle. Class relations dialectically define the modes of production which constitute successive social formations, corresponding to different levels in the development of the productive forces. But these classes are contained in a specific society, bounded by the borders of the state and, sometimes, of the nation.

Fourth thesis: societies constitute a system of social formations when they are so closely interrelated that their class oppositions and alliances can no longer validly be analyzed at the societal level but must be studied at the global level of the system. In particular, the contemporary world is a system, that of imperialism.

Fifth thesis: the social reproduction of capitalist society cannot be understood by looking only at the internal economic workings of the nation-states of the capitalist world system. To be understood, social reproduction involves the interference at the level of the state in the economic regulation and application of the class struggle-economic laws dialectic not to each nation-state but to the system as a whole.

Sixth thesis: the existence of nations raises the national question, and the process of unequal development makes this question particularly acute in the development of class struggles. Thus it is important to distinguish between bourgeois and proletarian tendencies with regard to how the national question is posed and resolved.

Seventh thesis: although the tendency to homogenization which characterizes the capitalist system operates by contradiction (homogenization and inequality), it has powerful ideological effects. The ideology of "universal culture" thus needs constant reexamination as it evolves through successive forms and phases.

I. The particular and the universal in history

1. The fundamental concepts of historical materialism have scientific value only to the extent that they possess universal analytical applicability. It follows that these concepts must be abstracted from universal history, and not from a particular segment of it. The concepts of mode of production, social formation, infrastructure, superstructure, social classes, and so on have this universal validity. On the other hand, the feudal mode of production is not necessarily valid universally, because it is abstracted from one part of history, that of Europe. To state in advance that feudalism is a universal category and to try to force the reality of other societies into this predefined mold is to turn one's back on the scientific spirit. The failure to use the whole of human history from which to derive universal concepts leads to talk of "the irreducibility of civilizations," talk which is irrational and, finally, racist.

From this perspective, the great lesson of history is the universality of the basic laws that govern human societies, European and others. Here Marx gave us only the first elements, although the basic ones, of historical materialism. The level of knowledge during his lifetime and the prevailing ignorance about the non-European world limited Marx's ability to develop these elements. He was also limited by his own experience of social struggles, struggles which only became really widespread after his death. I stress this in the belief that the major source of knowledge is action: any other position leads to rigid dogmatism and practical impotence.

Thus the participation of the peoples of Asia and Africa in capitalist and socialist history has enriched historical materialism. The struggle against narrow interpretations of Marxism, against West-centered reductionism, is part of the struggle for social and national liberation, of the struggle against ideological imperialism.

2. Historical materialism requires us to accept (1) that the development of the productive forces controls, in the final analysis, the relations of production, although it needs to be made clear whether we are talking about the actual development of existing productive forces or their potential development; and (2) that all human societies have gone through and will go through stages that, despite their diversity of form, are basically similar. The problem is correctly to identify these stages, on the basis of human history as a whole.

I propose the following schema: (1) All human societies have gone through three consecutive stages: (a) primitive communism, (b) the tributary mode of production, and (c) capitalism. They will all reach a fourth stage: communism. (2) Each of these three phases is separated from the one following it by a period of transition: (a) the period of communal modes of production, (b) the period of the transition to capitalism. And all societies are going through or will go through a third period (called socialist) of transition to communism. (3) Capitalism, like communism, is not an accident or an exception but an objective and necessary rule.

3. Primitive communism, as Guy Dhoquois has defined it, is

the "negation of necessary origin" (82-7).* It is impossible to conceive of the transition from animal to human without this stage. During this transition certain decisive transformations took place, the effects of which still remain and perhaps always will remain (that is, independently of social systems in that humans, as a species distinct from animals, transcend social systems). This means simply that certain of these characteristics may survive into communism. What are these characteristics? We know almost nothing about them, and anthropology has little to teach us on the subject because this stage is irrevocably lost. At best, certain recognizable elements in a handful of paleolithic societies may inspire philosophical and imaginative psychological speculation. But the danger of scientism is very strong here because we are and will remain unsure about the most elementary data.

4. The discussion of the stage I have called tributary is far more conclusive. If it is useful to compartmentalize by academic areas, this stage belongs to the historians and not the anthropologists. In it, we are dealing with the history of all civilizations based manifestly and indisputably on (1) considerable development of the productive forces—settled agriculture beyond the subsistence stage, a substantial and guaranteed surplus, and significant, rich, and varied nonagricultural activities (crafts) employing a range of technical knowledge and tools, although not machines; (2) nonproductive activities on a level corresponding to the size of the surplus; (3) division into social classes on this economic base; and (4) a developed state (city, kingdom, or empire) that transcends village reality.

A number of things can be said about this stage. First, it takes a wide variety of forms, all of which have common characteristics in that the extraction of surplus labor is controlled by the dominance of the superstructure within a society based on use value. Second, the basic mode of this stage is the tributary one, whereas the feudal mode is a variant thereof, and the so-called slave mode is an

---

*Figures in parentheses refer to listings in the References.

exception, usually located within another mode. Third, the complexity of formations at this stage (which explains its variety) implies that beyond the immediate relations of production, relations of both internal and external exchange are generating market relations. Fourth, this stage is not static but, on the contrary, is characterized by a considerable development of the productive forces based on tributary relations of production operating within complex formations. At this level of necessary abstraction and within this framework, Europe is no more "exceptional" than China, India, or Egypt, for example.

5. Capitalism is a necessary stage not only because it already exists, and exists worldwide. In fact, all tributary societies had to transform the relations of production underlying their development and to invent capitalist relations, which alone could enable the productive forces to further develop. Capitalism was not destined to be invented in Europe: it might also have been invented by the Chinese, Arabs, or others. The only reason it was not invented in Asia or Africa is that its prior development in Europe led to its impeding the other continents' normal evolution. Their subjugation did not begin with imperialism: it started with the birth of capitalism itself.

Many, including a number of Marxists, have attempted to prove that capitalism could have arisen only by chance and in the European context, which provided an exception to the static situation of the other continents. All these attempts betray the fundamental principles of historical materialism. They exemplify the West-centered perspective, which is the ideology of capitalism and imperialism.

The capitalist system, then, will always be divided into a center and a periphery. This is an inherent contradiction. Center and periphery have changed their form and function from the mercantilist to the imperialist era. They have evolved from one phase of imperialism to the other, but they always stand opposed, like the two poles of a contradictory whole.

We may note in passing that the level of the productive forces during the capitalist era and the laws that govern their development involve a homogenizing tendency. This is because the capitalist mode is based on exchange value, while the tributary mode is based on use value. Nevertheless, the homogenization remains partial. It does not occur everywhere, but only in the centers; the central capitalist formations become increasingly similar. This homogenizaton contrasts with the variety of formations remaining from the previous era. Thus we need deal with only one problem related to the capitalist phase: Why did capitalism appear earlier in Europe? The answer is that Europe was less advanced, was peripheral. This is the first major manifestation of the unequal development of societies.

6. The communist stage is also necessary. But is it the only possible necessary stage? Capitalist relations stop the development of the productive forces well short of their clear potential level. In particular, capitalism cannot resolve its inherent center-periphery contradiction. Must classes be abolished in order for the productive forces to develop? I am not completely sure that this is the case. The transition which begins with the overthrow of capitalist relations does not lead automatically to communism. This transition may lead instead to a new stage which would then appear as necessary, a stage characterized by a new social class structure. This stage, which I refer to as the Soviet mode of production (or state collectivist mode or, more simply, statist mode of production) can already be seen as a possible one. Things might evolve in this direction, both in the periphery and in the center. Were they to do so, state centralization of capital and the resolution of the center-periphery contradiction would make possible considerable development of the productive forces. For this reason, such a stage cannot simply be called capitalist.

Should such evolution occur, communism would remain the necessary subsequent stage, because the existence of classes would limit the development of the productive forces. But, clearly, the whole problem of the struggle for communism—the problem of the transition—would take on different dimensions.

7. Periods of transition are different from necessary stages because in the former elements of change prevail over elements of reproduction, while in the latter elements of reproduction are more prominent. This is not to say that during necessary stages reproduction eliminates contradiction, for without contradiction we could not understand change, that is, the reason why a necessary stage is not eternal. It simply means that during necessary stages class struggle tends to be integrated into reproduction, to become part of it. For instance, under capitalism, the class struggle tends—at least in the center—to be reduced to its economic dimension and to contribute to the functioning of the system rather than to its destruction. On the other hand, during periods of transition the class struggle really takes center stage. It becomes the motive force of history.

All necessary stages thus give the impression of being eternal and unchanging. In this respect, there is no difference between Europe and Asia, or even between the past and the present. All societies at the second, tributary, stage give this same impression of stagnation: what Marx said about Asia applies to European feudal society also, as Paul Sweezy has noted (50-2). In contrast to societies at this second stage, capitalism appears to be constantly changing, due to its basic economic law. But the permanent revolutionizing of the productive forces causes a no less permanent adaptation in the relations of production. This creates the impression that the system cannot be changed, an impression fostered by bourgeois ideology.

8. Each period of transition has its own very particular features. Each concrete situation gives rise to a specific articulation of all the contradictions. However, these contradictions ultimately are resolved by the creation of stable systems, corresponding to the necessary stages. Despite their variety, these systems do not have many concrete differences of the same type but rather share certain basic common characteristics. As Perry Anderson has argued, "the genesis of a mode of production must be distinguished from its structure" (40-1).

9. The first transitional period is from primitive, classless so-

ciety to tributary society. In the academic division of labor, this is the province of anthropology, the contribution of which is discussed below. The rise of social classes, the rise of the state, and the development of relations of domination and exploitation combine in as many concrete ways as there are cases, i.e., societies, however small. An appropriate expression for these situations is "communal modes of production," which emphasizes the fact that the formation of classes and the state is still incomplete and that forms of property are still collective.

10. The second transitional period is from tributary society to capitalism, and takes one of two basically different forms. The first is the transition to capitalism in the center, i.e., transitions (in the plural) in Europe and Japan. This is the area where West-centered views are at their strongest, even among many Marxists. The second is the transition to peripheral capitalism. Because of its initial domination by external capitalism—still external in certain respects—peripheral capitalism developed in a very distinctive way. In general, the societies subjected to external capitalist domination were tributary societies, some of which were highly developed. But certain minor societies have been integrated into the capitalist system while still in the communal stage, albeit rarely.

11. The third transitional period is the socialist experience. Up to the present, socialism has been introduced in peripheral areas (East Asia, Cuba) and semiperipheral areas (USSR, Yugoslavia, Albania, and countries of the European Soviet bloc). The Paris Commune provides an important exception to this generalization.

12. There is a big difference between studying past transitions, to the tributary mode and to the capitalist mode in the center, and studying present-day transitions, to the capitalist mode in the periphery and socialist transitions. We can understand the past only through the scientific investigations of anthropologists and historians. We understand the present primarily through action: this is the superior means to knowledge.

Of course, anthropologists and historians can try to adopt the perspective of the revolutionary classes within the history they study, but this is different from actually becoming a revolutionary. For this reason, we can understand the past better by beginning with present-day struggles than by the reverse procedure. Anthropology and history must therefore take a back seat to the lessons learned by activists in the anti-imperialist struggle (operating in the framework of the transition to peripheral capitalism) and in the process of socialist construction (operating in a transitional period the outcome of which is in doubt so long as the statist mode is not firmly installed).

13.   The above argument can be summarized as follows:

First necessary stage: primitive communism. Negation of necessary origin. Almost no knowledge about the transition from animality to humanity, although it is essential. Uniformity or variety?

First transitional phase: communal societies. Domain of anthropology. Incomplete class and state formation. Great concrete variety.

Second necessary stage: tributary societies. Tributary form dominant and variety characteristic of an economy based on use value. Slow but significant development of productive forces and impression of stagnation. Dominance of the base by the superstructure and forms of reproduction controlled by this dominance. Problems of particular situations (slavery) and of nondominant exchange relations.

Second transitional phase: the transition to capitalism. The transition to capitalism in the center: diversity of concrete situations related to the dominance of the elements of change over the elements of reproduction. Area where West-centered thinking is at its strongest. First manifestation of unequal development. The transition to peripheral capitalism: the basic lessons of anti-imperialist activity.

Third necessary stage: capitalism. Tremendous development of productive forces: permanent renewal of these and permanent adaptation of the relations of production. Elements of reproduction dominant and tendency to reduce the class struggle to its economic dimension. Economy based on exchange value and dominance of the economic factor. Inherent center-periphery contradiction and tendency to homogenization in the center only.

Third transitional phase: socialism. Second manifestation of unequal development. Diversity of historical experiences of this transition, always starting within peripheral or semiperipheral capitalism. Dominance of the class struggle and uncertainty about its outcome.

Fourth necessary stage. First possibility: the statist mode of production. Resolution of the center-periphery contradiction. Uniformity in that exchange value dominates the economy. Dominance of the superstructure (state centralization of capital). New contradictions and new conditions for the second transition, which will ultimately occur.

Second possibility: communism. Variety: reestablishment of use value. All else unknown (return to the original problems?).

14. The schema detailed here clearly raises basic questions about the method of historical materialism. At issue is whether one chooses Marx, Weber, or utopian socialism.

Although it is generally conceded that a mode of production consists of a particular combination of relations and forces of production, there has been a tendency to degrade the concept of mode of production by confusing it with the status of the producer (for instance, slave, serf, or wage laborer). Yet wage labor predates capitalism by several thousand years and capitalism is more than wage labor made universal. The capitalist mode combines wage labor with a certain level of development of the productive forces. Similarly, the existence of productive slaves is insufficient to constitute a slave mode of production: the fact of their existence means nothing, except in combination with a particular state of the productive forces. If the concept of mode of production is for certain people synonymous with the status of the producer, the misunderstanding is firstly a semantic one.

If we try to draw up a complete list of these statuses in the history of class societies, we cannot stop with the three modes of dependent labor: slavery, serfdom, and wage labor. Having *a priori* limited the list to these three types, West-centered Marxists have been forced to invent a fourth status, that of the producer in a so-called community ("asiatic") dominated by a state ("generalized slavery"). Unfortunately, this fourth mode does not exist. What does exist, however, and what furthermore is far more common than slavery or serfdom, is the labor of the petty peasant producer. This is neither completely free and commodified nor is it totally within the confines of communal property. Rather, it is subject to tribute. We need a name for this most historically common status and can find no other than the one I have proposed, the tributary mode.

Some people regard this mode as a useless oversimplification and insist on the need to locate in time and space the specific features of each precapitalist society. This is an example of how difficult dialogue is between historians, concerned to apprehend history in all its concrete details, and nonhistorians. The latter are perhaps too often in a hurry to generalize, to formulate so-called theories and laws. But the former suffer from empiricism and lack of perspective. What kind of progress can we make toward understanding social laws if we insist on defining one hundred, two hundred, five hundred modes of production? It is better to run the risk of finding diversity, which is real, elsewhere: in the articulation of a limited number of abstract elements, including modes of production, relations of production, productive forces, producers' statuses, degree of commercialization of the economy, base-superstructure relations, and so on. This is in keeping with the spirit of Marx's method: the concept is concrete because it synthesizes a number of determinations that articulate abstract elements.

We should not abandon theory simply because certain generalizations, such as the five stages or "two ways" (Asian and European), are incorrect. The strength of the formulation I propose is that it focuses on the deep similarities that characterize all precapitalist class societies. Many historians perceive only the differences among them. But the similarities are just as striking: Why were there corporations in Florence, Paris, Baghdad, Cairo, Fez, Canton, and Calicut? Why does the French Sun King remind us of the Chinese emperor? Why was interest on loans prohibited in various places? Doesn't this prove that the contradictions characterizing all these societies are of the same type? Only concrete analysis of specific cases enables us to understand why some went through the necessary transition to capitalism more quickly than others. We must therefore categorically refuse to reject the term "precapitalist" (which assumes the necessity of capitalism) in favor of the allegedly more neutral term "antecapitalist" (which assumes that capitalism was the product of mere chance).

The latter position breaks the connection between relations and forces of production. It substitutes Weber for Marx and the search for "ideal types" through a method of generalization based on outward appearances for the search for general laws of motion. We must uncover the basic characteristics of the historical dynamic connecting the development of the productive forces to several major, successive stages in the evolution of the relations of production. Only within the framework of research inspired by Marx's method can we avoid the ahistoricism of the structuralist alternative and the dogmatism of vulgar Marxism (the five stages and the "two ways").

I believe we can avoid the pitfalls of the major philosophy of history, economism, by correctly treating the connection between forces and relations of production. I have said that given relations of production always lead to a particular kind of development of the productive forces, whose orientation they shape. However, only superior relations (capitalist relations are superior to tributary ones and these latter to communal ones) can clear the way for progress beyond the level of development attained on the basis of the old relations of production. The abolition of classes is thus a logical necessity and not a preference for one value system over another. This is the difference between Marx and the utopian socialism that preceded him.

Is the motive force of history the class struggle or the development of the productive forces? My thesis is that the class struggle determines the direction and the pace of development of the productive forces and that this development is therefore not neutral. The distinction between the development of the productive forces on the basis of given relations of production and their potential further development on the basis of new and superior relations suggests this non-neutrality.

In *Imperialism and Unequal Development* and in *The Law of Value and Historical Materialism* I pointed out that the schemas of Volume II of *Capital* demonstrate that different dynamic equilibria are possible. Different combinations of technical coefficients, rates of surplus value, real wages, and rates of profit correspond to these different equilibria. The flexibility of the schemas of Volume II reminds us that class struggle directs technical progress. For the precapitalist era, I have shown how the class struggle between peasants and their tributary exploiters determined a form of development which involved eventual penetration by capitalism. I stated that the same determination was occurring in all developed precapitalist societies, in Europe as well as the Arab world and China before their subjugation by European capitalism. On this is based my reassertion of the necessity of capitalism. Moreover, while the class struggle is certainly in the final analysis the motive force of history, it is useful to distinguish between two types of class struggle. The first takes place within a system of relations of production (the economist struggle under capitalism, for example) which directs the development of the productive forces on the basis of the relations of production in question. The second type of class struggle, the goal of which is to overturn old relations and establish new ones, is the condition for unparalleled subsequent potential development. This struggle characterizes revolutionary and transitional periods.

Starting from this position, we can see how the thesis of unequal development becomes obligatory. In the system's center, where the relations of production are most firmly established, the development of the productive forces as directed by these relations reinforces the system's cohesion. However, in the periphery, insufficient development of the productive forces results in greater flexibility; this explains why revolutions occur sooner in the periphery.

The thesis of unequal development is certainly not economistic. However, those who have challenged the prevailing revisionist position, which is truly economistic, have tended toward anarchism and utopianism, particularly since 1968. In their somewhat facile antieconomism they forget that the economic base is ultimately determinant. This kind of antieconomism leads logically to structuralism and idealism: concepts of reason, progress, or imagination become the motive forces of history.

15. In conclusion, four points should be stressed from this discussion about the universal and the particular in history. First, the fundamental analytical concepts of historical materialism have universal validity. Second, the same basic forces in the form of the universal productive forces–relations of production dialectic have been and still are at work in all societies. These forces impel universal history to pass through three major, necessary stages. Third, this obligatory development has assumed a great variety of forms and types. Fourth, evolution works by qualitative leaps from one mode to the other. It works unequally and goes through concrete transitions which have particular features in each case.

II. Universality and particularities of unequal development

1. Universal history teaches us that development is always unequal. The regions that have the most advanced productive forces and relations of production at a given moment, are never or almost never the ones to move the most rapidly and radically to a more advanced stage. Unequal development has appeared with particular force twice in history: in our own time, during which the transition to socialism began in countries like Russia and China and not in Great Britain or the United States; and in the seventeenth and eighteenth centuries, when capitalism developed in feudal Europe and not in the older, more flourishing oriental

civilizations which had been more advanced for centuries or even millenia.

Within Europe itself, the transition to capitalism was uneven, as Italy, Spain, and England successively outpaced one another. Later in the development of capitalism, the United States surpassed Great Britain, Germany, and France. Today, in terms of the socialist transition, the USSR is retreating while China moves forward.

Is it possible to deduce a general law of unequal development from the fact of its universality? We must be careful not to confuse historical with natural law. In the natural sciences, a law is a discovery implying statistical repetition of the same cause-effect relationship. But this discussion is limited to two stages—capitalist and socialist—and two cases of unequal development, each having its own specific causes.

2. Yet the same pairs of terms—"center-periphery," "complete-incomplete," "advanced-backward"—recur through the whole of this analysis of unequal development in history. These terms will be explained in detail in subsequent chapters, particularly Chapters 3, 4, 5, and 6. The use of the same terms is not meant to imply that history "eternally repeats itself" and that a single, simple explanation therefore covers the whole of it. Rather, it is meant to suggest certain historical lessons, but these have meaning only if we grasp the originality of each of the two processes of unequal development in question.

Although the terms "center," "complete," and "advanced" are synonymous, as are the terms "periphery," "incomplete," and "backward," the area in which the development in question takes place is different for the two major stages, tributary and capitalist. It should be emphasized that in the capitalist mode the economy is dominant, while in the tributary mode, ideology (the superstructure) is dominant. Complete and incomplete are thus adjectives that apply in the former case to the economy and in the latter to the superstructure.

In the system of capitalist imperialism, the centers are economically dominant, the peripheries are dominated. The capitalist system, furthermore, is the first global economic system. The central-dominant economies are autocentered, that is, complete; the peripheral-dominated economies are extraverted, incomplete and hence backward. Economic domination blocks them, stops them from catching up. In this sense, the cause of backwardness is external, although it is internalized through the class alliances that reproduce it.

This is not at all the case with precapitalist modes, whether central or peripheral, complete or incomplete. The complete tributary mode (China, Egypt) is complete at the superstructural level, with a dominant class-state, state centralization of the tributary surplus, and corresponding forms of state and ideology. The feudal mode is an incomplete tributary mode because it is incomplete with regard to state centralization of the tributary surplus. But complete tributary societies did not impose external domination on incomplete ones. Egypt did not dominate Rome (rather, it was the opposite) or still less feudal Europe (which did not belong to the same system of formatiòns nor to the same era), and China did not dominate Japan. Consequently, external domination was not responsbile for blocking development in these cases. If feudalism, an incomplete and peripheral form of the tributary mode, was more suitable to the development of capitalism than the complete, central tributary mode this was not because tributary societies dominated feudal societies. There is no analogy with the correspondence between national liberation and socialism of our era. Obviously, we must seek the explanation elsewhere in the analysis.

Similarly, the European transition to feudalism resulted from a particular synthesis of the disintegration of the ancient, slave-holding Roman world and the development of the communal barbarian world. This barbarian world was backward compared to Roman society. In this sense, it was peripheral; it was in the process of transformation from a primitive classless society to a class society, while Roman society was a clearly recognizable class society. Among the barbarians, class society was embryonic, incomplete; in Rome, it was complete. That the less advanced sector initiated the synthesis accounts for the incomplete character of the resulting tributary mode (the feudal mode). Similarly, too, when we analyze unequal development in the European feudal system and in the transition to (mercantilist) capitalism, we see center-periphery relations inverted, although not necessarily by external causes. Thus we must avoid transposing the meaning of the terms "center" and "periphery" from one historical period to another.

I have expounded a theory of unequal development in terms of center and periphery, complete and incomplete. Is it possible to substitute for this theory a "general theory of the weak link"? Probably not. An analysis in terms of the weak link is appropriate to the capitalist system: the link is weak because the local alliance of revolutionary classes can prevail over the reactionary alliance, which is only one gear in the interlocking dominant alliances composing the imperialist system. The weak link assumes the dominance of the economic base. It would be pointless to generalize this particular analysis to all of history because the capitalist and the precapitalist weak links are different.

3. Thus there are no laws of transition. There are only lessons that reveal general and particular laws specific to each different mode of production and certain features particular to the conjunctures which produce unequal development.

Periodization of a system enables us to grasp the moments of transition in their specific configurations in relation to the characteristics of the mode of production which govern them. Of course, since the capitalist system is the first global system, we can speak of a general, world periodization based on the characteristics and tendencies of the system on a world scale. But there is no world periodization for past eras. History texts that equate the European, Arab, and Chinese middle ages are in error.

The periodization of European history, from the Roman and barbarian world to capitalism, is important because of the specific features of the feudal mode which dominated precapitalist Europe and of the birth of capitalism from this feudal society. There are three major divisions in this periodization: (1) ancient world

(Roman) and barbarian world (German), (2) feudalism/mercantilist and absolutist feudalism, and (3) competitive capitalism/monopoly capitalism. Since the division separating the ancient and barbarian world from feudalism and that separating mercantilism from capitalism represent transitions to new modes of production, each phase preceding the division can be considered a transitional one: transition to feudalism (first to eighth centuries), (mercantilist) transition to capitalism (seventeenth to eighteenth centuries). But does the current phase of monopoly capitalism represent a transition to socialism? The question calls for expanded analysis below (Chapter 7).

We can also see that the form a transition takes may account for subsequent long-range developments. For instance, the form of the transition to feudalism can explain the form of the bourgeois revolution (the peasant element in the bourgeois revolution, discussed in Chapter 4). Is this strong determinism, wherein the ancient past weighs heavily on the present, very different from the weak determinism of revolutionary periods? Can we therefore contrast evolutions (reformist) where the objective (synchronic) conditions predominate with revolutions where the subjective (or so-called subjective) conditions prevail by reducing the weight of the past?

4. Because the discussion of unequal development in Chapters 3-6 encompasses ethnic groups or nations at unequal levels of advancement, the national question will always be associated with it.

III. *The concept of nation*

1. I propose a concept of nation in contrast to that of ethnic group. The two share one extremely important characteristic, a common language. The distinction between them is based on the presence or absence of state centralization (on the state level and through state intervention) of the surplus product.

Thus, although state and nation are not identical, the national phenomenon cannot be separated from the analysis of the state. On this basis, I propose a systematic survey of the nation throughout history. In particular, the nation clearly appears in (1) complete tributary societies (China, Egypt) where the tribute was centralized by the state and the tributary class was a state class, in contrast to incomplete tributary societies (like European feudal societies) where tribute collection was not centralized, and (2) capitalism, where the competition among capitals (with the resulting equalization of profits) and the mobility of labor are controlled by the state through legislation, the monetary system, and state economic policy. I explained that the European situation—the absence of nations during the feudal era, the concurrent birth of the nation and of capitalism—accounts for the West-centered distortion of the concept of nation. This distortion appears not only in the works of Stalin but also in those of Marx, Engels, and Lenin. The question of the Arab "nation" should be studied from this perspective.

2. Class conflicts and alliances take place within social formations bounded by states, which may or may not be nations. This is because conflicts and alliances imply active interference on the political and thus the state level.

3. Thus the concept of nation clearly appears in complete societies, whether they are tributary (China, Egypt) or capitalist (European nations of the capitalist center). On the other hand, in peripheral, incomplete modes of production, ethnic identification is too weak to constitute a nation. This is the case for feudal Europe, because the feudal mode was only an incomplete tributary mode. It is also the case for contemporary capitalist peripheries. Similarly, the society-nation equation does not still hold during transitional periods. Thus in contemporary Europe (assuming we are in an ambiguous transition either to socialism or to a state class mode) new national problems are surfacing. For instance, French regions, France, and Europe are three levels of a rapidly changing reality. These questions will be taken up in the following chapters, especially Chapters 4–6.

IV. The concept of a system of social formations

I propose using the concept of a system of social formations when the class conflicts and alliances in one area (in one state) have a significant effect on the conflicts and alliances in the other. When this is not the case, the formations are autonomous, even if they maintain exchange relations between them.

The imperialist system is the model *par excellence* of a system of social formations. The alliances and conflicts among its different partners are interdependent: social-democratic alliances in the center, national liberation alliances in the periphery. This articulation of alliances and conflicts, wherein classes can be completely defined only in relation to their place in the system as a whole, indicates that value is being distributed systemwide. Value has a collective origin at the level of the system rather than the level of each (state) formation; value is a world and not a national category (globalization of the productive process); its distribution results, in the final analysis, from class struggles and alliances on a world and not a national scale.

V. State, nation, and economy in capitalist reproduction

1. The state instance is essential to an understanding of the way in which social formations operate. The latter are not simply modes of production, nor are modes of production merely infra-structural economic bases (relations and forces of production). This is because the state has been established as a tool of the exploiting classes.

Specifically, in capitalist formations the role of the state is essential for the reproduction of the concrete conditions of accumulations (including class alliances necessary to this reproduction, economic policies favoring them, etc.). Politics is the arena wherein the alliances of the hegemonic bloc form and dissolve. The same is true of the world system of capitalist formations. The

conditions for the reproduction of the world hierarchy are determined at the state level: international division of labor, class
alliances on a world scale, and so on. To separate the economy
from the state is to accept the artificial division between "pure
economics" and "political science" by which bourgeois scholarship
attempts to refute historical materialism.

2. A good way to approach the problem of the relationship
between the state and the economy (national and global) is to begin
with the original outline for *Capital*. Marx proposed to treat six
groups of questions in the following order: (1) capital, (2) real
property, (3) wage labor, (4) the state, the nation, political democracy, parties, and the class struggle, (5) crises, and (6) international
trade and the world market (82-9).

The four volumes of *Capital* (Volume I published during Marx's
lifetime, Volumes II and III by Engels, and Volume IV, concerning
theories of surplus value, by Kautsky) treat questions 1, 2, and 3.
The other questions are dealt with only tangentially and unsys-
tematically in the *Grundrisse* and in *Capital*.

I have elsewhere presented my interpretation of the place of
Capital in historical materialism in *Imperialism and Unequal
Development*, *The Law of Value and Historical Materialism*, and
will not repeat it here. Volumes I, II, and III consist partially of a
theory of the "pure" capitalist mode of production (two classes, the
bourgeoisie and the proletariat), and deals with fundamentals: the
law of value, accumulation and dynamic equilibrium, competition among capitals, and the equalization of profit. The rest of
Volume III begins to discuss the transition of the capitalist mode to
a standard capitalist formation with three classes: it deals with
capitalist ground rent. These volumes constitute Marxist political
economy, understood as a critique of political economy. They
define the boundaries which may not be transgressed without
sacrificing the scientific character of Marxism. These volumes
cover the first three questions.

By critique of political economy I mean the demystification of
the objective economic "laws" that certain political economists

claim to have discovered. Economic reality is not the sole determining factor but rather acts in dialectical relation with class struggles. The economy is only the immediate appearance; the deeper reality is located on the level of historical materialism. Thus economics is "the bourgeoisie's discussion of its own practice" (10-13). The bourgeois "scientific" formulations (of Ricardo or of neo-Ricardians such as Sraffa) correctly describe the manifest interrelations of price, wages, and profits, that is, questions 1, 2, and 3 of the outline for *Capital*.

But from such a limited perspective we cannot correctly understand the class struggle, which seems to be no more than the economic struggle between the bourgeoisie and the proletariat. If we want to understand the real dynamic of class struggles we must raise the questions contained in group 4 (state, nation, politics). It is the method of historical materialism, however, and not that of so-called economics, which raises these questions. What we need is a concrete analysis of a concrete situation, of the global (economic and political) history of a formation, of its blocs of class alliances as they function within a given political framework, with particular ideological mediations, and so on. On this level, state mediation is obviously required.

But this is not all. Bourgeois political economy claims to be able to answer questions 5 and 6 (crises and international economic relations) in economic terms. It proposes explanatory models for conjuncture and crisis, on the one hand, and for international exchange on the other; both models use the economic abstractions of price, wages, and profits. Can we criticize these theories in their own terms, replacing bourgeois models with Marxist models? Is this what Marx would have done had he written two more volumes in answer to these questions? Some think so and have tried to complete Marxist political economy along these lines. But I believe that these questions must first be answered in historical materialist terms; answers on a more basic level must precede answers in economic terms. I have stated that Marx did not write an "economics of crisis" and an "international economics" not because he lacked the time but because the scientific analysis of economic forms demanded prior advances in historical materialist thought.

3. Take the questions of group 5 (cycle and crisis), for instance. It is not difficult to propose a model of cyclical accumulation similar to the model of regular linear accumulation in Volume II of *Capital*. It can be discussed in Marxist terms (value, variation in the rate of surplus value) or in pragmatic Ricardian-Sraffan terms (prices, wages, profit). This is precisely what I did in *Unequal Development*. But this model has only descriptive value. To really explain things we must consider crisis as a means to regulate accumulation, that is, as the strategy of the bourgeois class.

In pre–monopoly capitalism, state control of money is the first means of regulation. I have emphasized the point that money is not a veil but is an active instrument in the accumulation process. State control of money and credit is thus the economic policy of the bourgeoisie as a class. Capitalism cannot function without the state, without centralized money and credit. It cannot be analyzed by looking only at the competition among capitals. The changes in the interest rate which implement this economic policy have two goals. First, they speed up accumulation and then "restore order" by means of a crisis; this is a time of heightened competition favoring big business and of organized pressure on the proletariat. Second, they manage external relations, that is, they maintain or improve the national position vis-à-vis competing centers in the international division of labor. (For a discussion, see *The Law of Value and Historical Materialism*.)

Thus, during the pre–monopoly capitalism era, accumulation is regulated by state management of two areas: management of money on the one hand and of the labor force on the other (by the changes it introduces in the unemployment rate). The two are linked through the management of crisis.

Of course, we must go further than this. The social formation contains other classes: real proprietors, peasants, small producers (crafts workers, merchants), and so on. The historical circumstances of the bourgeois revolution and the kind of state which resulted from it created a certain type of hegemonic bloc. Regulation must either reproduce the conditions that maintain these alliances (for instance, the antiworker peasant alliance), or create the circumstances to dissolve or transform them, to substitute a new bloc for the old one, and so forth.

Overall, during the pre–monopoly capitalism period, state regulation in the advanced centers took place within a political framework that was at best a parliamentary democracy (England, France under Louis Philippe) restrictive of the working class and at times an authoritarian bourgeois monarchy sympathetic to bourgeois interests (Bonapartism). During that period, the working class was largely excluded from political life, its organizations were not legal, suffrage was restricted, and so on. This limited bourgeois democracy was in fact more open to participation by the peasantry and the petty bourgeoisie.

4. Before seeing how this system of regulating the workforce changed in the imperialist era, we must try to answer Marx's questions. Let us take up the group of questions relating to international economics. These raise two types of problems, those relating to competition among centers and those relating to the center-periphery division of labor. These problems are different for the preimperialist stage and for our own imperialist era.

During the preimperialist era competition among centers was also subject to state regulation. Laissez-faire was never other than ideological. The state, expressing the collective interests of the bourgeoisie, had two major means of regulating competition: the control of money and the control of customs duties. In the control of money, the effects of state economic policy related to internal accumulation and to external competition are closely linked. (See *The Law of Value and Historical Materialism*.) In its infinite variations, the conflict between free trade and protection has always been a political question of the greatest importance and has had a decisive impact on internal class alliances. There are numerous examples: the abolition of the Corn Laws and the abandonment of the English aristocratic alliance; French and Italian protectionism and peasant interests; the protection of American farmers and American food aid policies, to name a few.

During the imperialist era, the automatisms which previously connected changes in the interest rate with short-term movements of international capital and of the balance of payments have been replaced by more complex mechanisms. Nevertheless, monetary policy still has a clear international dimension. It can be implemented by control of exchange and movements of capital in certain phases and always by state interference in money markets. The abandonment of the gold standard in favor of the Bretton Woods system and current monetary arrangements like the Smithsonian agreement indicate active intervention between national monetary policy and the conditions of international competition. Neoliberal policies such as the General Agreement on Tariffs and Trade (GATT) and the European Common Market and neoprotectionist policies, which are reappearing everywhere due to the current crisis, are still very important means of controlling international competition.

But with the advent of imperialism, whether in the form of imperial preserves or of a world ostensibly open to all, the international division of labor between centers and peripheries takes on a new dimension. My basic thesis is that this new division of labor ushers in the era of the social-democratic alliance in the imperialist centers. This alliance takes the place of old alliances based on dying classes, such as the peasantry and the old petty bourgeoisie. The alliance is often strengthened by the division of the working class into two sectors. The first is national and relatively privileged; it is the base of social democracy. The other is almost completely excluded from the system of privileges; it consists of immigrants, minorities subject to discrimination (blacks and Hispanic minorities in the United States, for example), young people, and women (especially temporary workers). There is also an attempt, which has met with varying degrees of success, to integrate the higher levels of the new petty bourgeoisie (including managers and technicians).

The natural complement to the social-democratic alliance in the center is the external alliance of the imperialist bourgeoisie with the exploiting classes of the periphery, either feudal and comprador classes or the dependent industrial bourgeoisie, depending on the era. On a world scale, this hegemonic bloc clashes with the bloc of national liberation forces, the composition of which varies with the class structure of each peripheral country.

The reproduction of this international structure involves imperialist ideological hegemony. It also involves the material corruption made possible by the superexploitation and looting of the periphery and by the economic impact this has on the center (full employment and combined growth of wages and productivity). This ideological hegemony makes it possible to extend electoral democracy to the working class, which had been impossible in the preimperialist stage. Nationalism, in its former national chauvinist guise or in its current panoccidentalist form, sustains this hegemony.

During the imperialist era, regulation by crisis and changes in the unemployment rate are no longer the main means of regulating accumulation. The substitution of the controlled conjuncture for the previous cycle expresses this change. Two main strategies, dictated by the international division of labor, are used to control the workforce: the reproduction of a growing reserve army in the periphery, and the division of the working class in the center, as explained above. National and international monetary and credit policies (such as those of the International Monetary Fund) reinforce this dual control over the labor force and the international division of labor. Control is exercised by states via political methods, not by the multinationals via their own independent actions, as some deviationist economists have claimed (71b).

Obviously, this control does not bring about harmony, contrary to the pretensions of economistic ideology (a two-pronged ideology of efficiency in the center and of development in the periphery, for which we must note the role of the World Bank in the production of its "third world action" component). It is fraught with class contradictions. But these contradictions are different from those of the past. The primary contradiction throughout the entire imperialist epoch is that between the imperialist bloc, including partners in the social democratic alliance and dependent alliances in the periphery, and the national liberation bloc. Thus the current crisis can be seen as a crisis of imperialism, i.e., a crisis of these blocs (for a fuller discussion, see Chapter 5 of *Imperialism and Unequal Development*).

Only by substituting historical materialism for political economy can we really understand problems of so-called international economics and fully criticize economism. It is not "comparative advantages" which determine the international division of labor, but the converse. And the international division of labor itself is determined by the reproduction of the class alliances underlying it.

By using historical materialism we can also analyze the economic operation of the system. We can see it as a system for determining the division of value created on a world scale through unequal rates of extraction of surplus labor and as a system based on the globalization of the previously national categories of the commodity form and of value.

5. In conclusion, it should be emphasized that accumulation, both on a world scale and on the scale of central and peripheral states, is a consequence of class alliances and oppositions within states and across state boundaries. Thus the state has essential functions: this level is decisive. But the state is not necessarily the nation. The two are basically the same in the center, where the nation-state was finally imposed by a twofold process of assimilation within the nation and destruction of multinational forms. But this is not generally the case in the periphery.

VI. The bourgeois and proletarian lines on the national question: ideology and material base

1. The bourgeois line, the line of all exploiting classes, recognizes the existence of every kind of social group (nations, ethno-

linguistic groups, races, tribes, religious groups, not to mention age, sex, and other groups) except classes. Thus, using a simple empirical definition derived from the observation of immediate appearances, sociology claims that there are only socioeconomic categories, derived from occupations. These are defined by the type of work and the sector of activity and are neither more nor less important than noneconomic social categories. Sociology seeks to establish possible correlations between different apparent social phenomena. It considers class distinctions based on an analysis of the mode of production to be "metaphysical," "vague," and "unidentifiable." This is similar to vulgar bourgeois economics, which deals only with price and considers the "metaphysical" category of value to be a pointless "detour."

Confronted with the various practical problems created by the existence of all these different categories, the bourgeois line takes one of two positions. The reactionary position denies the importance of rights and freedoms specific to the needs of each category. It believes that formal and individual liberty ("all men are equal") suffices. The democratic position recognizes the necessity for particular rights and freedoms, for instance, the right of nations to self-determination, the right of women to real equality with men, the right of minorities to use their own language, and so on.

2. The proletarian line, the line of all exploited classes, recognizes class division as more basic than national, religious, sexual, or other immediately observable distinctions. Class division is based on the mode of production. It results in conflicts between the exploited classes, which are forced to furnish surplus labor, and the exploiting classes, which appropriate this surplus labor. The proletarian line also recognizes that price is the phenomenal form of value.

Since in all societies the exploiting classes have ideological hegemony (the ideology of the dominant class is the dominant ideology of the society) we must distinguish between a class-in-itself and a class-for-itself. For, if social class is an objective reality, it only becomes a full and complete political reality to the degree that the ideological hegemony of the exploiting class is challenged by a clear and well-developed class consciousness. This consciousness develops through participation in the class struggle and through the recognition that other categories, although they also exist objectively, are less important than class exploitation.

Confronted with the problems which these various objective realities pose for the class struggle, the proletarian line also takes one of two positions, reactionary or revolutionary. The reactionary, or bureaucratic, formal position simply denies realities other than class. It denies the importance of sex, nations, religions, or other categories, regarding them not as realities but as phenomena artificially manipulated by the exploiting classes. This position results, moreover, in tactical concessions with regard to these realities. Indeed, it leads to practical failure in the class struggle because these realities are tenacious and subtly undermine the development of the class-for-itself.

The revolutionary position recognizes that all categorical differences have material bases and tries to understand how they interface with class differences. The revolutionary attitude does not distinguish between two worlds, the world of classes materially based on exploitation and the world of other categories based not on material reality but purely on circumstances and/or ideology. It recognizes only one world, wherein everything has a material basis which, in the final analysis, is class exploitation.

The revolutionary position thus always attempts to understand the dialectical interaction of all the elements of social life. It does not put all of these aspects on the same plane but always seeks out ultimate determinations and the ways in which these are expressed. On this basis, it develops a strategy and tactic of effective, revolutionary class alliances.

VII. *The ideology of universal culture*

1. Major debates, such as those about the state and the nation, lead us naturally to the formulation of conclusions about the

direction of humanity's cultural evolution—toward homogenization or not—and to the choice of a position with regard to this direction—active support for it or not. To do this we must understand how the productive forces develop and the impact of this development on the capitalist system.

2. My first thesis is that the tendency to homogenization, which underlies capitalist development, is blocked by the very conditions of unequal accumulation.

The material basis of the tendency to homogenization is the continual extension of markets, both in breadth and in depth. The commodity market extends progressively from one region to the country as a whole and then to the entire world. It also gradually envelops all aspects of social life. Capital markets, which were localized so long as capital could not be separated from the capitalist, tend to become global with the centralization of capital during the monopoly stage. The workforce itself, whose geographical mobility had been limited for so long by social, linguistic, legal, and other factors, tends to acquire greater—and even international—mobility.

Cultural life is not some mysterious, unfathomable domain, but is rather the way in which the utilization of use values is organized. Therefore, the homogenization of these use values through their domination by generalized exchange value must tend to homogenize culture itself. Nevertheless, this tendency is held in check by the effects of unequal accumulation.

First and most importantly at present, rapid accumulation in the center conflicts with curbed, biased accumulation on the periphery of the imperialist system. In the center, the tendency has been and is toward the disintegration of precapitalist modes and the integration of a proletarian labor force from which surplus value is directly extracted during the work process itself (real domination). In the periphery, the historical conditions under which capitalism attained a world scale have instead entailed a tremendous development of formal means of subjugation. This explains the survival of precapitalist forms, the superexploitation of labor in the periphery through the transfer of value, and the attendant distortion in the mode of accumulation. This fundamental inequality of imperialist development accelerates real homogenization in the center while blocking it in the periphery, where only a minority of the people can become modern consumers.

Second, accumulation is unequal in the centers themselves. This inequality was a major obstacle to the formation of these centers and to the acquisition of a unified national character by most of them. It continues to exist, surfacing again and again in the form of regionalism.

3. My second thesis is that this tendency to homogenization is not a necessary consequence of the development of the productive forces *per se*, but of the capitalist content of this development. The growth of the productive forces in precapitalist societies did not involve the domination of use value by exchange value. Thus, their development was not homogeneous but took a diversity of forms and methods.

The capitalist mode, which was historically necessary to the further growth of the productive forces, involved the dominance of exchange value and thus homogenization. But the capitalist mode is no more eternal than preceding modes. It has become an obstacle to the further development of the productive forces on a world scale because of the distorted mode of accumulation which it imposes on the periphery and which precludes the possibility of the periphery catching up. This is the major reason why capitalism is objectively obsolete on a world scale.

Can socialism, in its turn an historical necessity, overcome the legacy of the past and present by adopting models of accumulation similar enough to those of capitalism to succeed where capitalism has failed in homogenizing the world? Or must it operate differently? While socialism might bring about homogenization, the socialism in question in that case would be a new class mode, the statist mode. Since the nonstate path is equally "possible," i.e., based on real tendencies in the struggle, there is no obligation to regard the first possibility as being historically necessary.

The key to a scientific analyisis of these problems is a correct understanding of the question of technology. My view is that technology is not neutral in its effects on the relations of production, making it impossible to represent the productive techniques of a classless society by simple extrapolation from capitalist techniques. Under capitalism, technical development supports a division of labor separating conception from execution and thereby reproduces the material base of class division. And if classless society is founded on the abolition of exchange value and the reestablished primacy of use value there is no reason to think that the current tendency to homogenization would continue. It should, on the contrary, reverse itself, because communism implies variety.

4. The tendency to homogenization under capitalism is stronger in some areas than in others. In the area of industrial production techniques, in the realm of modes of consumption, "lifestyles," and so on, its force is virtually irresistible. It is somewhat weaker in the domain of ideology and politics. And when it comes to the use of language, its impact is very weak.

During a long period, the linguistic unification of newly forming nations took place by force of circumstance (including force pure and simple) rather than by systematic design. For this reason spoken popular languages and official administrative languages continued to coexist. The spread of schools, corresponding to the practical demands of a considerably more integrated market, has only really succeeded in establishing national languages within the modern era. Each time the authorities tried to use the schools to impose a foreign language on a newly forming nation, they met with generally successful resistance. Many nineteenth-century socialists had hopes of rapid assimilation (see Kautsky's predictions for the Austrian empire, or Strasser's about the Czech language) but these have proved false.

5. How should we evaluate this tendency toward homogenization? Obviously, it is pointless to cry over what has already taken place and is historically irreversible: the Gallicization of the Languedoc, the widespread adoption of private automobile transportation in the West, or of Coca-Cola by the Cubans, to take

random examples of unequal importance. All emotion of this sort is foreign to Marxism, which does not believe in the immutability of societies in any area.

But the real question concerns the future. Should we celebrate this capitalist tendency toward homogenization, as we would celebrate the growth of the productive forces? Should we support it and view opposition to it as being as reactionary as smashing machines? Should we only regret that its class character limits its effectiveness? Or should we conclude that socialism will lead in the same direction, though more rapidly and less painfully?

Two tendencies have always coexisted within Marxism with regard to this question. Marx himself, at least in the first part of his active life, always spoke admiringly of the growth of the productive forces, the achievements of the bourgeoisie, and the tendency toward homogenization which freed people from the narrow confines of village life. But he gradually came to have doubts about this and in his later writings substituted a more nuanced perspective for his original onesided view.

However, the dominant tendency of the workers' movement evolved in the opposite direction. Praise for "universal civilization" and a naive belief in the blending of cultures (and even of languages) were dominant in the Second International: we have only to think of Esperanto. Belied by the First World War, this naive cosmopolitanism reappeared after the Second World War, when Americanization emerged as a synonym for progress, or at least for inevitable modernization.

In fact, the tendency toward homogenization renders the superstructure more suitable to the needs of the capitalist infrastructure. It weakens the contradictions in this area and is therefore reactionary. The spontaneous resistance of people to this homogenization must be encouraged and strengthened with a view to overturning the underlying relations of exploitation. *Homo consumens* is not an inescapable necessity but only a necessity of capitalism. Indeed, the ideology of universal culture is a bourgeois ideology, child of the enlightenment ideology which held that the growth of the productive forces mechanically and automatically determines the growth of civilization, the progress of liberty and equality, and so on. This ideology obscures the class contradictions whereby the productive forces develop.

6. Whatever the case, has the tendency toward homogenization had important repercussions in the political arena, i.e., an impact on the class struggle in the contemporary world? Certainly. Until the wars of 1914–1918 and 1939–1945, the tendency toward homogenization seemed to be at work only in the nations of the center and especially in the great nation-states. It developed simultaneously with the constitution of monopoly capital on this national basis. It reinforced the deep chauvinist tendencies which served the interests of fiercely competing national imperialisms.

But things seem to have changed since 1945. Imperialist countries have been too unequal to escape the dominance of American imperialism and have relegated contradictions among themselves to the background. Fear of the USSR and of a widespread colonial revolt have reinforced this tendency. At the same time, the imperialist economic sphere became globalized and the construction of a European community began. The nature of this construction is ambivalent: will it result in a Europe united against the United States or in a Europe integrated into the Atlantic community via German mediation? Now, with the end of Gaullist illusions, a Germano-American Europe seems the more likely. And, as it has already done in America, economic growth has begun to homogenize European social life.

Under these circumstances, we must ask if the old type of nationalism is not about to disappear, to be replaced not by internationalism, but only by a pan-European neonationalism (panoccidentalism) with racist overtones and defining itself primarily by opposition to Asia and Africa. Its counterpart, tolerated and regenerated, would be microregionalisms without political significance.

Chapter 2

Communal Formations

1. If we accept the view that anthropology is the study of societies in the process of class formation, what can we learn from it? Anthropology, like all the specialized disciplines of social science, artificially divides social reality. It also has a twofold ideological objective: (1) to create a realm outside the fundamental laws of historical materialism (determination in the last instance by the economic base); and (2) to distinguish between "primitive peoples without a history," especially those of Africa, and "peoples with a history," or even "with a great history" (Europeans), and thereby to provide a moral justification for imperialism. Given these circumstances, it is obvious that the work of anthropology generally has not been scientific, even though the evidence gathered by its best researchers can be used, following critical inventory, to enrich historical materialism. Thus the plethora of resources available to Anglo-Saxon anthropology, which rejects Marxism, has not made up for the inadequacy of its theoretical bases. It is worth noting that amidst this ethnographic jumble the most interesting contributions of non-Marxist anthropology have been made by researchers sympathetic to Marxism (cf. 10-9).

This oppressive legacy enhances the importance and value of the contribution of the Marxist minority in France that over the past fifteen years has rediscovered historical materialism. How can we forget that Engels' *The Origin of the Family, Private Property, and the State*, a work of genius given the level of knowledge during his time, failed to inspire a tradition of inquiry and remained a sort of intellectual curiosity, a decorative luxury object for the workers' movement? This deplorable situation may be changing.

2. Marxist anthropology already has to its credit the clarification of the problem of the dominance of kinship in societies in the process of class formation. It has shown that the low level of development of the productive forces necessitates forms of co-operation within the village collective and between villages, forms which are the material key to understanding the function of family, lineage, clan, and tribal organizations. It has thus effected a radical and salutary return to the best of Engels.

By demonstrating that the economic base is determinant in the last instance, some Marxist anthropologists have dispelled the confusion created by their structuralist colleagues, notably Maurice Godelier (10-14), in their attempt to treat kinship as part of the infrastructure and of the superstructure at the same time. Important in this regard are the contributions of various French Marxist anthropologists, particularly the distinction therein proposed between dominance and determination in the last instance (10-5, 10-6, 10-7).

3. I do not conclude from this that economic anthropology has thereby taught us how the dominance of the noneconomic realm functions in societies in the process of class formation, based on what Alain Marie calls "the ideology of the family (or of kinship)" (10-4). Indeed, if we want to see this dominance at work, tributary societies provide material which is not only richer but also more directly related to the questions raised by the struggle against capitalism and for the construction of socialism. For in these far more advanced societies, the dominant ideology is no longer that of kinship, to which our modern world is rather indifferent, but is one conveyed and imposed by the major absolute institutions, whether religious or civil. Consideration of the role of the Christian church in feudal Europe, the ideology of absolute monarchy in mercantile Europe, of Islam in the Arab world, of Confucianism in China, and so on, seems

much more useful to an understanding of the exact place of ideology in historical materialism.

In fact, the role of ideology has been obscured by the economistic reduction of Marxism. This reduction is evidence of the reintegration of the dominant Marxist tendency into the tradition of bourgeois philosophy, the philosophy of the Enlightenment, itself the ideological expression of the dominance of the economic instance in the capitalist mode. But it was not anthropological discoveries that led to the reexamination of this economistic reduction and of the theory of ideology-reflection which it inspired. Rather, it was prompted by political thinking about Soviet society and the construction of socialism, which in turn, promoted the growth of better anthropological thinking.

This fact underlines the primacy of the contribution of militant action over the best academic contribution, especially since it was not intellectual analysis of socialist problems but rather the enormous practical and theoretical movement brought about by the struggles in China that inspired the best anthropology. Maoism, not anthropology, has enabled us to reestablish historical materialism in every area. As a summary formulation I suggest that the centralization of capital in the statist mode ends the dominance of the economy (based on the transformation of surplus value into profit, Volume III of *Capital*) and reestablished the dominance of ideology (here, statist, *consumismo* nationalism). It is for this reason that the statist mode does not seem to me to be simply a form of capitalism but a new term in the necessary alternative required for the transcendence of capitalism.

4. However, progress always involves the risk of subsequent regression. For the resolution of certain problems creates new ones. Thus anthropology, having clarified the question of kinship, today faces a new and still unanswered question, namely, how male-female relations and the social relations of domination (which are on the level of superstructural instances) interrelate with exploitation (that is, the extraction of surplus labor). Particularly striking is the power of Alain Marie's substitution of the term

"women" for that of "commodities" in Marx's text (10-4). This seems to be the best possible description of women's status through the ages—not that of an exploited producer but of a commodity.

The particular nature of this problem stems from perhaps the fact that the question of the relations between the sexes and the dominated status of women dates in part from primitive communism, the transition from animal to human, and in part from the subsequent phase of early class formation. We may know how family organization interrelates with different modes of production. But we cannot conclude from this that women are a social class (exploited by men) except if we both confuse relations of domination with relations of exploitation of the one hand and on the other reduce to a single category the extraction of surplus labor from women throughout the ages (thereby denying the particularity of the interrelation between the family and the mode of production in different modes of production).

This formulation of the woman question results from an economistic interpretation of historical materialism. Or, worse, it comes from extending the domain of historical materialism to an area outside its purview: that of anthropology in the literal sense, the definition of the human being in relation to the animal species. Such a formulation opens the door to psychologistic and biologistic follies based on the "myths of origin" that sustain certain feminist tendencies to the detriment of the struggle for the real liberation of women (11-3).

Here once again it is not intellectual speculation (anthropological or otherwise) but the eruption of women's movements that has raised these issues. The fact that these movements have at times been quite remote from Marxism, as in the United States and northern Europe, and at others very close to it, as in the period just after the Russian and Chinese revolutions, neither adds to nor detracts from their relevance and importance.

Is it useful to reformulate these problems in terms of a so-called domestic mode of production, interfacing with other modes of production (11-1, 11-2)? I do not think so. In trying to prove that the source of the profits monopolies extract from immigrant workers is to be found in domestic exploitation, one clouds the specific effects of monopoly domination over the peasant societies from which these migrant workers come (cf. 11-2). The correct way to analyze this problem is, it seems to me, to look at the domination of the capitalist mode over peasant modes. This line of inquiry was probably opened by Marx himself, in his brief consideration of the effects of the integration of the Russian peasantry into the capitalist system, followed by Lenin, Kautsky, and even Chayanov (10-10). Once again, it was the peasant movement, especially in France, and anti-imperialist peasant struggles that gave rise to these ideas (cf. 73b).

Marx never posited that the value of labor power was that of the worker taken in isolation, but insisted it must take account of the cost of reproduction under the conditions characterizing any given society. These social conditions are familiar to us: they include the organization of the family, the sexual hierarchy, the sexual division of labor, and the assignment of domestic labor to women. This is why it is important to rediscover the true meaning of the value of labor power in the capitalist mode and the implications of this for the oppression of women. The fact that in the West the women's revolt occurred first in the United States and in Northern Europe has not been without its effect. The widespread ignorance of Marxism in these regions has led to some ahistorical formulations, feminist versions of the feminine mystique (11-3).

We have to see the problem in a new light. I have argued that the notion of a domestic mode of production is confusing, since a mode of production cannot be transhistorical, accounting for everything in all times and places. With regard to the household division of labor an older phrase, "the oppression of women," is clearer. The confusion stems from reducing all relations of domination and exploitation to a single category, that of relations of extraction of the surplus. The correct way to formulate the question of the interrelationship between women's oppression and capitalist exploitation is this: women's subjection enables capital to reduce the value of labor power; men dominate women, but they are exploited together. Bruno Lautier was, as far as I know, the first to develop systematically the idea of the interrelationship between formal and real forms of subjection and to reject the concept of a "chain" of exploitation, i.e., exploitation of women by man and of man by capital (73-3).

Doubtless the "historic defeat of the female sex," to use Engels' expression, is so ancient that the oppression of women has been a permanent feature of history. But in that case it cannot be analyzed as a mode of production. As Alain Lipietz has noted, this oppression never exists in an isolated manner, which proves that it does not have the status of a mode of production in the true meaning of the term (82-10).

5. Oriented toward the past (the transition to class society), anthropology is poorly placed to profit from the experience of class struggle, and may end up in a number of blind allies. The first of these comes from the tendency to forget that it *is* about the transition to class society. It is worth remembering that the societies it studies are necessarily societies wherein the level of development of the productive forces is very low. The lineage, clan, and tribal organizations are themselves obstacles to the further development of these forces, obstacles which cannot be overcome except through state tributary organization.

Of course, in order for class formation to begin, an initial development of the productive forces is necessary. This corresponds to the transition to settled agriculture. Contrary to the neoclassical economic theory which stupidly equates earth and nature, agronomists have known for a long time that agricultural land is a means of labor and not an object of labor. But other branches of the social sciences have not read agronomists because they are supposedly too earthy and empiricist. Economists, historians, and anthropologists have thus thought they were discovering what they were in fact only rediscovering. As to the myth which confuses the development of the productive forces with gains in the productivity of labor, Ester Boserup, although not a Marxist, dispelled it in a work published in 1965 (10-11). She argued that the transition to intensive agriculture under the impact of demographic pressure brought about greater per capita production (and thus ultimately a more dependable surplus) thanks to the greater annual quantity of labor and not to the higher daily productivity of labor.

Every time we encounter the dominance of kinship, this is an infallible sign that we are still at the first stage of a long evolution, an embryonic stage in the process of class formation. And on this particular point, the criticism that Meillassoux pays too little attention to the level of the productive forces seems justified (11-4). Africanists too easily forget that the sub-Saharan societies they study had neither the plow nor a written language (except in Ethiopia and the Sudan). This conjunction is not accidental. The development of the productive forces, a necessary condition for the constitution of a surplus large enough to lead to irreversible state formation, occurs through the transition from human energy (hoe agriculture) to animal energy. Similarly, it is hard to imagine a state without the use of writing for census taking, dispensing information, and transmitting orders. The imperial Ethiopian state and the Mahdist state in the Sudan were forming at the same time that the use of the plow and of writing were becoming widespread.

Analysis of the productive forces implies analysis of the technical process of production, but the latter obviously cannot be separated from the superstructure. François Pouillon emphasizes this point, reminding us that the category of abstract labor is a category of the capitalist mode (10-4). When classes are forming, the relations of domination and the embryonic relations of exploitation are still inextricably bound together. To disentangle them, it is necessary to make a radical distinction between them. As Marie suggests, "exploitation is not a necessary correlary of domination," although the two are linked: the birth of the state parallels the birth of classes (10-4). Because Meillassoux refused to make this distinction, he confuses the peasant mode of production and the domestic mode of production. Based on his study of the Guro, in West Africa,

Meillassoux states that neither control of a surplus product nor control of the means of production exists and that the control of labor power (but why?) operates via that of the reproducers (the women). Here he is confusing relations of cooperation and domination, already established to a certain extent (sufficiently to enable the gerontocracy to organize cooperation within the village and between villages), but not yet completely (no state, no power at its disposal), with relations of exploitation not yet established at all. For if there is no state, it is because there is no need for one. There is general acceptance of the gerontocracy because it brings about the necessary cooperation. The lack of social classes does not necessarily mean that a society is idyllic.

And if there are no classes, the modes of production of this transition must be characterized as communal modes. I use the plural because at this stage of human evolution, ecological, demographic, and other conditions bring into being a great variety of organizations. Nevertheless, this variety is created not by the level of the productive forces (which is everywhere very low) but by the relations of production and juridical and political relations.

The task of historical materialism, therefore, is to find the common denominator in all this variety. This is the communal ownership of the primary means of production, the land. Communal ownership is organized in a great variety of specific ways, in which individual, family, lineage, and other uses are combined. If we emphasize specific details, we run the risk of forgetting the basic common characteristic, that of collective ownership. We may confuse the plane of the economic base with the plane of political organization (prestate), emphasizing the gerontocracy (relation of dominance) and attributing to it effects of a mode of extraction of surplus value which it is not.

6. The second blind alley into which anthropology may stray intensifies the negative effects of dogmatic rigidity. Given the circumstances under which academic anthropology has developed, this once again opens the way to the aberrations of West-centeredness.

The persistent search for a "slave mode of production" seems to be a deviation of this sort, one which recalls the "five stages" of the Stalinist vulgate. Among the extreme variety of forms taken by the transition from communal to tributary modes of production, slavery seems to be neither obligatory, nor even widespread. And the persistence of the search is due exclusively to the importance of Greek and Roman antiquity in the development of the West.

The confusion between the status of persons and that of producers is a case in point. West-centeredness reaches caricature proportion on this subject: fifty words from fifty different languages describing different situations in different areas are translated by the same term, "slavery." Then a way out of this impasse is sought. In fact if these words have different connotations, it is because they describe different realities. Slavery constitutes a particular and rather exceptional labor status, which becomes really widespread only in highly mercantilized situations, which are clearly the situations just preceding the completion of the capitalist mode.

7. The third blind alley has serious consequences. If under the pretext of the primacy of the relations of production, it excludes the analysis of circulation from the realm of historical materialism, circulation will be treated as having no effect in its turn on the relations of production. Is this a dialectical vision?

Elsewhere I have argued about the importance of Volumes II and III of *Capital* and the danger of reducing Marx to Volume I alone. Here I will merely state that the refusal to consider circulation is rather suspect, and acts as a blind for imperialism. It is precisely this obstinate refusal to even consider the existence of commodity circulation and the exclusive concentration on the relations of production, thus reduced to the immediate labor process, which has led to considering slavery as a necessary and general state in the succession of modes of production.

8. Questions about the transition from antiquity to European feudalism belong to the intersection of history and anthropology. I will return to this point to emphasize the importance of the interpenetration of barbarian communal modes with the class

modes of antiquity in the establishment of feudalism as a special and peripheral form of the tributary mode.

Marx and Engels created a Marxist anthropology based on questions about the history of Greek and Roman antiquity and about the establishment of Christian feudalism. Marx thought this particular development of the state and classes was different from that of "Asia" (in the *Grundrisse*). Engels, on the other hand, in *The Origin of the Family*, emphasized the universal characteristics of evolution, by analogy with the Greek *gens* and that of the Iroquois.

Marxist exegesis having replaced Marxism, the *Grundrisse* has inspired a literature which is prolific but lacking in scientific spirit. I will return to this debate in the following chapter. As Meillassoux notes, we must study reality in all its variety if we wish to make progress (10-5). Without doubt, it is on the basis of concrete anthropological studies, particularly those about Africa, that progress has been made toward a better understanding of communal societies.

Chapter 3

Tributary Formations

1. The period between the definitive establishment of social classes and the state in a given society and the entrance of that society into the central (complete) or peripheral (dominated) capitalist era varies in length. At times it is long (five thousand years for Egypt, three thousand for Greece), at others short (fifteen centuries for Europe). Occasionally, imperialist integration does away with this period entirely (for several African and Oceanic societies). Clearly, even a superficial view reveals the immense variety of social organizations that characterize this period. Given this situation, is it scientific to try to find a common denominator?

Marxist tradition in this area is contradictory. Academic Marxism has insisted on emphasizing the particularity of each case. At times, it has even become empiricist and refused to use the same terms for societies belonging to different cultural areas; for instance, it has reserved the term "feudal" for Europe (with, as always, the Japanese exception) and refused to use it for Asia. On the other hand, the militant Marxist tradition has always used a global terminology, using the term feudal, for instance, for all great precapitalist societies: China, India, the Arab world, and even clearly less developed societies (in Africa, for instance).

If we approach this question with Marxology rather than Marxism, we can attribute either tradition to Marx. As Rodney Hilton states, Marx certainly gave the term "feudal" a general and broad connotation which was completely understood by his contemporaries (50-2). He used it to cover all of European history at least from the barbarian invasions to the English and French bourgeois revolutions. His view of feudalism was not that of later bourgeois historians who, by restricting it, have narrowed the area of its sway to the region between the Loire and the Rhine during four centuries. But Marx also invented the phrase "asiatic mode of production," and—in his erstwhile unpublished writings, including the *Grundisse*—adopted certain theses of Montesquieu and Bernier that contrast Asian "stagnation" with the eventful and dynamic history of Europe.

These two tendencies have consistently generated controversies which have always passionately interested activists. Overall the dominant tendency in the Euro-American academic world has stressed the diversity and exceptional character of European history. Elsewhere, the prevailing tendency has attempted to play down the particularities.

In the course of this discussion there have been slack times, for instance from the end of the nineteenth century to 1917, followed by the period of apparent unanimity imposed by the theory of the "five universal stages." There have also been moments when the stylish view prevailed, as with the asiatic mode of production. The flagrant West-centeredness of the end of the last century or the gospel of the five stages led to conclusions which seem absurd to us today. But it is probably equally erroneous to try to find the "asiatic" mode everywhere, in protohistory, among tribes around the world, and in the "great historical" empires. Ultimately, what purpose is served by generalizations based on a feeling of vague similarity imposed by a unitary conception of a generalized mode of production, be it feudal, asiatic, or tributary? How can we avoid being blinded by the many details of immediate reality (slavery here and not there; a highly monetized economy in one place and an almost natural one elsewhere; nonexistent or complete urbanization, etc)? How can we use the same concept of mode of production to analyze societies at so many different levels of development of the productive forces? It is well for those who wish to defend the unitary viewpoint to spell out the field of unity in order to avoid serious misunderstandings. Two observations seem relevant here.

2. First, the search for an ultimate unity beyond diversity applies only to societies wherein the level of development of the productive forces is the same. Of course, this does not mean exactly the same: the level is not the same in France and in the United States, but we can nonetheless agree that both are capitalist countries. It is necessary to consider three steps in the development of the productive forces and three corresponding sets of relations of production. If we do not try to link the essential content of the relations of production with the level of development of the productive forces, we are rejecting the very essence of historical materialism, which is the determination in the last instance by the economic base.

On the first step of the development of productive forces, the surplus is too small to permit more than the beginnings of class and state formation. This is why it seems absurd and non-Marxist to use the same term (asiatic or other) for lineage, clan, or tribal and state formations. Still, this is what the Hungarian scholar Ferenc Tökei, whose theses are better known in the West through Godelier's interpretation of them (30-3, 30-4), tries to do. Tökei locates the "asiatic" mode (which he uses to characterize the great civilizations of the Orient) in the transition to class society. How can China, which in the eleventh century produced as much iron as Europe in the eighteenth and had five cities of more than one million inhabitants, be classed as being at the beginning of class society, and Europe, which was at the same level of development of the productive forces, be classed as being on the brink of industrial revolution?

It seems obvious that on this first step the low level of development is inextricably linked with lineage, clan, and tribal relations. It is these relations that enable the productive forces to begin developing beyond the phase of primitive communism (the transition to settled agriculture) and at the same time block their development beyond a certain point. Thus, wherever we find these relations, the level of the productive forces is necessarily low, and where we do not find them, it is necessarily high. The existence of these relations is furthermore the expression of the dominance of kinship (and the absence of the state). The forms of property that accompany this first step always—and necessarily—have basic traits in common: property is always communal and its use is regulated by the systems of kinship that control the dominant instance.

The second step corresponds to a level of development of the productive forces which makes the growth of the state both possible and necessary. That is, it necessitates the end of the dominance of kinship (which can continue to exist but only as a vestige dominated by another rationality). The forms of property corresponding to this second step are those which enable the dominant class to control access to the land and by means of this to extract tribute from the peasant producers. The extraction of this tribute is controlled by the dominance of ideology, which always takes the same form: state religion or quasi religion.

The high level of the productive forces under capitalism corresponds to the third step. This level involves capitalist property. That is, at one end, monopoly control by the bourgeoisie of the means of production, which are no longer mainly land but machines, equipment, and factories; and at the other end, free wage labor, the extraction of the surplus (here, surplus value) by means of economic exchange (the sale of labor power). Concretely, the development of agriculture beyond a certain point necessitated machines and fertilizers, i.e., industry and therefore capitalism. Born in the agriculture of the transition, capitalism thus had to expand elsewhere before returning to agriculture. This point is essential to an understanding of the particular features of peripheral capitalism (90-2).

Thus we have very general and abstract definitions of three forms of property—communal (of the land); tributary (of the land); capitalist (of means of production other than land). These stress the content of property understood as social control, rather than its juridical and ideological forms. The same conceptual framework will be used to investigate the problem of transcending capitalism. Each form of property necessarily corresponds to one step in the development of the productive forces. On the first step, organization of production remains at the lineage and village level. On the second, the organization of production is, at least in part (in fact, in its decisive part, not quantitatively but qualitatively) determined at the level of a state society, which is more or less extensive but always much bigger than the village. The circulation of the surplus (not necessarily in the form of commodities) accounts for the importance of specialized crafts, nonproductive functions, the state, the cities, commerce, and so on. A higher level of development necessitates a general market, a capitalist market.

On this level of abstraction, each step is universally necessary. Not to look for unity at this level is to reject the abc's of Marxism. If we do this, history becomes not necessity but chance, and its explanation can be only idealist, structuralist, or psychologistic: the "genius of peoples," and the like. West-centeredness involves this kind of explanation (the "destiny" of Europe) and therefore must negate the unifying principle.

3. The second observation relevant to this inquiry is that the unifying principle of each step should be sought on the level of the basic mode of production rather than the social formation. Theorists like Perry Anderson (40-1) and others who refuse to make this conceptual distinction, use the argument of the variety of formations to negate the unifying principle (of the mode of production). To the extent that I emphasize this conceptual distinction, I am rejecting the argument based on the variety of immediate reality (90-1).

4. What then are the basic, common characteristics of the mode of production (in the singular) of this second step of development of the productive forces? The first is that the surplus product is extracted by noneconomic means. This characteristic differentiates this first class mode from the communal mode preceding it. There the surplus product—which already exists—is not appro-

priated by an exploiting class. It is centralized by a ruling group for collective use and redistributed according to the needs of reproduction. The confusion between relations of cooperation and dominance (functions that oppose the governing and the governed, even without a state) and relations of exploitation underlies the failure to distinguish between the surplus product used collectively and the surplus product appropriated by an exploiting class. The confusion stems from the desire to reject those naive simplifications equating the communal mode with idyllic primitive communism. The extraction of the surplus product is thus like tribute to the profit of the exploiting class. This is why I propose to call this basic mode of the second step the tributary mode.

5. The second characteristic of the tributary mode is that the essential organization of production is based on use value and not on exchange value. The product kept by the producer is itself directly a use value meant for consumption, in general, for the producer's own consumption. But the product extracted by the exploiting class is also directly a use value for this class. The essence of this tributary mode then is a natural economy, without exchange but not without transfers (tribute is one) and redistributions (50-2).

Still, there is in tributary formations what seems to be commodity exchange, which is sometimes nonmonetary (barter) but more often monetary. How can this be reconciled with the statement that use value is dominant? Here I will merely note that exchange, even monetary exchange, in these formations is not always nor even primarily commodity exchange; that is, it is not based on exchange value (the law of value) but on use value (comparative advantage). Maurice Dobb, followed by Kohachiro Takahashi, Rodney Hilton, and many others, because they forget this difference, have not arrived at an acceptable conceptual definition of the tributary mode (or of its feudal variation) (50-2).

For this is what is needed. The argument in favor of variety and particularity rests on the confusion between mode of production and social formation and the subsequent rejection of the abstract character of the concept of the mode of production. And yet this is what Marx taught us (reduction to two classes defined as two poles of a contradiction, absence of noncapitalist property, especially of land, etc.). No capitalist formation, however advanced and complete, can be reduced to this mode. The existence of landed property and of a third class of landed proprietors having a third kind of income (rent) proves this point. Exchange in tributary formations is subject to the fundmental law of the tributary mode just as land ownership is subject to the fundmental law of the capitalist mode in capitalist formations.

6. The third characteristic of the tributary mode is thus the dominance of the superstructure. Although there is general agreement on this point, a few comments are in order.

Tribute can never be extracted solely by means of violence: some social consensus is necessary. This is what Marx meant when he said that "the ideology of the dominant class is the dominant ideology of society." In the tributary mode this ideology takes the form of great religions: Christianity, Islam, Hinduism, Buddhism, Confucianism, and so forth. It is worth recalling that this domination aids in the extraction of the surplus, while the ideology of kinship in the communal mode, where ideology is also dominant, aids in the reproduction of relations of cooperation and domination but not of exploitation. Furthermore, local religions correspond to the communal modes and the dominance of kinship, in contrast to the state religions of the tributary mode. This is why it is not anthropology but the history of great precapitalist societies which has the most to teach us about the dominance of the superstructure. For in the communal mode there is no class struggle (except an embryonic one), while in the tributary mode the class struggle takes center stage. In addition, the fact that this struggle is connected in the precapitalist peripheral formations of our own time with the struggle for socialism explains the deep reasons for the contribution of Maoism.

In fact, the dominance of the superstructure is the first consequence of the dominance of use value in the economic base. The functioning of this dominance of class ideology has an impact on the class struggle in the tributary mode. The exploited class does not generally struggle for the total elimination of exploitation but only for its maintenance within the "reasonable" limits necessary for the reproduction of economic life at a level of development of the productive forces where the surplus product is collectively used. The theme of the emperor who can lose a heavenly mandate if exploitation exceeds these limits supports this. In the West, an alliance of the absolute monarchy against the feudal lords and in favor of the peasants had the same import.

Of course, this characterization of the class struggle in the tributary mode excludes neither class struggle nor steps toward the total abolition of exploitation: we find peasant communism every-where, in Europe, the Arab world, and in China, as P.-P. Rey (10-6) and Jean Chesneaux (31-6) have pointed out. Generally, the class struggle in these circumstances took the form of challenging ideology on its own grounds: the Christianity of the state churches was challenged by Albigensian and Protestant heresies; Sunnite Islam was challenged by Shiism and Qarmat communism; and Confucianism was challenged by Taoism.

7. The fourth characteristic of the tributary mode is its appear-ance of stability and even of stagnation, the second consequence of the dominance of use value. This is a characteristic common to all tributary formations, including European feudalism, and not unique to the mythical "Asia" of Montesquieu, Bernier, and the anthropologists who want to revive the asiatic mode. This charac-teristic, which is highly relative, is a false appearance deriving from the contrast with capitalism. Based on exchange value, the basic internal law of capitalism functions on the level of the economic base: competition among capitalists necessitates accumulation, that is, a permanent revolution in the productive forces. This is an additional reason why I hesitate to equate the capitalist mode with the statist mode (a possible development), characterized by the centralization of capital and control over it. The tributary mode, based on use value, has no similar internal exigency on the level of its economic base.

And yet tributary societies are not stagnant. The very idea of nonmovement is foreign to Marxism. In fact, all tributary societies, whether in Egypt, China, Japan, India and South Asia, the Arabian and Persian East, North Africa and the Sudan, or Mediterranean or feudal Europe, have made great progress in the development of their productive forces. But progress does not imply qualitative change in the tributary relations of production. In the same way the United States of 1970 and England in 1780 represent two extreme moments in the development of the productive forces on the basis of the same capitalist relations. New relations of production grow up to overcome the block imposed by the resistance of old relations and, in their turn, bring about further development of the potential inherent in the new relations. However, the dynamic underlying the mechanism of development of the productive forces in the tributary mode lies in an area that simultaneously involves the base and the superstructure (which here is dominant).

8. How then is the class struggle carried out in the tributary mode and how does it necessarily lead to capitalism? The class struggle between peasant producers and their tributary exploiters spans the entire history of tributary formations, in Asia and Africa as well as in Europe. There is, however, an essential difference between this struggle and the struggle between proletarians and bourgeois under capitalism. The second can end in the victory of the proletariat and the establishment of a classless society. The first cannot end in a peasant victory. Each victory won by the peasants in these circumstances weakens the exploiting tributary class in favor of a third, nascent class, the bourgeoisie, and thus opens the way to capitalism.

This bourgeoisie grows up partly alongside the peasantry, on the basis of commerce and merchant capital, and partly within the peasantry which when even partially liberated becomes internally differentiated along the lines described below. This difference, which prevents us from schematizing and mechanically transposing the functions and perspectives of the class struggle from the capitalist to the tributary mode, is closely related to economic vs. ideological dominance.

Nonetheless, the class struggle in the tributary mode is also the motive force of history because it is the contradiction that leads to the transcendence of this mode in accord with the objective necessities of the development of the productive forces. Along these same lines, we should examine the class struggle under capitalism to see if it can lead to the displacing of capitalism by a statist mode which would bring about the new development of the productive forces and also operate to the benefit of a "new class."

Thus it is also class struggle which accounts for the changing character of the tributary mode and which impels the development of the productive forces within it. The search by the tributary class for a greater surplus is certainly not an inherent economic law analogous to the pursuit of capitalist profit. But it is the search for increased tribute—or even for the maintenance of tribute—which compels the tributary class, under the impetus of the peasant struggle, to improve production methods. For this reason I have tried to refute, since 1957, the then current thesis of external technical progress in precapitalist formations by analyzing the dynamic of rent in peripheral capitalism.

Finally, class struggle within the tributary mode explains, at least in part, the external policy of the tributary class. This class seeks to compensate for what it loses inside the society it exploits by an expansionist policy aimed at subjugating other peoples and replacing their exploiting classes. This is the motivation behind all tributary wars, including feudal wars. At times the tributary class has even been able to mobilize the people for this type of venture. This may be compared with the dependence of external policy on internal class struggle under capitalism, even though the capitalist law of accumulation is of a different type. And it can also be compared with the alliance of the bourgeoisie and the proletariat of an externally oriented country under imperialism, following the prediction of Marx and Engels for England and the plan of action drawn up by Cecil Rhodes.

9. These characteristics are common to all precapitalist class formations. They are sufficiently defining to merit a common designation, for which I propose the concept of tributary. The particular features—those of feudalism, among others—follow on the recognition of these common characteristics. But in order to approach the question of the particular features of different tributary formations correctly, it is necessary first to elucidate a series of theoretical questions concerning the relations of exchange and of circulation.

10. In the concrete, there is virtually no such thing as autonomous, "simple petty commodity production." The conceptual definition of this mode, which involves no exploiting class but only small, specialized producers owning their means of production and exchanging their products (in their entirety, in principle) according to the law of value, indicates its particular epistemological status relative to other modes.

Marx pointed to the conditions necessary for exchange to take place according to the law of value: exchange must be not occasional but systematic, not monopolistic but competitive, not marginal but of sufficient quantity to permit adjustments in supply and demand. These conditions do not usually obtain in the societies studied by anthropology (10-4). In 1957 I made a similar statement about tributary formations, which are characterized by the absence of a generalized market in the means of production (land and labor power) and by the importance of self-subsistence. From this I concluded that in these formations exchange generally operates—and paradoxically, to all appearances—in accordance with neoclassical value theory (comparative advantage) rather than with the law of value which applies to a different form, to capitalism. This reflects the dominance of use values in precapitalist modes.

There is much confusion and ambiguity in the controversy about whether exchange in precapitalist societies has a "dissolving" effect. Perhaps this is because of the too frequent failure to recognize that exchange, which involves only a fraction of the surplus, is dominated by the law of the tributary mode. Under these circumstances, historical discussions about the relative and comparative importance of exchange flows, market organization, urban agglomeration, and so forth are not pointless but do not address the essential questions. The fact that no tributary economy has ever been "natural" proves nothing in favor of or against the notion of the dissolving power of commodity relations.

I do not underestimate the importance of commodity relations. I have stressed their role in Arab formations and shown that they had in their turn a decisive impact on the tributary mode by assuring its expansion: for instance, in Iraq during the great Abbasid epoch. And I have gone so far as to account for certain civilizations by the importance of these relations. The existence of these relations makes it necessary to examine the dynamic of relations between tributary societies. As a parallel, we would similarly be unable to examine central and peripheral capitalist formations in isolation from each other. Here we need to analyze the dialectical relations between internal and external forces in the dynamic of tributary socities and particularly in the transitions to capitalism.

Paul Sweezy notes, for instance, that the disintegration of feudal relations in Europe (the reasons for which will be examined below) ushered in a transitional period of precapitalist commodity production governed by the law of value, before the expansion of capitalism (50-2). He shows that this disintegration was produced by the transformation of payment in kind into monetary payment under the combined impact of the internal class struggle and the effects of large-scale commerce.

In 1957 I noted the even more striking case of New England, model *par excellence* of the precapitalist commodity mode. This is incomprehensible as an isolated case but completely understandable when its functions in the world system of the time are considered. Ignoring this aspect of reality is always a mistake. In the change from feudalism to central capitalism in Japan can we eliminate external forces and their interaction with internal forces? Is this interaction not decisive for the establishment of peripheral capitalism? And even more generally, beyond strict economic interactions, should we ignore those which operate on the super-structural level? Can we explain the particular forms of feudalism in Eastern Europe ("second serfdom") without invoking both commercial relations with the West and the transfer of political and ideological structures: the borrowing, for instance, of the form of absolute monarchy from the West? As to the periphery of the capitalist system, can we exclude from our analysis ideological and cultural domination, borrowing in the areas of models of consumption, and technical and political organization?

11. Another problem which it is probably useful to examine before discussing the particular features of feudalism is the question of slavery. In my view the Greco-Roman exception is the source of a series of major confusions. I have already commented on the methodological questions raised by works that look for slavery on all continents and in all centuries, and in the doubtful nature of the supposed "slave mode of production."

My first observation is that the publication of the *Grundrisse* led to an explosion of Marxology, which grew increasingly distant from Marxism as erudition took on the subject. Tökei's exegesis, carried further by his students, always comes down to the same thing (30-2). With the emergence from the primitive community, two paths were open. The first was that taken by Asia: communities continued to exist and a despotic state superimposed itself on them. The communities remained the owners of the land, over which the producers, organized in families, had only a tenuous hold. This path was a dead end which blocked the development of the productive forces and reduced the history of Asia to an unchanging repetition of one superficial scenario.

The other path entailed the dissolution of the community and the assertion of individual private property in land. First, it engendered an initial, radical class division, fostering the reduction to slavery of those who had lost their agrarian property. From this came the Greek miracle, followed by its extension to the Roman empire. Then came the transformation of slavery into serfdom and the unique composition of feudalism. Seigneurial property, always private, fostered the development of the contradictions (autonomy of the cities, struggle of the peasants for peasant private property, etc.) which engendered capitalism. This is the path of constant change, of incessant progress. This was Europe's path, which originated in Greek antiquity. In this unique path, slavery had a decisive role from the outset.

This theory is false from beginning to end and is based on nothing other than nineteenth-century Europe's almost total lack of information about and strong prejudices with regard to a mythical "Asia." There has been no communal, collective ownership of the land in Egypt (for the past five thousand years at least) nor in China (at least since the Han), nor probably in India (with some qualifications). These societies have long had private property in land in the same way as had feudal Europe. They have never had slavery on a large scale and rarely serfdom in the European sense. Were the majority of caliphs and of Chinese emperors any more despotic than the absolute monarchs of Spain, France, or England? And everybody knows today that the development of the productive forces in Asia was on the same level as and at least as rapid as that which took place in the West over the centuries from Homer to the Industrial Revolution.

And so? The theory reflects a West-centered teleology, inspired *a posteriori* by the capitalist development of Europe, which implies that no other society could develop capitalism on its own. If all this were true, we would have to conclude that the laws of historical materialism apply only to the West, that Western history is the incarnation of reason. This so-called Marxism is similar to the cultural nationalism of ideologues in the contemporary third world who reject Marxism because "it does not apply to our particular societies." At one end, West-centeredness produced by imperialist ideology and posing as Marxism; at the other end, cultural nationalism: these are true twin brothers.

12. The only interest this Marxology holds is as a curiosity of West-centeredness. Suffice it to say that slavery was exceptional because of the small number of societies it affected. Moreover, it

coexisted with very different levels of development of the productive forces: from the city of Athens and from Roman Sicily to Lower Iraq under the Abbasids, to the plantations of America and, for all intents and purposes, to the mines of South Africa. Can relations of production be totally independent of the productive forces, as this suggests?

On the contrary, slavery always yields a commodity (a marketable product): in Classical antiquity, in Lower Iraq, in America. But commodity production was the exception in the precapitalist world. Thus the areas where slavery prevailed cannot be understood by themselves: they were only dependent parts of a much greater whole. Athenian slavery can be understood only by considering the Greek cities as part of the whole area with which they traded. For their specialization extended to an area which included the Orient—where slavery did not penetrate. In the Roman west slavery was limited to the coastal zones, the product of which could be commercialized. In Gaul and Spain the cost of transport stopped its extension, proof that slavery is linked with commerce. And America had no existence of its own; it was the periphery of mercantilist Europe.

Yet another characteristic makes slavery a necessarily exceptional mode: it barely reproduces the labor force. It thus almost always entails—and that quite early on—external raiding and dies when the source dries up. This is illustrated by the examples, farflung in time and place, of Roman raids among the barbarians and European raids in Africa. Of course, we must not confuse this kind of slavery with other forms which go by the same name. In reality the latter are a different phenomenon, and involve the reduction of the status of persons within diverse types of societies: for example, communal (without exploitation), or tributary (where the so-called slaves are domestics and state servants).

13. The feudal mode has all the characteristics of the general tributary mode as set out above. But it has the following additional characteristics outlined by Sweezy: (1) the organization of production within the framework of the domain, involving payment in

labor; and (2) the exercise by the lord of political and jurisdictional prerogatives, which implies political decentralization. At least this was the case in the beginning (50-2). These characteristics are a precise reflection of the origin of the feudal formation in the barbarian invasions, invasions by peoples still in the stage of class formation as they were taking over a more advanced society. Thus the feudal mode is simply a primitive, incomplete tributary mode.

Feudalism did not grow out of slavery. The temporal succession is here perhaps an illusion. It reproduced the general law for the transition of a society without classes to a class society: after the communal stage comes the tributary stage (without the passage through slavery). The history of the West is no different from that of the East in this regard. And myths about asiatic communal property and so on can quite as easily and incorrectly be applied to the West. In addition, Japanese feudalism also left the communal stage without going through slavery.

It is a well-known fact that the barbarians were at the communal stage. Are the variations among these communities—Slavic, German, or Indian—of a different sort than the innumerable other variations discovered since then: Inca, Aztec, Mayan, Malagasy, pre-Islamic Arabian, plus a good thousand African varieties? Is it also an accident that, passing from this stage to the tributary stage, the Germans abandoned their local religions to adopt an imperial religion, Christianity? Is it an accident that the same thing happened in Africa with Islamization?

Feudal property is not radically different from tributary property. Rather, it is a primitive form of tributary property, a form resulting from the weak and decentralized character of political power. To contrast "eminent state ownership of the land" in Asia with seigneurial private property is to mix truth and falsehood. For the eminent ownership of the state functioned on the superstructural level—to justify taxes—but not on that of the technical organization of production. In European feudalism, eminent ownership by the Christian God functioned in the same way (the land must be worked, the peasants have a right to use it), in a weaker version corresponding to the rudimentary character of the state. Thus, with the development of the productive forces original political decentralization gave way to centralization. And the absolute European monarchies became very similar to complete tributary forms.

Those who espouse the asiatic mode of production try to reconcile things which are irreconcilable: the primitive character of the asiatic mode (chronologically the first, corresponding to the transition to classes) and the development of the productive forces in Asia, which development has finally been acknowledged. Thus they hypothesize an evolution from the tributary to the feudal mode (despite the survival of the state!). I believe exactly the opposite occurred: the primitive feudal mode evolved toward the tributary mode; the tributary mode is not the exception but the general rule and the feudal mode is a particular and exceptional variant of the tributary set.

Some think they can save the theory of the "Western miracle" (and of its counterpart, Asiatic desolation) by inventing a Chinese feudalism, assumed to have followed the asiatic mode. Would this Chinese feudalism be different from (and inferior to) Western feudalism because it followed not slavery but the asiatic mode, in conformity with Tökei's schemas? But Western feudalism came out of the barbarian invasions and the Germans also went from the community to protofedualism, then to feudalism, without going through the intermediary stage of slavery. Godelier then tries the ultimate explanation: oriental feudalism did not engender capitalism because it was not "accompanied by a great development of commodity production and of money" (due to the tenaciousness of "peasant communities") (10-14). But the survival of these communities exists only in the minds of those who talk about it. As to the development of a market, facts support the contrary position, that it was much more advanced in the East (Arab, Indian, and Chinese, among others) than in the feudal West. The reason for the early appearance of capitalism in the West lies elsewhere: by the time European feudalism attained the tributary stage under an absolute monarchy, it was too late.

Precisely because of its poor origins, European society traversed the tributary period more quickly. This is the thesis of unequal development: European society was more flexible because it was peripheral. It thus resolved its contradictions more quickly. These were the same as in other tributary societies and had necessarily to be resolved in the same way: by capitalism. But elsewhere these contradictions were better controlled and therefore developed less quickly. This is the general framework in which to place the history of the transition to capitalism.

Before analyzing this transition, it is useful to review these controversies about the uniqueness of feudalism and the asiatic mode. Those who deny that the primitive and undeveloped character of European feudalism was responsible for its more rapid transition to capitalism do so for ideological reasons. Refusing to accept the thesis of unequal development, they are forced to construct an alternative: hence the asiatic mode. But the notion is not based on reality. What is the difference between peasant communities in the Orient and the West? We know that the Western serf, like the Eastern peasant, had the right to use the land, that during the feudal period he could not be ejected by his lord. Although according to Tökei it was only in the asiatic mode that the individual needed to go through the community in order to get land, in fact this was also true of feudalism. As to eminent ownership by the Eastern state, the feudal lord also had this. And under absolute monarchy, when the king became the lord of all lords, his eminent property was very similar to that of the pharoah of Egypt or the emperor of China.

But, if Tökei's schemas are without scientific value, I agree with Chesneaux that they have a clear ideological import (30-4). Godelier expresses this when he claims to have proven that "European feudalism was the only one to have made capitalism possible." Not the only one: just the first one.

14. The history of the transition to capitalism underscores the practical importance of the primitive, peripheral character of original feudalism. The first series of controversial questions concerns

the feudal cities, their importance, and their autonomy. There is no doubt that the cities, like the countryside, were less controlled by the central power. But arguments must go beyond immediate appearances, which are contradictory to begin with. Max Weber has been accused of exaggerating the autonomy of European cities and Rodney Hilton correctly observes that the most important city of the West, Paris, was tightly controlled by the monarch (50-2). John Merrington observes that cities became "refeudalized" when their bourgeoisies invested in landed property as in Italy, or allied with the feudal lords against the peasant revolts, as in France in the seventeenth century (50-2). He adds that the new capitalism rose outside the cities and to escape the guilds put its factories in the countryside, in Manchester and Birmingham. It was only very late, in the nineteenth century, that triumphant capitalism "ruralized" the countryside by destroying its craft production and limiting it to farm production alone.

Furthermore, the urban phenomenon is older than European feudalism. Classical antiquity was urban *par excellence*. Were its cities autonomous? Less than it seems: on the one hand, they were cities of landed proprietors and on the other, as they grew under the direct and indirect effects of large-scale commerce (onto which slave craft production was grafted) their domination over the distinct and foreign rural areas which they indirectly exploited remained precarious because it only operated through commercial flows and uncertain alliances.

Arab cities were in a generally analogous situation. As to Chinese cities, which were very important, they were contained within a complete and very advanced tributary mode and reflected the complexity of its rich, secondary distributions of the surplus (flourishing crafts and manufactures). But like the Arab cities, Chinese cities were under the effective supervision of the central tributary power. This was the case throughout Chinese history. In the Arab world, when the tributary power weakened, the cities proliferated. By contrast, Japanese cities were important and autonomous for the same reason as in the West, namely, the weakness of the central feudal power. But they proliferated because the lack of external expansion, from which European cities benefited, obliged the Japanese merchant class to look toward the countryside and to invest in land purchase and usury.

Thus we can see the common thread running through this multiplicity of forms. The exceptional, accelerating role of feudal cities whether old (dominated by guilds strong in relation to the central power) or new (having neither guilds nor central power) stemmed from the weakness of the central power. When this latter asserted itself with the absolute monarchies, feudal relations already had more than begun to disintegrate even in the countryside.

15. The early disintegration of feudal relations in the countryside was due also to the fragmentation of feudal power. This fragmentation allowed the class struggle rapidly to transcend the manorial economy, to impose petty exploitation through payment in kind and then in money. This transformation lightened the weight of tribute, accelerated peasant accumulation, and initiated differentiation within the peasantry. By the time the feudal class reacted, via the absolute monarchy they constructed to stop the liberation of the peasantry, it was too late (40-1). Serfdom had disappeared, the peasantry was differentiated, and the market had begun to grow.

The dialectic of the two paths of capitalist progression rests on this essential foundation. At one end was the establishment of manufactures and the putting out system, organized by merchant capital grafted onto long-distance trade. At the other end was the establishment of small industrial enterprises based on the kulak peasantry. Between these two paths have been contradictions, doubtless secondary but nonetheless important, particularly when the big bourgeoisie won over the feudal monarchy, obtained protections in exchange, and profited from these to fight against competition from the dispersed bourgeoisie of the towns and countryside.

16. It is not my intention to go into more detail about the transition, which took a great variety of concrete forms. There are no general laws of transition, only concrete, specific conjunctions

of all the contradictions of the mode which is beginning to disappear and their interaction with external forces. The same is equally true for the socialist transition.

This is why "causes" may seem here to be "effect." As Anderson has emphasized, Italy suffered from the too early appearance of embryonic capitalist relations, Spain from its too early and disproportionate domination over America. In the West (France and England), the absolutist feudal state was established to compensate for the end of serfdom and was strengthened by advanced urbanization. In the East, absolutism found an urban void and was the means of establishing a serfdom required by the low level of the productive forces and by unoccupied land (40-1). Andre Gunder Frank (50-10), Oliver Cox (50-11), and Immanuel Wallerstein (50-4) complement more than they contradict this analysis based on the formation of absolutism with their own based on the formation of the world system and the dialectic of center-periphery relations. Finally, the study of the Japanese case is always instructive, first because the genesis of feudalism was different there and also because Japan did not benefit from a periphery as did mercantilist Europe.

Generally, all transitions are very instructive; this includes belated transitions, that is, those which have led today to dependent, peripheral capitalism. Subsequent history often depends on the form taken by this essential transition to capitalism. I agree with Anderson that in the West the absolute monarchy was toppled by the bourgeois revolution, that in central Europe the monarchy carried out this revolution from the top down, that in the East— already a semiperipheral situation—the monarchy was ousted by the proletarian revolution. I should add that from this time on this is the only possible path for the periphery: a "bourgeois revolution" is no longer possible. Thus we see the second manifestation of unequal development operating within the transition to socialism.

17. If feudalism had its particular features, so did each one of the other great tributary civilizations. I have discussed the particularities of Arab civilization in my recent book *The Arab Nation*

(76b-6) and elsewhere those of the Ottoman Empire, in which the Balkan area yields striking parallels (76b-7).

Controversies about so-called asiatic societies, when they have gotten beyond Marxology to a Marxist analysis of reality, have contributed precious data of the dynamics of change through the comparative study of China, India, Africa, Malagasy, South Asia, and other areas. For there is no doubt that a Marxist must try to identify the forces and mechanisms that govern the movement of each of these cases, a movement which is irresistible. Those who try to identify in these areas so-called mechanisms of immutability are not doing scientific work. They are doing idealist and West-centered ideological work, like the bourgeois economists who analyze the "immutable" laws of "pure economy."

Every tributary society looks different. But all of them can be analyzed by using the concepts of tributary mode of production and the class opposition between tributary exploiters and exploited (peasant) producers. The Indian caste system is a case in point. This false concept is a passive reflection of Hindu ideology (which here functions precisely in the same way as state ideology exercises its absolutist dominance, like Confucianism in China, for instance) and masks social reality: this can be seen in tributary appropriation of the land by the exploiters (Kshatriya warriors and the sacred Brahmin class), the exploitation of the Sudra, the redistribution of tribute among the clients of exploiting classes (the jajmani system). The remarkable work of Louis Dumont and Meillassoux' subtle and pertinent critique of it (31-9) show that Indian castes had scarcely any existence except ideologically. In reality, what was at work was a system of tributary exploitation (here Meillassoux sometimes uses the word "seignorial," so strong is the analogy with feudalism; at others he uses the more debatable term "slavery").

The Chinese gentry type of exploitation and the Confucian ideology which accompanied it certainly had their particularities. But on the basic level of the class struggle between exploiters and exploited and the dynamic between them, the analogy is very great. The analogy is also very close with the Muslim Arab and Ottoman East, to the point where the interrelation between basic tributary relations and market relations functioned there in the same way: formation of merchant-usurer classes and private appropriation of the land, for example.

Bourgeois historiography about precapitalist societies has little to offer in the way of analysis. We have only to look at how the arbitrary definition of feudalism given by the authors of *Feudalism in History* (50-18) (feudalism is a method of government, not an economic system) allows them to skip from the Hittites to Sumer, from Shang and Chou China to the Parthians, from the Rajputs to Byzantium, and so on, thanks to a method which consists of looking for certain facts regardless of context. And yet in this abundant literature we can find much useful material if we are willing to rearrange it.

18. If slavery is recognized as exceptional and the communal modes are relegated to the distant past, only four formulations about the great class societies remain: (1) the "two ways" (European feudalism and the asiatic mode), (2) generalized feudalism, (3) the generalized tributary mode, and (4) the particularity of each society. The fourth position simply evades the theoretical problem and the first is false. The old formulation of generalized feudalism is not fundamentally wrong. In fact, my formulation of the tributary mode is nothing more than an improvement on it. But it emphasizes the incomplete character of the feudal variant of the tributary set. Its incomplete, peripheral character is due to the effects of the barbarian invasions and seems to explain better than any other theory the early development of capitalism in the West.

I have learned from an article published in *La Pensée* (no. 122, 1965) that the Japanese Marxist Jiro Hoyakawa proposed the term "tributary mode of production" in 1934. I do not know the exact content of the Japanese controversy, except through several brief book reviews published in Western languages. In the 1950s I began to make a distinction between "feudalism in its general form" and in its "European type" and I substituted "tributary" and "feudal" for these unwieldy expressions for the first time in 1957. In another issue of *La Pensée* (no. 132, 1967) I learned that the Rumanian Ion Banu also uses the term "tributary." But he and I use this word in very different ways. For me, the tributary mode is the general form of precapitalist class society, of which feudalism is a particular type. Banu discusses the ideology of oriental philosophers from a perspective which seems to me close to that of the European revisionists who believe in the asiatic mode (Tökei, Godelier, etc.), that is, who are above all concerned to stem the Maoist tide.

I have attributed the incomplete character of the feudal mode to the lack of centralization of the surplus and to the fragmentation of power. Based on this, I stated that the European feudal mode evolved toward the tributary mode, with the establishment of absolute monarchies. This general direction did not preclude effective regressions, which took place here and there, from advanced tributary modes back toward feudal fragmentation. The centralization of the surplus implies both the real preeminence of the central power and a relatively advanced mercantilization of this surplus. Circumstances have made one or the other of these recede, and they have often done so in correlation. The feudalization of Arab formations is an example. This occurred, furthermore, in conjunction with the progressive domination of incipient European capitalism over the whole of the mercantilist world system and illustrates my thesis that the potential appearance of Arab capitalism was forestalled by that of Europe. In a certain way, the feudal mode is thus also a decadent tributary mode.

The opposition between the central, complete tributary mode and the incomplete character of the feudal peripheral mode is not on the same level as that between center and periphery in the capitalist system. In tributary formations, ideology is dominant and thus it is on this level that the complete or incomplete character of the mode underlying these formations is to be identified. An example is complete, tributary China: Chinese national unity was expressed in the common use of the written Mandarin language (linked to the state, which centralized the surplus), whereas diverse regional languages continued to be spoken in everyday use, and this linguistic unity went along with Confucian state ideology. This is why I speak of a nation only with regard to complete tributary formations.

Chapter 4

Unequal Development
in the Capitalist Transition
and in the Bourgeois Revolution

1. One can hardly avoid asking whether the road of capitalist development has exhausted its potential in our modern world. To be precise: Can currently underdeveloped countries still catch up to the advanced capitalist countries, still become like them, by following the capitalist road?

A survey of the past, of events and of their interpretation, of what really happened and what was predicted, shows that capitalist development has always been unequal. There have always been some countries and regions that were more advanced and others that were backward. Today's most advanced countries were not always so. Thus we must continue to analyze the concrete forms taken by the unequal development of capitalism in advanced and retarded, peripheral and "peripheralized" countries.

I. The different capitalist roads. The peasant component of the bourgeois revolution. Unequal development at different stages in history.

Marx and Lenin always believed that there were different roads of capitalist development and that these were related to class struggles and to hegemonic class blocs: the French road was different from the Prussian road, for instance. We can list an almost infinite number of roads and have something different to say about them from one day to the next. Is the English road, for example, responsible for the current decadence of Great Britain? Is there a Brazilian road and what are its particular features and perspectives? All cases are equally interesting.

It is usual to make a distinction between the revolutionary and the nonrevolutionary roads of capitalist development. Historical materialism will not permit us to conceive of capitalist development as an economic fact, that is, as an isolated transformation of the relations of production through the evolution of the productive forces, without the active intervention of political transformations.

Doubtless, new capitalist relations of production appear first within the previous system, whether tributary or feudal, and thus initiate the process of capitalist revolution. But, as long as political power remains feudal, they cannot develop fully. At a certain stage, then, power itself must change. This change constitutes the bourgeois revolution, strictly speaking. This is why in every case the development of capitalism is preceded by a change in the class content of the state. The revolution of 1688 in England, that of 1789 in France, German and Italian unification, the abolition of serfdom in Russia in 1861, American independence and/or the Civil War, the Meiji revolution in Japan, the fall of the Manchus in China, the Mexican revolution, the revolution of Ataturk, that of Nasserism, and many others represent qualitative breaks. Before them, power was precapitalist (feudal, for instance); after them, it was capitalist. But are all of these really revolutions? Marxists believe that 1688 in England and 1789–1793 in France were revolutions, while the abolition of Russian serfdom and the Meiji and Nasserian coups d'état were not.

If we want our words to have precise meanings which do not vary with the context and if we want to incorporate the Marxist-Leninist discovery about the conditions of revolutionary change necessary to the abolition of capitalism, we must define the "bourgeois revolution" as the abolition of the old state and the creation of a new one. In contrast to the adaptation of the old state for new purposes, its abolition involves not only violence (that is, in fact, the destruction of its legitimacy by means external to its own legal framework) but probably also the mobilization of massive (and therefore popular) and powerful social forces.

In this respect, it is obvious that the revolution in France, 1789–1793, was violent and popular, but so was the Mexican revolution, for instance. On the other hand, 1688 in England was scarcely more so than the Meiji revolution. The process of German and Italian unification, like the civil and foreign wars of Ataturk, was certainly violent and in a sense radical. But were these popular movements? And how much less so than in France?

2. In reference to the capitalist content of the era ushered in by these revolutions, we can define its popular content by its peasant component. A bourgeois revolution thus would be one which culminates in a violent class struggle between peasants and feudal elements in the countryside. The peasants win this struggle, impose the abolition of feudal rights and the division of land. Thus they impose themselves on the rising urban bourgeoisie, generally pushing the old merchant and financial big bourgeoisie into the counterrevolutionary camp and allying with the new potential bourgeoisie of artisans and petty producers. This opens the peasant road of capitalist development by accelerating differentiation within the peasantry and, ultimately, by creating a rich, exploitative kulak peasantry.

But by this definition there has only been one real bourgeois revolution: the French. The English revolution was scarcely one. The Mexican revolution took a similar form to the French revolution but it did not generate vigorous capitalist development: Mexico remained underdeveloped. Why? Probably because its revolution did not take place in the same period of global history, as we shall see.

The American road also diverged from the above pattern. From the beginning, it had a colonizing peasantry free from any feudal restrictions. This was true in the North of North America (British nonslave colonies), in Australia, and in New Zealand. To develop on this foundation, capitalism did not need an antifeudal revolution.

The above considerations finally lead to a question too often ignored: Is it correct to speak of a bourgeois revolution? Should we not restrict the term "revolution" to cases where the exploited classes challenge the global order, rather than use it to designate struggles between exploiting classes as well? If so, we can speak of a peasant but not of a bourgeois revolution. When a peasant revolution takes place, it opens the way to capitalist development; but it is not the only road this development can take. For capitalism had already developed within feudalism. Similarly, feudalism had developed within the slave system of the ancient world. Slave revolts and revolutions accelerated its development, but we cannot speak of a "feudal revolution." Is the expression "bourgeois revolution" not an invention of bourgeois ideology?

The transition to capitalism does not necessarily involve a revolution because it is a transition from one class society to another. This is why we cannot apply the lessons of this transition to the socialist transition. The abolition of classes involved in socialism presupposes a revolution carried out by the exploited. However, if such a revolution does not take place, the contradiction between the productive forces and the relations of production continues to operate within capitalism—and ultimately engenders, by evolution and not revolution, the transition to another class mode, the statist mode, which is discussed below. Reformist theory confuses this evolution, which cannot abolish classes but which can substitute new for old ones, with the abolition of classes, or socialism. At the limits, the revolution of the exploited may fail and engender this evolution toward the statist mode.

3. Thus the model of a bourgeois revolution is for all intents and purposes limited to France. From this a question arises: Will the revolutionary (exceptional) or nonrevolutionary (general) character of the capitalist road have differential effects on the subsequent class struggle, the one which becomes determinant in capitalist development, that is, the struggle of the proletariat against the bourgeoisie?

Three aspects of this question need to be considered. The first concerns the development of Marxism. Yes, it seems as if the revolutionary character of the transition to capitalism in France did affect later class struggles: Babeuf and Buonarrotti were not French by accident. And French socialism was one source of Marxism. But it was not the only one. The lack of revolutionary maturity in Germany accounts for German philosophy (Hegel in particular) and the character of English capitalist economic development, wherein ideology and politics played a minor role, accounts for Ricardo.

The second aspect of the question concerns the pace of subsequent capitalist development. This is a very controversial question. One view, based on the pace of capitalist development in France compared to that in England and Germany, holds that the French peasant road was an impediment to accumulation. According to this view, the bourgeois revolution should not be a peasant revolution and becomes one only rarely, due to a particular conjunction of class struggles and alliances. But this view has not always been accepted. Another view has it that the peasant road adjusted the relations of production to the needs of the development of the productive forces in the most radical and therefore the most appropriate way, giving them their maximum potential for later development.

The third aspect of the question concerns the class struggle in today's imperialist era. There is no question of adopting a historical determinism which goes back so far into the past as to negate the importance of the impact of more recent circumstances on the class struggle. These new circumstances, those involving social-democratic ideological hegemony in relation to imperialism, for instance, have an infinitely more decisive impact.

4. Today, as in the past, capitalist development remains unequal and follows different roads. On the world scale we can distinguish at least between the central road of the imperialist centers and the road of peripheral, dependent capitalism in the countries dominated by imperialism and therefore underdeveloped. The question remains as to whether the latter are in a stage or in a permanent condition.

The analysis of unequal development can be enhanced by the method of comparative history. But it is important not to lose sight of the period in which particular developments take place. Thus, unequal developments in the beginning of capitalism (from the thirteenth to the sixteenth centuries in Europe), in the mercantilist era (1660–1800), in the preimperialist period of industrial capitalism (1800–1880), and in the imperialist period (since 1880) have neither the same meaning nor the same perspective.

II. Unequal development in the ancient and feudal world

5. Feudal Europe was not a homogeneous entity. Its regional social formations were of qualitatively different kinds and played different, unequal roles in their interrelationship. For these formations interacted and constituted a true whole, which because of its dominant feudal nature we are justified in calling global.

I characterized the feudal mode as a peripheral, tributary mode, meaning that in contrast to other, more advanced tributary societies the feudal European mode was an early, incomplete, and complex variant. The proximity of the more or less primitive barbarian community (Iberians, Celts, Germans, Slavs) explains its incomplete character: the absence of state centralization and redistribution of the tributary surplus, its "feudal fragmentation." We can see its particular character clearly if we compare it to a pharaonic Egypt or imperial China. In the complete tributary mode (1) the fief was administrative and (2) the state generally coincided with a unified national formation.

The complexity of the European situation is certainly due in part to the fact that Christian feudalism arose from the disintegration of the Roman Empire. The imperial formations, first Hellenistic and then Roman, constituted in that part of the world the first tributary imperial constructs. In the ancient East, the transition from the primitive community to the tributary mode, the general form of advanced precapitalist class society, occurred very early. Having achieved its complete form in Egypt and Mesopotamia, the tributary mode progressively developed in rougher forms elsewhere, among the Hittites, the Medians, the Persians. But the region remained divided into relatively small states, separated by still primitive zones. The attempts at empire building (of Egypt, Assyria, and Babylonia in Persia) were too superficial to make of the Orient a single, national unit like China. In the interstices of this unequally developed and divided Orient, commercial societies had found a place: Phoenicia, then Greece. Slavery had spread in these societies along with the development of the market. The empire of Alexander, the successor Hellenistic states, then the Roman Empire repeated the imperial pattern without substantially advancing it. These empires remained heterogeneous in ethnic terms and tributary centralization remained unequal. Within them coexisted diverse modes of production, from the primitive community to the complete tributary mode, with some commodity exchange. Along with this slave enclaves developed.

In its turn the Roman Empire might have evolved into a complete tributary form and have gradually become more homogeneous. At any rate, it fell before doing so. Three entities grew up on the ruins of Rome: the Christian West, Byzantium, and the Arab-Islamic state. These latter two groups probably went further than the Roman Empire toward constructing the tributary mode, although they did not become complete. This progress was visible on the level of national unification, which has left its traces in our own day, at least in the Arab area (cf. 76b-6. 76b-7).

On the other hand, the West remained marked by the primitive societies of barbarian Europe. This is precisely the reason why feudal Western Christianity offered the most favorable conditions for the transcendence of the tributary mode and the rapid growth of the capitalist mode. Unequal development manifested itself in this manner. The long history of the ancient East, of Greek, Hellenistic, and Roman antiquity, of the Western, Byzantine, then Ottoman, and Arab-Islamic successors, is the history of the gradual development of the tributary mode and of its transcendence by capitalism beginning in its least advanced periphery: barbarian, then feudal, Europe.

To suggest that the empires of oriental and Roman antiquity were evolutionary stages in the establishment of a complete tributary formation is to say that the tributary form is superior to the forms of antiquity. It is also to contradict the thesis which places the asiatic mode of production before the slave mode and thereby contradicts the comparative level of the development of the productive forces. It is probably inaccurate to suggest that these attempts at empire might have homogenized the Mediterranean area as had occurred in China. Among other things, this fails to take account of the ethnic diversity of the region. The obstacles were such that imperial attempts to homogenize the area failed.

Nonetheless, striking progress toward homogenization was made extremely quickly in the course of several centuries, or even several decades. In the Asiatic Orient linguistic unification on the basis of Aramaic laid the foundation for subsequent and rapid Arabization. In the West the Romanization of Italy, Gaul, and Iberia testifies to the power of the tendency toward homogenization. It is possible to draw too strong a contrast between the fragmentation of Europe and the Middle East on the one hand as against Chinese homogeneity on the other. The linguistic unification of China was limited to writing, closely related to state unity and tributary centralization, while regional diversity of spoken languages—which still exists—threatened imperial unity during several millenia. In the West the tendency toward homogenization never ceased working: Beyond the variation of history, Arabization and Islamization at one end, and the establishment of absolutist national monarchies following the feudal fragmentation caused by barbarian and other invasions at the other, both illustrate this tendency.

6. The history of Western Christianity should be reexamined in terms of this global framework. The feudal mode, as an incomplete tributary form, dominated the whole of the Christian West. But it did not spread evenly throughout the region. One can distinguish three unequally developed subregions of feudal Europe. The most

developed of these was Italy and the regions that make up the area known today as the Languedoc (Spain was conquered by the Muslims). In this relatively developed region feudal forms did not expand because they came up against a more solid ancient heritage, particularly in the cities which were more important here than elsewhere. The second region, including northern France, England, Holland, western and southern Germany, and Bohemia, was partially developed. Feudal forms grew and capitalism found its most fertile soil in this region. Farther east and in the north (eastern Germany, Scandinavia, Hungary, Poland, and Russia) the original level of development was not as high and the pretributary community was quite close. Feudalism appeared later and took particular forms related on the one hand to the modalities of integration of these regions into Europe (the Hanseatic League, Scandinavia, Prussia, and Poland) and on the other hand to the modalities by which relations of external domination functioned (Turkish occupation of Hungary, Mongol occupation of Russia, Teutonic occupation of the Baltic regions, etc.).

7. Returning to the feudal mode, which dominated the area, three aspects of its history should be emphasized: (1) feudal fragmentation and its meaning in relation to the specific phenomenon of the church, (2) the persistence of market relations, their origin, and their effects, and (3) the ways in which feudal societies expanded.

Feudal fragmentation, unlike the centralization of the complete tributary form, was characterized by a particular set of relations between the economic base (tributary) and the ideological superstructure. In all the modalities of the tributary mode ideology was the dominant instance, in the sense that social reproduction operated directly on this level. However, in the complete tributary mode, this ideology was the ideology of the state, even though it may have taken a religious form. In this case the superstructure was perfectly adapted to the relations of production.

Conversely, in the feudal mode the ideology, which was Catholicism, did not act as a state ideology. Not that anything in Christianity precluded this. Under the Roman Empire, Christianity became a state ideology as it did in Byzantium and in the Russian orthodox world, i.e., precisely in those regions closest to the complete mode. But, in the feudal West, Catholicism was resisted by the fragmentation of the tributary class and by peasant resistance, evidence of the survival of the spirit and ideology of the original communal societies. The independent organization of the church reflected this less perfect adaptation of the superstructure to the relations of production. This created a more flexible and therefore a more favorable climate for subsequent evolutions and adjustments to the exigencies of the transformation in the relations of production. These adjustments took two forms: the modification of the ideological content of religion (Protestantism), and the elevation of religion to the place of state ideology (in the form of Gallicanism or Anglicanism, for example), as royal absolutism gained strength in the period of the mercantilist transition.

8. Since external and internal market relations continued to exist, we cannot conceive of feudal Europe as a subsistence economy composed of a series of fiefs. Long-distance trade with Byzantine and Arab areas, which had been more advanced for a long time, Monsoon Asia, and Black Africa, and the impact of this trade on internal European and local trade gave structure to feudal Europe. The coexistence of predominantly rural zones, which were less urbanized, and zones of commercial and artisanal concentration testifies to this particular structure. Italy, with its artisanal and merchant cities (Venice, Florence, Pisa, Genoa, etc.), and southern Germany and the Hanseatic League have a place in medieval Christianity which can only be understood in terms of these market relations. By reference to the later characteristics of the European mercantilist world economy Wallerstein speaks here of "mini world economies" (50-4). In these regions, particularly Italy, not only were the productive forces more highly developed (manufacturing) but also embryonic capitalist relations appeared sooner. However, it is not these advanced regions that ultimately became the centers of capitalist development but the partially developed regions described above.

9. The expansion of the feudal system took place differently from that of complete tributary empires and led rapidly to the mercantilist transformation of forms of social organization. The complete tributary systems showed a remarkable capacity for geographical expansion without a qualitative transformation of their internal organization. This type of expansion, under appropriate geographical and other conditions, may have continued for centuries: Chinese history provides the best example of this.

In contrast, the homothetic expansion of feudal Europe was brief—a century and a half from 1150 to 1300 (cf. 40-3, 40-4, 40-8, 50-4). This expansion without change, carried out by breaking new land and by colonization, underwent a crisis from 1300 to 1450, propelled by decreasing output from existing technology. This led to a series of technical revolutions in agriculture, facilitated by the flexibility of the relations of production, which also underwent change: serfdom was lightened or abolished, payment in money was substituted for payment in kind or in work, and so on. A second wave of expansion, which already had new characteristics, followed: the search for food products or wood through the colonization of new lands, whether reconquered from the Arabs (Spain and Portugal) or located on the Euro-Asian steppes (the Ukraine and Siberia) or the islands of the Atlantic.

This occurred not only on the initiative of the feudal lords, whose income had diminished due to the effects of the transformation in the relations of production; through a class struggle which was particularly sharp—perhaps due to the proximity of the primitive community—the peasants forced feudal tribute to be lightened. It was at once the initiative of the merchants and monarchs. This expansion initiated the establishment of the economic system of the mercantilist world, which formed the transition to capitalism. And it was precisely in this system that the old advanced regions (Italy and the Hanseatic League) lost their advantage and dominant position to the new centers of northwestern Europe.

III. Unequal development in the mercantilist transition

10. A series of questions arises concerning the nature—feudal, capitalist, or transitional—of the mercantilist system. There are two contending viewpoints. The majority position sees in the three centuries from 1500 to 1800 a transitional period during which the capitalist mode gradually established itself within the feudal system. Based on certain analyses of Marx and Engels, historians who adopt this position believe that the absolute monarchies were able temporarily to constitute themselves as a power above classes by exploiting to their own ends the feudal-bourgeois conflict. The minority tendency, whose best known exponent is Perry Anderson (50-1), holds that the dominant character of the economic and political system remained feudal and that the absolute monarchy was a means by which feudal elements responded to the threat of the rising bourgeoisie.

Of course, the answer to this question is related to the class struggles of the period, the interrelation between them (peasant and bourgeois struggles), and their relation to the development of the productive forces. The debate about the respective roles played by the disintegration of feudal relations of production and by the development of the Atlantic market economy with the birth of capitalism must be placed within this framework. Here also three viewpoints emerge. According to the first the disintegration of feudal relations under the impact of peasant struggles was alone responsible for the birth of capitalism. According to the second the mercantilization of the economy, following from the import of American gold and silver, was decisive. Finally, according to the third these two poles are part of a dialectical unity.

The facts do not speak for themselves with regard to any of these questions. Facts are chosen to serve theoretical hypotheses and are interpreted in the light of them. In addition, the facts are extremely varied. The most serious studies prove only one thing: that class struggles were not the same in France, Italy, or Russia, the development of the productive forces was unequal, and the effects of the Atlantic economy manifested themselves in different ways.

11. Thus we need to develop an overall theory of the mercantilist system. A theory (and not simply a history) of the mercantilist system must answer the central question, i.e., whether the mercantilist period was still feudal, already capitalist, or transitional. If the latter, the theory must make explicit the play of forces which made the growth of capitalism inevitable. But at the same time it must also account for the inequalities and asymmetries that developed during this period, both between Europe and its colonies, dependencies, and overseas partners and within Europe itself.

There is an extensive literature on these questions, which the reader would find useful; notably the volume edited by Rodney Hilton (50-2), the recent work by Perry Anderson (40-1), and the studies of the mercantilist world system by Wallerstein, Cox, Frank, Vilar, and others (50). As long as we deal in general terms with the overall effects of the explosion of Atlantic commerce on European societies, we will not make much theoretical headway, for the reactions to these effects were different in every area.

The first example concerns economic effects in the strictest sense of the term (prices and wages). Of course, everywhere inflation followed the influx of American silver (not because of the sudden rise in the quantity of coin, as Bodin thought, but because of the reduced price of its production, as Marx understood). But the price-wage distortion evolved very differently from one region to the other of Europe, changing the relative profitability of manufacturing activities, the relative real weight of ground rent in money, and the real income of the small commercial peasants and/or the gentlemen farmers.

Both Wallerstein and Pierre Vilar correctly trace the gradual movement of inflation from the West to the East. While in 1500 the price differential between the Mediterranean and Eastern Europe was 6 to 1, by 1750 it was 2 to 1. But Wallerstein notes that the price-wage distortion at times favored and at others discouraged nascent capitalism. In Venice the too rapid rise in wages ate into the profit margin. In France and Spain on the other hand, real wages dropped too much and as a result the market for manufactured goods was insufficient. In England it seems that a sort of optimum condition was created by the stability of wages, which did not return to the 1250 level until six centuries later in 1850.

These distortions brought about an important result: the modification of the international division of labor. Wallerstein remarks that the decisive change which took shape in the seventeenth century was not in technological progress but in the localization of activities. The old manufacturing regions (Italy and Flanders) declined because their prices were too high and because they were unable to overcome French and English protectionism. On the other hand England, up till then an exporter of wheat and wood, became a manufacturer and exporter of manufactured goods.

The second example concerns relations of production. All European societies responded to the call of the market, but in such different ways that it is not correct to say that money everywhere destroyed feudal relations. In some places it did destroy them, but in others it strengthened them. In the West, particularly in England and also in France to a lesser extent, old feudal relations gave way either to a small landed peasantry (although still subject to seigneurial rights, albeit in a lightened form), or to a land tenure system which was less disadvantageous to the tenants. To the east of the Elbe the opposite took place, serfdom was strengthened and the corvée made heavier. In America, although commodity production was much more important than in Europe, slave, quasi slave, or serf relations prevailed in the plantations, the mines, and the encomiendas. This illustrates the point about the correlation between slavery and commodity relations.

The third example concerns political and ideological evolution. The monetarization of the economy and the impact of this on the development of the transformation in the relations of production taken as a whole at times strengthened the state and at other times undermined it. Wallerstein proposes an attractive thesis to deal with this question: in the centers (where the commercial balance was favorable due to their growing capacity to export manufactures) the influx of monetary means facilitated the creation by the monarchy of a bureaucracy which in turn made higher taxes possible. In the periphery, where the situation was reversed, the first transfer of money closed a vicious circle which weakened the state. This much is true. But Poland nonetheless was caught in this vicious circle and disappeared as a result, while Russia was able to avoid it and strengthen its state apparatus. Whatever the case, and even if this somewhat too economistic and mechanistic argument seems unsatisfactory, the other attempts to deal with this question are unacceptable. The Protestant ethic (Weberian idealism) is an illusion, as Wallerstein has stated. If we compare Italy and Poland, Spain and Hungary, we can see that Catholicism, like Protestantism, could be adapted to very different situations. To invoke nationalism to explain the establishment of strong nation-states and regionalism to account for the lack of such states is tautological. We are reduced to narrative history, which does nothing more than explain the immediate flow of events.

The debate about the feudal vs. the capitalist character of the mercantilist period gets us nowhere because the question is incorrectly posed. The real question is: What were the existing classes, how were their struggles and alliances organized, and how did the economic struggles of these classes, as well as their ideological expression and their effect on political power, interface?

There is probably general agreement that the period was a transitional one, wherein feudal and capitalist relations coexisted. There is probably also general agreement that the dominant character of society was feudal in England until the revolutions of the seventeenth century (Cromwell, then 1688), in France until 1789, and in Germany and Italy until nineteenth-century unification. The feudal nature of political power was a sign of this dominance. But it would be formalistic to view bourgeois revolutions as absolute breaks with the past. For the class struggle between feudal and bourgeois elements began before and continued after this break, becoming involved in the organization of power and modifying its content. Cromwell's radical revolution was followed by a restoration, then by a second mild and incomplete "revolution" (I hesitate to use the term) carried further by the peaceful extension of the franchise in 1832. In France, the revolution that culminated in 1793 was followed by a long restoration. The revolution in 1848 was still part bourgeois, part proletarian (but already in 1793 embryonic proletarian demands followed on the heels of the bourgeois revolution, as Daniel Guérin, following Marx, notes [51-3]) and was followed by a second restoration. German and Italian unification were not revolutionary but created the conditions for sweeping social change. Was the abolition of serfdom in Russia in 1861 the bourgeois break? Or was it February 1917? Moreover, history has shown that the socialist revolution is no different: the class struggle continues after it, although it creates a point of no return in the process of social change.

The mere existence of the feudal reaction is insufficient to allow us to characterize Western absolutist power as feudal. At the same time there was the development of a free peasantry, initial differentiation of capitalist classes within this peasantry ("laborers," "*bras nus*," yeomen, and agricultural workers), the expansion of manufacturing, and differentiation within the crafts as they threw off the guild restraints.

12. Thus I propose the following five theses relative to the transition to central capitalism.

(1) Each mode of production is characterized by its own contradictions and thus by its own specific laws of motion. The feudal mode, as one member of the large tributary set, is characterized by the same fundamental contradiction (peasant producers–exploiting tributary class) as all the other types of the tributary mode. But there are no laws of transition. Each transition involves the working out of a historical necessity—the transcendence of the old relations of production so that the latent and mature development of the productive forces may take place on the basis of new relations—through the concrete interrelation of numerous specific contradictions within a social formation (and not a mode of pro-

duction). There are no laws for the transition to central capitalism any more than for the transition to peripheral capitalism or to socialism. There are only concrete situations.

(2) The feudal mode, as an incomplete, primitive, peripheral form of the tributary mode (which existed in complete form elsewhere, including China and Egypt) had a profound inherent tendency toward completion. In this sense, the movement from the feudal fragmentation of the Middle Ages to royal mercantilist absolution is not a chance occurrence. The primitive character of the feudal mode resulted from the combination of the disintegration of the Roman Empire, which was evolving toward a tributary form, and the acceleration of the transformation of the barbarian communal mode. Perry Anderson has made this point beautifully (50-1). The greater flexibility deriving from the incomplete character of the feudal mode made for its more rapid transcendence through the early growth within it of embryonic forms of the capitalist mode.

(3) The class groups present during the mercantilist period were therefore three: the peasants, the feudal lords, and the bourgeois. The tripartite class struggle involved shifting blocs of two against one. The struggle of the peasants against the feudal lords led to differentiation within the peasantry and to the development of petty agrarian capitalism and/or to the adaptation of feudalism to an agrarian capitalism of large proprietors. The struggle of the urban bourgeoisie (merchants) against the feudal lords interacted with the peasant struggle and gave birth to manufacturing, the putting out system, and so forth. The bourgeoisie tended to divide into an upper fraction which tried to compromise (royal protection of manufactures and merchant companies, enoblements and assumption of seigneurial rights, etc.) and a lower fraction which was forced to become radical.

(4) The tendency for feudal fragmentation to evolve toward absolutist power took place on the basis of these struggles. Depending on the relative power of each group (and subgroup) this evolution sped up or stopped, took a certain form and content (support of

a given principal class). Power thus gained a certain autonomy, to which Marx and Engels called attention. It was ambiguous and switched its support from one to the other. If the establishment of centralized states (which some too simply call feudal) did not forestall but rather accelerated the evolution to capitalism it is because class struggles intensified within them.

Here my thesis is that by the time the tributary mode acquired its complete form in Europe (with the absolute monarchies) it was too late: the new class contradictions (agrarian capitalism and manufacturing capitalism) were already too far advanced for the state to arrest their development in any real way. In relation to these combinations, which have particular features in each case, we must analyze: (a) the movement of the international division of labor (between the regions of mercantilist Europe and between certain of them and the overseas peripheries they created) and (b) the content of the great ideological currents (Reformation, Renaissance, Enlightenment) which have to different degrees a big bourgeois, a petty bourgeois (agrarian and/or artisanal), a peasant, and even at times an embryonically proletarian (where the bourgeoisie is born, so is the proletariat) character.

(5) At the end of the period there emerged a world conditioned by the results of a new type of unequal development, different from the results of the unequal development of previous eras (tributary, feudal): the unequal development of the mercantilist period. In 1800 there were capitalist centers on one side and peripheries on the other, the latter for the most part created by the emergence of the former. But among capitalist centers some were complete (England and to a lesser degree France) and others were not; we must trace their subsequent history.

13. With this theoretical apparatus we can now make sense of the different evolutions which took place within mercantilist Europe. Let us return to Wallerstein (50-4), Cox (50-11), and Frank (50-10), who have made an analytical advance on the basis of the center-periphery distinction. By emphasizing the effects of center-periphery relations on the dynamic of the centers, they

have made a decisive contribution to a field previously distorted by Eurocentrism. Unfortunately, Perry Anderson's almost total neglect of the center-periphery problem reduces the significance of his work.

Wallerstein's distinction, based on the introverted or extroverted nature of central and peripheral economic development, beginning in the mercantilist period as a prelude to the subsequent establishment of the complete capitalist system and of contemporary imperialism, has remarkable synthetic power. Of course, the introversion or extroversion results from the combination of class struggle in the different regions of the system during the period.

England is the model *par excellence* of a mercantilist center. Wallerstein observes that this nation was not only commercial but manufacturing and commercial. It tightly controlled its imports in order to strengthen its autocentric development; it was not autarchic but conquering. He remarks that the true religion of this absolutist state was not Protestantism but nationalism, as the existence of Anglicanism indicates.

The French model is analogous (including on the religious and ideological plane: Gallicanism), except for its diverse external attractions (Paris and the north were pulled toward Anvers; the west toward the New World; the Midi toward the Mediterranean). These attractions were the internalization of external struggles: Huguenot and Catholic alliances with foreign powers, England and Spain, which the king finally broke after protracted struggles; the attempt of François I to thwart Charles V in his drive to establish a continental empire; and pointless battles in Italy and Flanders.

At this stage, the other regions of Europe failed to become complete mercantilist centers. The previously more advanced regions (Italy and Flanders) declined. The Italian cities declined not because the establishment of the Ottoman Empire dried up their trade (on the contrary, it brought a new expansion of West-East commerce) but precisely because they were more advanced (we have seen the effects of their advanced character on the prices-wages-profits dynamic). The same applied to Flanders. Holland took the place of these countries. It remained a commercial and maritime power whose prominence hung in the Anglo-Spanish balance: the Dutch kept their place so long as England did not yet control the seas and Spain, fearing English depredations, was less afraid of Holland. This accounts for the short-lived rise of Holland, followed by its stagnation and retreat until its belated industrial awakening, based essentially on colonial pillage.

Spain and Portugal, which were the first to create a periphery, paid for this advance with their subsequent backwardness. They rested content with monopoly profits from the pillage of America and used them to pay for the import of English and French manufactures. Thus they became economically extraverted and dependent. Their parasitical role and underlying poverty became suddenly apparent when they lost control of America. At the same time, they helped to strengthen the introverted and aggressive autonomy of the English and French centers.

Russia reacted to the threat of peripheralization by creating its own periphery in Asia and by strengthening its state. When in the nineteenth century it was integrated into the world system as an exporter of wheat and an importer of manufactured goods, it escaped the fate of semicolonization thanks to the strength of its state, which actively intervened to promote autonomous industrialization of the country. The same was true for Prussia. On the other hand, as a wheat exporter, Poland quickly became peripheralized. Its state grew weak and then disappeared. Sweden, unsuccessful in its initial attempt to use foreign conquest to compensate for the weakness of its agriculture and the strong resistance of its peasant communities to feudalism, just managed to escape Poland's fate. Turned inward, it was integrated into the world system only very belatedly but directly as an advanced, autonomous industrial center.

Thus the division of the capitalist world took place during the mercantilist period. The industrial centers (through the growth of their manufactures and the flourishing of petty rural and craft capitalism) satisfied their own needs (and in that were autocentric) and thus acquired a decisive capacity for external aggression. The peripheries, created as incomplete, extraverted economies complementary to those of the centers, furnished wheat, sugar, and precious metals. The wheat, sugar, and metals were produced within modes that were precapitalist in form (serfdom or slavery) but were new in the sense of having been established directly by or for the metropoles because this made possible the superexploitation of labor power.

But by the end of the mercantilist period vast regions of the world were still not part of this center-periphery division. Certain European countries were not deliberately peripheralized but rather were blocked, retarded, and still could have evolved in either direction. This was the case for Spain, Portugal, Italy, Germany, Austria, Hungary, and Russia. Poland disappeared to their profit. All these countries became autonomous centers during the nineteenth century. Relay points of the center-periphery system also became autonomous centers: New England took over almost all of English America, for example. Other regions were still exterior, to use Wallerstein's terminology: Japan, the Ottoman Empire, China. These countries were involved in world mercantilist commerce but remained completely autonomous. They exported and imported—in small quantities and in a completely controlled way—what their ruling classes wanted to exchange, generally rare products. In the Indian Ocean trade did not foster accelerated accumulation in the center as did Atlantic trade. India and Indonesia, partially subdued by military conquest, had not yet been made into peripheries. This did not occur until the Industrial Revolution, when the English systematically destroyed Indian manufactures and crafts and the Dutch established semislavery plantations in the Indies. Finally, Black Africa, despite its apparent autonomy, had already become peripheralized during the mercantilist period as a provider of slaves for the American periphery.

IV. Unequal development in the bourgeois revolution

14. Unequal development within mercantilist Europe resulted from combinations of class struggles particular to each formation. Studies of the peasant component of these struggles (50, 51) have inspired four theses.

15. *First thesis:* the struggle between exploited peasants and their tributary (feudal) exploiters is the decisive one in the combination of struggles leading to the capitalist transition. Where the complete character of the tributary mode made this struggle more difficult, the (urban) bourgeoisie lacked the ally it needed to force the power to deal with it; this slowed the transition to capitalism. The reverse was true for feudal societies, that is, incomplete tributary societies (Europe and Japan). This is the expression of the unequal development of systems. Obviously, when the bourgeoisie was too weak, peasant struggles failed because in themselves they could not produce capitalism. This was the case for the peasant wars in Germany, while peasant struggles in England and France cleared the way for capitalist development.

The peasant-tributary class struggle certainly characterized all precapitalist class societies. It was their primary contradiction, just as the proletariat-bourgeoisie contradiction is primary in the contemporary capitalist system. The peasant revolt is to precapitalist class societies what the strike is to the capitalist system.

But just as proletarian struggles vary greatly in intensity and radicalization from one country and one period to the next, so too do peasant, antitributary struggles. The objective (perhaps determining) framework fostering or dampening this intensity lies in the origins of tributary society. The modalities of the transition to feudalism in the regions still close to primitive communalism were probably the decisive factor in fostering intensity. There people could still remember, and were perhaps still experiencing, feudal dispossession, at the same time as the new class struggle against feudalism was beginning.

However, this general framework was not determining in an

absolute and mechanical way. Diverse circumstances accentuated or reduced its potential impact. Among these circumstances was the extent of external market relations: long-distance trade. It is highly likely that the mercantilization of the Atlantic economy (especially the transition to payment in money and the attraction of new consumer products which the feudal class had to purchase) sharpened the basic class struggle in Europe. Peasant and bourgeois struggles interacted and mutually reinforced one another in an escalating historical spiral. The development of trade gave the peasants an ally and at the same time an outlet for their independent commodity production when they extracted concessions from the feudal lords. The development of petty agrarian capitalism freed a labor force and thus increased the possibility that manufactures, urban commerce, and so on would develop. Conversely, where the bourgeois or peasant element was weak, a reverse spiral put a brake on the necessary movement of history.

Other circumstances also intervened. The external expansion of the tributary mode attenuated peasant struggles (similarly to the effects of imperialist expansion on the proletarian class struggle). This expansion took the form of the colonization of "empty" lands (by the Portuguese, the Spanish, and the English in America; by the Russians in Siberia and the Ukraine—there is an analogy with the effects of proletarian emigration to North America and Australia). But it also took the form of colonizing foreign peoples (Germanization of Slavic lands, etc.), in which case national struggles obscured the class content.

For all these reasons, the political play of classes in relation to power as well as the content of the related ideologies acquired a certain autonomy. Generally, the great ideological currents that accompanied the transition to capitalism were ambiguous: they contained a peasant and a bourgeois component (for instance, Protestantism). The fact that the peasant component was rarely completely independent (it was so only in the religious form of millenarian "communism") shows that additional development of the productive forces was historically necessary before a classless society could become possible.

16. *Second thesis:* the more intense and radical the peasant struggle, the more revolutionary the process of overthrowing the feudal state and the purer the bourgeois character of the successor state (this is almost tautological). Does it also follow that the process of capital accumulation will be more rapid? This is debatable.

As we know, Marx distinguished between the revolutionary road of the transition to capitalism and the Prussian (we might say reformist) road. In the first the peasants freed themselves from feudal tutelage, establishing a "simple petty commodity" economy of free peasants. Differentiation was taking place among them and resulted in a kind of diffuse agrarian capitalism. In the same way crafts workers, freed from guild restrictions, created small, dynamic industrial enterprises. "The producer became a merchant." The reverse took place where commercial capitalism became merchant-entrepreneurial, manufacturing, and then industrial (putting out) capitalism and/or when the feudal lord became a merchant lati-fundiary. The second road, then, did not result from internal necessity but from external factors, from integration into the mercantilist and capitalist (though pre–monopoly capitalist) system. "Revolution from above" or even reform rather than revolution, although with the necessary participation of social forces from below?

The French revolution is the model of the radical bourgeois revolution. As analyzed by Albert Soboul, the bloc of free peasant and petty craft producers stood against the bloc of the oligarchy of great feudal proprietors and the commercial and financial big bourgeoisie (51-1). Later the empire and then the Restoration tried to impose a compromise to safeguard the interests of the big bourgeoisie and the great capitalist proprietors descended from the feudal lords. However, the abolition without compensation of seigneurial rights and the sale of national goods, which could not be reversed by later reactionary forces, strengthened the position of the small peasantry, particularly its kulak sector. According to a widely accepted thesis, adopted by Eric Hobsbawm, the weight of this small peasantry slowed the subsequent development of capitalism in France (51-6).

The English revolution was, in fact, less radical. In this country the free small peasantry and its rich yeoman sector were older and had been the champions of the Cromwellian revolution (followed by the Levellers, whose revolutionary ideology was radical in a way unparalleled at the time). Here reactionary forces were able to impose a compromise more favorable than in France to the big bourgeoisie and the great landed aristocratic proprietors who had begun the agricultural revolution. This was a form of capitalist modernization similar to that effected by the Prussian Junkers and the great Russian, Polish, and Hungarian proprietors. The revolution of 1688 testifies to the nature of this compromise, under which England lived until in the mid-nineteenth century the abolition of the Corn Laws destroyed the standing of agrarian capitalism to the exclusive profit of industry.

My interpretation of the different paces of subsequent industrial development (fast in England, slow in France) differs from that of these two conflicting theses. In France, the factor that slowed industrialization was not the existence *per se* of a tenacious group of petty peasant proprietors, because a process of internal differentiation could rapidly have destroyed such a group. It was the power of the proletariat that forced the peasant alliance on the bourgeoisie. The French proletariat had this power not because of its numbers (which in the nature of things was in proportion to the level of industry) but because of the radical antecedents of the revolution. The peasant alliance had its price: agricultural protectionism, which put a brake on the internal differentiation of the peasantry and checked industrial growth both by slowing the rural exodus and by limiting the means of industrial accumulation.

England overcame this obstacle sooner. Differentiation within the peasantry accelerated before the Industrial Revolution, in conjunction with the modernization of the great estates. The Industrial Revolution therefore had at its disposal a bigger proletariat than it had anywhere else. This proletariat almost became radicalized after the Industrial Revolution, during the time of Chartism. Perhaps the safety valve provided by massive emigration explains why this failed to happen. Whatever the case, the bourgeoisie could not make the internal peasantry into its ally against the proletariat. It therefore turned to an alliance with the external peasantry, the American farmers. In the process it sacrificed the great English proprietors, although they were modern. Furthermore, it resorted to the pillage of India and brigandage in Ireland, with its deplorable ideological consequences.

The third road, the American road pointed out by Lenin, also involved rapid industrialization. Here, the small peasantry did not come out of an antifeudal revolution. I maintain that New England was a byproduct of English mercantilism and was characterized by exceptionally widespread simple commodity production within its social formation. The example of the United States, even more than that of England or France, shows that this mode contained the seed of rapid capitalist development, in accordance with Dobb's thesis (50-3). It is true that other exceptional conditions favored this development, namely, the extent and wealth of the country, immigration, and the surplus from the internal slave colony.

The Prussian road does not necessarily slow subsequent industrialization. The means of accumulation extracted by the super-exploitation of the peasants was large enough to accelerate industrialization, particularly as the unified German state made sure it was not absorbed in overly high ground rent. Here we can see clearly the manner in which the emerging new economy fit into the world circuit. Where the ruling class became an exporter of agricultural products, the country was led into a process of dependence and unequal exchange to the detriment of internal accumulation. But where the ruling class became an industrial exporter, financing industry from the agrarian surplus, the Prussian road was very effective. The first possibility occurred in Hungary and Rumania, for example; the second in Germany, Japan, and Italy. Russia was somewhere between the two.

Thus the speed of industrialization does not depend mainly on whether the bourgeois revolution takes a revolutionary or a reformist road. The class struggle and the alliances made by the bougeoisie after the bourgeois revolution are the prime determinants of this speed. Often a strong proletariat slows down accumulation. Inversely, accumulation may accelerate after a serious defeat of the proletariat. A good example is the economic growth of Germany after the Second World War. Defeated in 1933 to reemerge on the political scene only in 1945, the German proletariat had very difficult working conditions. In 1965 the wage bill in German industry was still only 55 percent of that in the United States and 74 percent of that in France. But the rapid growth that resulted from this in the period 1950 to 1970 allowed salaries to catch up. In 1974 the same percentages were 99 percent and 83 percent, that is, the relationship between Germany and France was reversed. * The accompanying surplus in the external balance accentuated this tendency by the overvaluation of the mark and the devaluation of the franc. This took place within a rightwing social-democratic political framework perfectly controlled by capital. Other outcomes are possible from a conjuncture of effective resistance on the part of the exploited: high salaries may lead to either stagnation or intensive technical progress. But this parallel is instructive in that it reveals how the French peasantry, strong in its alliance with the bourgeoisie, was responsible for the slow pace of accumulation.

17. *Third thesis:* in radical bourgeois revolutions, the radical peasant component goes beyond capitalist demands. It calls into question class society as such. Albert Soboul notes that the poor peasants in France did not want the division of communal lands which the rich ones were demanding (51-1). Thus communal lands were maintained in large regions and disappeared only slowly and gradually during the nineteenth century, as the rich peasants

---

*These figures are derived from a recent study by the Ministry of Research and Industry, GRESI, *La situation des Etats-Unis au début de l'administration Carter*, July 1977, p. 30.

acquired the means to take advantage of land improvement contracts with the municipalities under their control.

We can find poor peasants resisting the objective necessities of capitalist development elsewhere; in contemporary northern Portugal, for instance. Should we consider this resistance to be reactionary because it impedes capitalist development of the productive forces? This would reflect a bourgeois class viewpoint, for as we have seen, proletarian resistance also curbs capitalist growth. On the contrary we must stress the progressive character of this resistance, which anticipates the resistance of the class on whose back capitalist development of the productive forces takes place: the proletariat (10-5). Daniel Guérin's insistence on the embryonic proletarian character of the struggles of *"bras nus"* and poor peasants has met with violent criticism, which seems to me to be social-democratic in inspiration. For the struggle of poor peasants is certainly a struggle against class society *per se* (50-3).

18. *Fourth thesis:* radical or not, peasant struggles in the transition to central capitalism, that is, *before* the imperialist era, have always ultimately served the interests of the bourgeoisie and not the peasantry. Depending on their modalities they favor one or the other section of the bourgeoisie: the kulak petty agrarian bourgeoisie formed in the differentiation of the peasantry; the great capitalist landed proprietors integrated into the market and using modern technology, i.e., the agrarian big bourgeoisie; or the industrial bourgeoisie itself. But the goal of the radical wing of the peasant movement—an egalitarian, communal peasant society without classes—was never realized.

This failure shows that while further development of the productive forces required a society with new relations of production, this would still be a class society, capitalist society. This is an expression of historical necessity.

Today, however, in the framework of the imperialist system, the same capitalist mode is no longer able to realize the full potential of the productive forces on the periphery of the system, due to the effects of the domination, superexploitation, and distorted development caused by capitalism. In light of this, radical peasant struggles can no longer be seen objectively as part of the bourgeois revolution but rather are part of the socialist revolution. The poor peasantry opposes class exploitation and this time has the ally which it lacked in France in 1793: a real proletariat.

Doubtless, the countries of the contemporary periphery are not all weak links in the imperialist system, nor are they the only weak links. Southern Europe is perhaps a weak link in the center of the contemporary system. If so, it is not for the reasons given above, which apply only to the periphery. The peasantry is disappearing in the center, and thus can no longer be the main reserve of revolution.

V. *Summary of conclusions*

19. The contrast between the European world economy that developed during the mercantilist transition and the expansion of previous tributary empires underlines the uniqueness of the transition to capitalism and thus forces us to rethink the fundamental questions of historical materialism.

Territorial expansion in other advanced societies never took this form. The centralized tributary Chinese state integrated newly colonized southern regions as ordinary provinces, subjected to the same system of tribute collection centralized by a prebendary bureaucracy. On the other hand, European expansion created for the first time a real periphery based on unequal specialization of production. While an empire is a political unit, the world European system is an economic one; that is, the links between its different parts are economic and not necessarily nor primarily political. This is not a chance coincidence. On the contrary, it reveals essential facts about the function of relations between the base and the superstructure in different modes of production.

I have developed the thesis that the tributary mode was the more general form of precapitalist class society; that slavery was exceptional and, like the simple commodity mode, marginal; that feudalism was a peripheral form of the tributary mode and that, precisely for this reason—because it arose earlier, it was still marked by the characteristics of original communal society—it could be transcended more easily. Thus Europe was endowed with its singular destiny.

The tributary mode defines at once relations of domination (class-governing state and governed peasants) and relations of exploitation (extortion of a surplus in the form of tribute). The transparence of the relations of exploitation implies the dominance of relations of domination, that is, of political ideology. Such a mode, in its complete form, is highly stable. It can bring about development of the productive forces without disrupting the relations of production (combination of relations of domination and exploitation). This is a reminder that the view of the mechanical determination of the relations of production by the level of development of the productive forces is not a Marxist one but a vulgar economist one.

The type of progress made in the productive forces is not immaterial and neutral but in fact is determined by the relations of production. Technology is not an autonomous prime mover springing from progress in human understanding in some lay version of God in Enlightenment philosophy, but is subject to the requirements of the relations of production. For instance, the complete tributary mode in Egypt and China was able to direct the development of the productive forces toward considerable technological advances in irrigation and construction (financed by agricultural progress) and in communications (roads, postal service, etc.), and thus to stengthen the tributary mode itself.

Slavery is not an autonomous mode of production. It is a political concept which defines a type of domination, just as personal dependence, serfdom, or bourgeois right are other personal statuses which constitute a framework of relations of domination. The existence of slavery does not necessarily imply a slave mode, which would mean a relation of exploitation of the slave. But this relation is exceptional and in general appears only where slaves produce a commodity for their masters. The slave mode is therefore associated with another dominant mode of production: either a communal mode (lineage), or a tributary mode (Classical antiquity), or a capitalist mode (the United States in the nineteenth century).

In principle, the tributary mode, like the communal mode, precludes commodity relations. These appear in the interstices of nonmarket societies as an associated, dominated mode or, more often, in the external relations of the communities or tributary empires (long-distance trade). And it is precisely in such exceptional circumstances, wherein commodity relations predominate at least sectorally, that the slave mode develops.

These conceptual clarifications increase our understanding of the nature of European feudal society, the reasons for the particular forms of its expansion, and the genesis of capitalism. If feudal Europe was not an empire, this is because the feudal mode was a peripheral form, an incomplete form, of the tributary mode. The dismemberment of state power and the noncentralization of the surplus originated in the distant past: in the nature of the takeover of the Roman Empire by barbarians who had scarcely left communal modes. The primitive forms of the tributary mode are thus more flexible than its complete forms. It was backward Europe that went through the capitalist transition from the tributary mode and not the advanced Orient. This expression of unequal development disproves the thesis of linear and continuous development of the productive forces and of their determination by successive modes of production.

From 1150 to 1300 territorial expansion of the feudal mode took place without difficulty, thanks to the abundance of virgin territory (we see a similar phenomena in Africa). Its contraction from 1300 to 1450 (demographic expansion met falling outputs of the current technological level) reduced feudal income and brought on a crisis. The lords' attempts to find new lands led to the enormous expansion of Iberia into America and of Russia into Siberia. At the same time extremely violent forms of labor exploitation were

introduced: once again slavery appeared (in America), contradicting
the mechanistic thesis that it is a more backward mode of production than feudalism. Serfdom reappeared in Eastern Europe, always in conjunction with the birth of capitalism.

The attempts to establish a European empire nevertheless failed,
always for the same basic reason: feudal resistance, heritage of the
old freedoms of communities which were far less subjugated than
in the more advanced forms of the tributary mode (China and
Egypt). Again this contradicts the assumptions of the asiatic mode
of production. The failure to establish such an empire led to a
capitalist solution to the problem: the juxtaposition of central,
national absolutist states, free cities, and autonomous provinces
and the establishment of the periphery (America) of the European
economic system as a prelude to the unequal capitalist development of modern times.

Just as essential was the opposition between the center and the
periphery of the system. Since the system is an economic one, it is
in the economic realm that new divisions arise. The economy of
the centers is autocentric; that of the peripheries is extraverted and
constrained by the unequal division of labor to produce a lower
order of merchandise at lower remuneration. The roots of unequal
exchange go back to the first centuries of capitalism.

20. The nature of unequal development prior to the establishment of the capitalist system—notably in the transition to feudalism, in feudal expansion, in the mercantilist transition, and finally
in the bourgeois revolution—is different from the kind of unequal
development familiar to us in the imperialist era of capitalism. The
universality of unequal development does not mean that we can
derive a few simple laws according to which history eternally
repeats itself. Center and periphery, complete and incomplete are
concepts different in content and plane from one period to another.

Thus it is not possible to offer a general periodization for universal history prior to imperialism. The specific periodization of
European history outlined above only highlights the different and
unequal forms of capitalist development in Europe. In this history,

the central pivot of the analysis is the class struggle among the three elements of the society—feudal lords, peasants, and bourgeois—and the interrelation of these struggles with the evolution of the state.

21. The national question developed gradually in the course of this unequal development out of the capitalist transition and the bourgeois revolution. During this process nations in the modern sense of the term appeared only in the centers that bourgeois revolutions had made complete: England and France. For the rest of Europe, the national question was not yet settled at the dawn of the nineteenth century. It was gradually settled during the particular process of unequal development, the subject of the next chapter.

Chapter 5

Unequal Development
in the Capitalist Centers

The break represented by the emergence of central capitalist nations during the eighteenth century is so important that 1800 marks the decisive turning point of universal history, the birth date of universal history. Nevertheless, the gradual consolidation of the central zone of the world capitalist system (Europe, North America, Japan, Australia) and the definite division of this system into central and peripheral zones took an entire century. During this century the national question was gradually resolved in Europe, as the central capitalist formations under consideration emerged. A series of questions known as regional questions were still outstanding; this is related to the problem of unequal development.

I. The national question and the emergence of
central capitalist formations

In 1848 revolution broke out in France and appeared likely to enflame all of Europe. The Communist Manifesto proclaimed the socialist revolution. However, except for the Paris Commune, during the following three-quarters of a century and until the Russian revolutions of 1905 and 1917, capitalism was not in jeopardy. Although violent struggles rocked and transformed Europe, they were all national struggles.

In 1848, then, there were only three nation-states constituting more or less complete capitalist formations: England, France, and the United States. These three more or less national states had emerged from the long history of the maturation of capitalism and of unequal development during the feudal and mercantilist periods. In France and England the class struggle involved three groups— the feudal lords, the bourgeoisie, and the peasantry—and even three and a half, insofar as in rare moments (Cromwell, 1793) the nascent proletariat sounded a discordant note. In the United States (at least in the northern states) a capitalist formation without feudal antecedents was born. After the Industrial Revolution, the compromises resulting from the series of bourgeois revolutions and the Restorations that followed them became stabilized and the bourgeois-proletarian struggle came to the forefront.

This class struggle was unequivocally on the national level. Bourgeois and proletarians belonged to the same nation, a self-satisfied nation, formed gradually during the three preceding centuries. Certain unresolved national problems—most importantly, that of Ireland—surfaced later and had an effect on these class struggles. But they were minor in that they did not determine the basic form taken by the most important question, the social question, to use the contemporary expression. Witness English Chartism and the Paris Commune.

These three nations aside, what was Europe like at that time? There were small bourgeois nations—Holland, Denmark, Sweden —which had not yet entered the industrial era. There was Portugal, a nation blocked at the mercantilist stage. There was Spain, only partly a nation, where the same blockage had destroyed the historical possibility of amalgamating Castillians, Catalans, and Basques (be it by "iron and fire," as in France the Languedoc had been Gallicized). But beyond the Rhine and the Alps was a conglomeration of principalities and empires that were neither national nor capitalist. Here the belated emergence of capitalism coincided with the emergence of nations instead of following it. Thus in this part of Europe class struggles (which constituted in the final analysis the motivation for all the battles that took place there) were bound up with national struggles. More precisely, class struggles to a large extent took the form of national struggles. Thus the twenty-five years following 1848 were primarily given over to German and Italian unification and the four decades after that to the break-up of the Russian, Austro-Hungarian, and Ottoman empires. Of course, German and Italian unification and the establishment of the Danubian and Balkan national states were bourgeois revolutions, but well-disguised ones.

There is a vast literature, notably by Marx and Engels themselves, devoted to these questions. It has been seriously analyzed and commented upon in studies which are neither Marxologistic nor pure and simply laudatory exegeses, and by Marxists from the regions in question: Karl Kautsky, Rosa Luxemburg, Otto Bauer and all the Austro-Marxists (Karl Renner, Josef Strasser, Otto Strasser), Anton Pannekoek, Lenin, Trotsky, Stalin, and so on (60). These analyses are all well presented and developed. I would simply like to draw the reader's attention to several points.

1. European history during the decades 1850-1914 was in fact primarily the history of national struggles. This was so much the case that Marx and Engels not only wrote extensively on these questions but also found it necessary for the proletarian movement to take a position about them. They were correct on the principle, although certain of their positions are debatable.

Marx and Engels considered classes to be more important than nations. Thus they adopted a pragmatic attitude toward national struggles and subordinated self-determination to the exigencies of what they saw as the longer term interest of the proletariat. Confronted with the absence of clear class struggles and the violence of national struggles, they sometimes substituted nations for classes, "investing nations with the role of classes" (60-1). They spoke of progressive and reactionary nations. It is true, as we will see, that the nations in question were progressive because of their possible contribution to the bourgeois revolution, while the reactionary nations were feudal. In this discussion there were no proletarian nations.

For the moment, let me make the following remarks without commentary. Marx and Engels did not discuss the division of the world into imperialist nations and nations dominated by imperialism, a division that appeared only later. But if today we were to use the language of Marx and Engels and to state that England, France, Germany, or the United States were reactionary while putting the Egyptian, Arab, Cuban, or Vietnamese nations in the revolutionary role, many objections would be raised.

2. Marx and Engels based their classification on the famous distinction between "nations without history" and "historical nations." The latter are those which were able to establish a state, that is, which had their own ruling classes. They were nations of the nobility (Russians, Poles, Hungarians) or the bourgeoisie (French, English, Germans, Italians). The former included those that did not succeed in establishing a state, and were thus dominated by exploiting and foreign classes (feudal). These were peasant nations (Czechs dominated by feudal elements and the German bourgeois, Croats by Hungarian feudal elements, the Balkan peoples by Ottoman feudal elements, etc.). At times there are certain simplifications, not to say errors, in this area: there was a Croatian feudal class in Croatia, for instance. But this is unimportant. At times there was a nascent local bourgeoisie (Czech, Greek) but it was very weak. Nations "without history" are thus peasant nations to the extent that they really correspond to the classificatory criteria of Marx and Engels.

Marx and Engels had no sympathy for these peasant nations, which they judged incapable of making a bourgeois and *a fortiori* a proletarian revolution. Due to this the worst feudal reaction was able to manipulate them. The example which haunted Marx was the behavior of the armies (in large measure Czech and Croatian) that massacred the 1848 revolutionaries in Austria. This convinced Marx and Engels that the Slavic peasants of the Danube and the Balkans were subject to tsarist manipulation by means of Pan-Slavism used in the most reactionary way against the German people, potentially more advanced as they were divided into bourgeois and proletarians.

Today we can easily recognize their error in judgment. Marx certainly foresaw the development by stages from the bourgeois to the socialist revolution in Germany (and later in Spain). He had the brilliant insight of unequal development, an insight which Lenin was able to clarify. But he did not envisage the development by stages from a peasant to a socialist revolution—although it was a peasant rather than a bourgeois revolution that broke out in Russia. And yet elsewhere, in France, Marx understood very well that the bourgeois revolution was radical only to the extent that its peasant component was strong.

Insofar as the bourgeois revolutions of 1848 had no strong peasant component, they could not become radicalized, for the bourgeoisie already feared the proletariat and made sure to suppress the peasant component. Marx should have asked if the failure of the Czechs and Croats to support the Germano-Austrian revolution was due to their feeling that this revolution had nothing to offer peasants like themselves. But he did not ask this question.

I see two reasons for this. The first is circumstantial and lies in Marx's veritable phobia about Russia. This clouded his mind to such an extent that certain of contemporary China's foreign policy judgments seem subtle by comparison with Marx's errors about Russian diplomacy. Marx thought Palmerston was a Russian agent and accused England of playing St. Petersburg's game in the Ottoman Orient. He went so far as to support the Ottoman yoke against states made independent by the Russians. He was in error about the Pan-Slavic Congress of Prague (on which point Bakhunin was correct; cf. 81b-5), endowing the anti-Russian Poles with revolutionary virtues which they did not possess and which he would not grant to the Czechs.

The second reason is less circumstantial and thus more serious. Despite his remarkable analysis of the peasant and bourgeois components of the French revolution (the distinction between the revolutionary and the nonrevolutionary roads of capitalist development), Marx believed that the peasant revolution could occur only under the leadership of the bourgeoisie. He did not see that when this is impossible (and this he does say), the revolution must take place under the leadership of the proletariat, even where the latter is embryonic. Nonetheless, we must excuse Marx on this point: in his time the proletariat was less than embryonic in peasant societies (except in Bohemia). Fifty years later Lenin did not hesitate to take issue with Marx about this vital problem.

Under these circumstances Marx preferred the bourgeoisie to the peasants and thus came up with some strange options. He made a sort of eulogy of the "civilizing mission" of the bourgeoisie: the German bourgeoisie in the East (Engels struck an almost pan-Germanist note) and the English in India. Marx celebrated the annexation of Texas by the "civilized" Americans from the Mexican "savages"; in reality the abolition of slavery there in 1823 created problems for the American southerners. He held onto certain illusions, countered adroitly by Bakhunin, about the advantages of a centralized state—but he changed his mind fifty times on this problem, as seen in his eulogy of the Paris Commune. Marx had a firm conviction that there was nothing to hope for from the Russian (peasant) people who, even if they set off a revolt, would not be able to carry it further except with the support of a revolution in the West. Trotsky inherited this error in judgment.

Two erroneous conclusions, proven false by history, derived from Marx's and Engels' judgments on these questions. First, Marx and Engels did not foresee that these same peasant nations would be much more revolutionary in the socialist transition than many others: thus the Yugoslavs, Greeks, Albanians, and Czechs, in contrast to the Hungarians and Poles. The contradiction they did not perceive is that in the historical nations where national feudalism and then the bourgeoisie were strong, the peasantry had much more difficulty in aligning with the proletariat than in the nations without history, where these exploiting classes were weak because they were foreign.

Secondly, Marx and Engels believed that nations without history were going to be gradually assimilated into the superior culture of their conquerors. The same thing would happen to them as happened to other ethnic groups (Bretons, Scots) that were assimilated and absorbed by the French and English nations and were no more than ethnographic fragments devoid of political importance. The question of regionalism in the developed centers is taken up below. But Marx and Engels underestimated the time it took for these assimilations to occur (they are still only partially complete) in the history of the most advanced mercantilist centers. And the pace of capitalist development among the peoples of eastern and southeastern Europe was going to be far more rapid than that of any possible assimilation.

I discovered in the work of Alexander Koyré (80d-4) that the expressions "historical nations" and "nations without history" were first used in 1837 by the Russian writer Polevoi, who attempted thereby to offer a justification in the slavophile spirit for the destiny of Russia. Whatever the case, subsequent developments, contrary to Marx's predictions, once again demonstrated the universality of unequal development. For these peasant nations, backward in the bourgeois phase of their development, appeared more advanced in the subsequent struggle against capitalism when it was forced upon them and eventually entered the socialist transition under more favorable conditions.

3. However, Marx understood the Irish question perfectly. At first he encouraged the Irish to renounce nationalism and to join the English proletarian movement, Chartism. Later he did not hesitate to take up the cause of oppressed Ireland unconditionally, and to affirm that, so long as the English proletariat did not rid itself of chauvinism, nothing could be expected of it. This position is all the more remarkable in that the Irish were not oppressed by a barbaric Tsar but by liberal England.

This judgment largely redeems the errors Marx made about eastern and southeastern Europe. For in England Marx was an activist whose position directly affected the movement. And he understood the problem and the correct attitude from the first. He did not feel involved in the struggles of eastern and southeastern Europe, where the workers' movement was moreover as yet nonexistent. He observed this from outside, as a journalist, on the basis of secondhand information derived for the most part from reactionary sources.

4. These discussions continued after the death of Marx and Engels and took a new turn in eastern and southeastern Europe due to the emergence of socialist parties (60). Four observations should be made about these discussions.

First, the great majority of socialists in this region were preoccupied by the danger of the great states breaking into qualified and nonviable micronations. To avoid this break-up, Otto Bauer and Karl Renner invented the strategy of "personal and cultural autonomy." It seemed to them important to safeguard for socialist society, which would soon come into being, an adequate framework for the productive forces. In this period, Rosa Luxemburg observed, the framework suitable to the needs of these productive forces was no longer the nation-state but the conquering, imperialist state. The same logic led Otto Strasser to demand freedom of emigration for workers.

Second, a great many socialists of the region continued to think that the process of assimilating peoples of diverse races would quickly diminish the importance of nationalities. Kautsky believed that the Czech language, which had become a peasant language, would disappear along with the growth of urbanization, as workers and bourgeois alike adopted German. Moreover, he looked forward to this in the name of the universalization of culture, the progressive work begun by the bourgeoisie and completed by the proletariat. On this base, Otto Strasser thought that the national question had no importance for manual workers; it was only important for those sectors of the petty-bourgeoisie that "made a living through language" (teachers, lawyers, etc.). For them, language was a means of production, while for the worker it was only an accessory, the means of production being the tool.

Third, on this same basis, Rosa Luxemburg questioned Marx's positions with regard to Poland. She who defended the Balkan peoples against oppression by the backward Turk saw no need to defend Polish independence against the Germans or even the Russians. In her mind, the Polish movement was far from being the only serious revolutionary manifestation in Russia: the Russian autocracy would be overthrown by a revolution in Russia itself.

Fourth, and a bit at countercurrents, there is the Leninist position, grounded in the basic distinction between oppressing and oppressed nations, a distinction that is sometimes forgotten. For this reason, Lenin did not adopt Rosa Luxemburg's position with regard to Poland, although he knew that the Russian revolutionary movement was far from negligible.

5. The definition of the concept of nation emerged gradually during nineteenth-century European history. Marx was not particularly interested in it. On the other hand, the Austro-Marxists were led to ask the question in the following way: When bourgeois and proletarians speak the same language, do they have the same culture, a common culture which in fact defines the nation? Some (Otto Strasser, for instance) thought not, claiming that the life experiences of the exploited and the exploiters were too different to constitute a common culture and almost a nation. These people played down the importance of the national reality. Others (Pannekoek, for instance) believed to the contrary that the national reality was undeniable because the classes of a single nation shared a common experience, be it only that of struggle.

Without taking the analysis very far, Kautsky suggested that the concept of nation appeared only with capitalism. For him, to speak of a peasant nation would be a contradiction in terms. It would fall to Stalin to make explicit what was only implicit here: the unifying element of the markets in capital, commodities, and labor power. As I have said, the simultaneous emergence of nations and of capitalism is unique to European history (although perhaps an analogous problem exists in the contemporary third world) where capitalism overcame feudal fragmentation. But this does not necessarily occur.

II. Questions of "regionalism" in the advanced centers

Development has always been unequal in all class societies. Due to the character of the alliances-compromises made in the course of its evolution, the bourgeois revolution itself engendered subsequent inequalities in the development of capitalism. These inequalities developed on several planes simultaneously. Internally (within a national or multinational state) they took the form of regional inequalities, which sometimes coincided with national conflicts. Internationally they took the form of unequal paces in the accumulation of capital from one country to the other within the group of central capitalist formation on a world scale. Beginning at the end of the nineteenth century, the division of the planet into dominant imperialist formations and dominated, incomplete colonial or semicolonial capitalist formations assumed its definitive, contemporary shape.

The absolutely general character of unequal development can lead to confusion. If the analysis is too vague, if it equates all manifestations of unequal development regardless of context (inequality between center and periphery, or between centers, or within a center) and reasons by analogy, it will miss the particular features of each case. These are on the level of the structure of the class blocs particular to each situation: alliances within blocs, classes assuming the leadership of blocs, the extent of the opposition of blocs, the determination of subordinate classes, the interrelation with foreign class alliances and oppositions in a system of formation. This structure is not fixed; it evolves under the impact of its internal and external contradictions.

Thus in each case we must (1) analyze the historical establishment of the blocs that created the situation, starting with relevant class struggles; (2) analyze the direction which this structure would take on its own, that is, if the initiative were left to its ruling classes, whose relations would be modified as accumulation took place; and (3) define (this is the goal of the exercise) the strategy used by the exploited classes to make the structure evolve differently, to make it break apart, to put in its place an effective bloc of exploited classes which would bring about the end of exploitation.

This is the direction of the foregoing analyses of the unequal formation of capitalist centers on the one hand and of the unequal formation within the world system on the other (theory of the center and the periphery and of the class alliances and conflicts on the world scale during the imperialist epoch). The history of unequal development thus did not end with the bourgeois revolution. It continued during the Industrial Revolution of the nineteenth century, finally assuming its contemporary, complete shape during the imperialist period. The contrast between dominant imperialist centers and underdeveloped, dominated peripheries thus became the predominant form of unequal development. The door to the establishment of new capitalist centers is henceforth closed, while the era of the stages of the socialist revolution is opened.

What follows will not deal with this determining form of the division of the imperialist system but with the emergence of unequal development within the central social formations during pre–monopoly capitalist industrialization.

The Italian case

The Italian case is exemplary for two reasons. First because it is particularly clear. Second because much more than others it generated discussion on a high scientific level. The figure of Antonio Gramsci dominates this discussion. But it should be pointed out that Gramsci's great thesis has been called into question or significantly added to by such authors as E. Sereni, Rosario Romeo, Sergio Romano, Benedetto Croce, Nicola Zitara, Capecelatro, and Antonio Carlo (61).

1. *First thesis:* having been blocked during an earlier period, Italy was globally threatened with peripheralization at the beginning of the nineteenth century (it lost its advance over the rest of Europe from the thirteenth and fourteenth centuries and became even more backward during the entire mercantilist period). Italy

escaped this fate through the initiative of the northern agrarian and particularly the Piedmontese bourgeoisie.

The Risorgimento and unification, up to the establishment of the protectionist tariff of 1887, were the work of this northern agrarian bourgeoisie. It is not adequate to characterize this unification, as is often done, as a compromise that sealed the class alliance between the northern bourgeoisie and the feudal elements of the south, excluding the peasant element (of the south especially) from the bourgeois revolution. It must be added that what I call the northern bourgeoisie was at the time of Cavour still primarily an agrarian bourgeoisie. It had been produced by a twofold process: internal transformation of the old feudalists into capitalist gentlemen farmers and differentiation-kulakization within the peasantry, partially freed by the French revolution. The bourgeoisie of the time was not yet industrial. And even its merchant function had been undermined by the long decline of Genoa and Venice and the integration of the latter into the Austrian feudal system.

The agrarian bourgeoisie feared that the radicalism of an anti-feudal peasant movement would challenge its own well-established power in the Piedmont. This is why it preferred the more tractable alliance with the southern feudal elements. It favored free trade also—not only because freedom of trade allowed it to emerge as a bourgeoisie by destroying feudal relations or forcing them to modernize, but also and especially because it envisaged its integration into the (young capitalist) European system as an agrarian bourgeoisie. Had it persisted on this path, the whole of Italy would have been peripheralized just as Hungary was.

It is interesting to compare Italian with Prussian and Russian history. In the latter countries also the latifundiary agrarian bourgeoisie predominated. In Prussia, to the east of the Elbe, they were called Junkers and monopolized state power. But the annexation of the Rhineland by Prussia, while it did not modify the class content of the state, gave it a nascent industrial economic base. This contributed to putting the German Bismarckian state on the road to accelerated and autonomous industrialization. In Russia, although state power was also completely aristocratic (latifundiaries in the process of integration into the capitalist system, especially after 1861), the state promoted and strengthened industry. From this resulted the mixed character of subsequent Russian evolution—neither totally peripheralized (as a wheat exporter) nor openly evolving toward autocentric industrial predominance.

In contrast, what we can call the agrarian bourgeoisie of the Balkans and the Ottoman Empire was integrated into the world system as a peripheralized, exploiting class. The most typical example is probably Egyptian large proprietors, who themselves shifted to cotton production for England after the failure of autocentric industrialization by Mohammed Ali under the Ismaili Khedivate during the War of Secession (77c-1). The Greek and Turkish agrarian bourgeoisies acted similarly, especially with regard to tobacco (76b-7). The combination of great latifundiary capitalist property (or, in Greece, small capitalist property) with a commercial and financial bourgeoisie which became a comprador bourgeoisie typifies the evolutionary course that Italy might have taken.

2. *Second thesis:* the autocentric industrialization of Italy was initiated by the Italian state and financed by a levy on ground rent in the north and especially in the south of the country. Four questions arise here: (a) Did the protectionist tariff of 1887, maintained until Italy joined Europe and its common market beginning in 1950–1958, promote or impede this evolution? (b) Was the surplus extracted from the south responsible for the new and growing unequal development between north and south? (c) Was this form of industrialization more or less rapid than other possible forms based on a peasant revolution might have been? (d) Has contemporary European integration modified these perspectives?

3. Italian historians are unanimous in their agreement that the industrialization of Italy was initiated by systematic state support, which brought about the formation of finance capital. State responsibility for the rapid construction of rail and road networks, the creation of a monetary system and a credit network, and the

formation of an important merchant marine supported by the state meant that Italian capitalism had, from the beginning, a relatively more concentrated structure. Somewhat like Russia, Italy entered the monopoly stage without really having gone through the prior stage. The intensification of this characteristic following the 1930 crisis, with the creation of the Institute for Italian Reconstruction and its affiliates to rescue Italian industries, gave a strong state bias to contemporary Italian capitalism.

Protectionism was an essential means, a condition for the process of industrialization, which would not on its own have been able to prevail over competition from more advanced countries within its own national market. The liberal rhetoric of contemporary ideologues of imperialism, who claim that protectionism slowed down development because it imposed costs and distortion unfavorable to optimalization, totally lacks historical perspective (71a-11).

4. Was Italian industry financed by the surplus extracted from the south? Gramsci's analysis does not preclude this possibility, despite certain over-hasty deductions. Gramsci merely noted that the northern (agrarian, then industrial) bourgeoisie achieved unification without calling on the southern peasants but by concluding an alliance with feudal-style landed proprietors. The question of whether these proprietors were feudal or not has been raised only recently, so far as I know. But this was not Gramsci's basic question. His thesis was only that an agrarian revolution in the south would have (1) accelerated capitalist development and (2) made development less unequal between the north and the south. While the second point is certainly valid, I have some hesitation in agreeing on the first.

Contemporary historians of Italy's south have undertaken to demonstrate that industrialization was largely financed by a surplus extracted from it, thanks to the state which the northern bourgeoisie monopolized through the unification of the fiscal and public finance systems. To prove this, Nicola Zitara and Capecelatro and Carlo have compared the fiscal burden on the north and south, respectively, and the distribution of public finances. They have also studied the effects of the liquidation of the Banco di Napoli in favor of a centralized credit system (61-5, 61-6).

The question of protectionism is related to that of the surplus. Is Sereni spelling out what was implicit in Gramsci when he claims that protectionism represented the convergence of northern industrial and southern agrarian interests because it allowed the rate of ground rent to rise (61-2)? This is very debatable, because the agrarian interests protected in this case were northern rather than southern. Zitara, Capecelatro, and Carlo have in fact shown that unification destroyed southern self-sufficient cereal agriculture, which could not compete with the modern cereal and animal agriculture of the north. This led to southern specialization in agricultural exports (wine and oil).

Can we speak of true conquest and colonization of the south by the north, as do the Italian Meridionalists? Colonization during the contemporary imperialist epoch fulfills a precise function: to promote the acceleration of accumulation in the dominant centers by the extraction of a considerable volume of surplus labor through the maintenance and reproduction of forms of exploitation that were originally precapitalist but have been subjugated. The resulting extraverted distortion of dependent development conditions the reproduction of this superexploitation. I accept this analysis, which is not incompatible with Gramsci's thesis. But it extends his analysis in a way which he himself could not do, given his ignorance of the problematic of formal domination through which the surplus labor of precapitalist modes is transformed into surplus value and profit for dominant capital. In this sense, southern Italy played exactly this role; the thesis of the Meridionalists seems correct.

Moreover, the Italian case is not unique of its type. Did not New England have an analogous internal colony, the slave South, which specialized in the export of cotton thanks to the superexploitation of the slaves' work?

5. Returning to Gramsci, can we claim that an agrarian revolution in the south of Italy would have accelerated the development

of national capitalism? Rosario Romeo thinks not (61-3). His thesis, which is also Hobsbawm's, is that the survival of feudal relations enabled pressure to be maintained on the peasants' income (60-8). The surplus product, extracted by means of rent, was used for rapid accumulation via fiscal measures. An agrarian revolution would have destroyed this model of accelerated accumulation.

I have already stated that the agrarian revolution can boost capitalist development because differentiation within a peasantry subjected to market exchanges can occur very rapidly. If industrialization was curbed in France, this was for a different reason: the antiworker bourgeois-peasant alliance.

Let us give Gramsci his due. He was not interested in the pace of capitalist growth (which is a bourgeois preoccupation) but in the style of its development as it affected the anticapitalist struggle. On this level he was completely correct: the road taken by Italian unification brought about unequal development between the north and the south, while an agrarian revolution would have created the conditions for a different, homogeneous, and thus truly unifying development. Gramsci noted that unequal development impeded the anticapitalist struggle because it kept the rural masses of the south outside the proletarian battle. How can we contradict him when we know the support given to fascism in southern Italy?

Today, the Meridionalists are only carrying the same line of reasoning a bit further. Why do the southern masses support the Right? Is it not because what the northern-based Left has to offer them does not match their aspirations? The Meridionalists are not unfaithful to Gramsci when they treat north-south relations in terms of the center-colony problematic; nor when they recall the nature of the social-democratic alliance and the complicity of the northern proletariat, which supports its bourgeoisie in the superexploitation of the southern "external proletariat," a proletariat of small producers subjected to the formal domination of capital. But they make certain people uncomfortable.

6. This is ancient history, however. The immaturity of the northern social-democratic (and/or anarcho-syndicalist due to its

weakness, some would say!) proletariat, its defeat in 1920–1922 have been transcended since 1945. Furthermore, Italy's decision to join the European Common Market, a decision which is now irreversible, put an end to the old protectionist measures. Finally, the massive emigration from the south to the northern factories, the establishment of industry in the south, undertaken on a large scale with the rapid modernization of the last quarter century, have completely changed the givens of the situation. The old Risorgimentist alliance no longer has any meaning and the conditions for pan-Italian proletarian unity have been created.

I am reluctant to be so optimistic. Is Zitara wrong in pointing to the bourgeois character of the working-class position, an apologia for the development of the productive forces (which are capitalist in this case)? In the past, he reminds us, the working class did nothing (except verbally) to support an agrarian revolution in the south. Some have suggested that they feared this would diminish the productive forces. Today the working class sees in the establishment of industry in the south the means for the creation of a southern working class. Zitara sees in it the appropriation of southern space by big capital, under conditions analogous to those of the imperialist export of capital. I might add that the European discourse remains disquieting. For once again, in the name of the development of the productive forces, which is the bourgeoisie's concern, what will not be accepted? And how will escape from the claws of "Germano-American" Europe be possible if we support this discourse?

7. *Third thesis*: southern Italy was no more backward in 1860 than northern Italy. Colonization was entirely responsible for its backwardness. It would be necessary to make a thorough study of Italian history before judging this thesis of Capecelatro and Carlo. But the ravages of West-centered historiography elsewhere give reason to take their arguments seriously.

These authors claim that Sicilian agriculture ceased to be feudal in the second half of the eighteenth century. Under the impact of the influx of American silver via Spain, the great proprietors modernized and became large-scale producers of wheat for the market. Rent was paid in money. Advanced rural proletarianization had led to urbanization and to the establishment of manufacturing, as the exports from Palermo indicate. As the abolition of feudalism by Murat at Palermo conformed to internal forces, the Bourbons, on their return, were unable to reinstate it. Southern Italy was nonetheless integrated into the world system as a periphery in England's wake. English imports had killed the silk industry but encouraged wheat export. Moreover, the same was true at this time for the north, where the bourgeoisie was still exclusively agricultural. This was the meaning of the 1820–1821 revolution, followed by the Bourbon method of initiating industrial expansion, i.e., protectionism and appeal to foreign capital. The collapse of the Bourbons was due to the attitude of the free-trade agrarian bourgeoisie, which abandoned its king to support the King of Savoy. Thus it was southern reactionary forces that welcomed unification.

If these theses are correct, do they contradict those of Gramsci? I believe not. In fact, Gramsci in no way confused capitalism and industry nor believed that the northern bourgeoisie was already industrial when it brought about unification. But it was destined to become so. Of course, Gramsci underestimated the contribution which the superexploitation of the south made to industrial accumulation because he was unaware of the problematic of formal domination. But this development extends Gramsci's analysis rather than contradicting it.

In any event, whether or not southern Italy was as advanced as northern Italy in 1860, the devastating effects of unification are hardly debatable. China or Congo, the consequences of imperialism are everywhere the same.

8. The unequal development of capitalist Italy is related in certain respects to the more general problem of the unequal development of centers and peripheries during the imperialist period. I would not draw this conclusion for all forms of unequal development within centers. First it would be necessary to examine in more detail examples such as French regionalism (Brittany,

Languedoc), Ireland, and the South of the United States, where we should ask whether blacks constitute a nation or not.

The case of Brittany

9. The history of Brittany is an interesting case of unequal development within an advanced formation that became a nation through a long process of transition from feudalism to the absolutist-mercantilist tributary form. This transition was capped by a radical bourgeois revolution, which cleared the way for accelerated accumulation after the Industrial Revolution. If the French nation at the head of the Federation in 1790 was not yet a totally complete reality, its establishment was already well advanced. The Languedoc, the Basque country, Brittany, and even Corsica and Alsace-Lorraine had been undergoing Gallicization, in some instances for a very long time. That the peasants kept their original languages for another century until the primary school of the Third Republic imposed French on them; that Alsace-Lorraine had its process of Gallicization interrupted by its integration into Germany in 1871–1918; that in lower Brittany and in Corsica, Breton and Corsican had not yet disappeared—these facts only indicate that even in the advanced capitalist centers assimilation is less rapid than certain Austro-Marxists thought it would be. The bourgeois classes and the urban world were already Gallicized in 1790.

The dominant bloc that established itself on the national level during the revolution and the compromises that ensued are not abstractions. This bloc was reproduced concretely at different levels, both regional and local, of the national reality and took on different colorations according to its local functions.

It is thus useful to analyze how it functioned in Brittany, as Yannick Guin does (62-1). The general lines of his analysis of the class struggles and of their interrelation with class struggles on the scale of France as a whole are convincing. According to Guin, in 1789 Breton feudalism was of the poor type: relative fragmentation of the small rural aristocracy, large zones of small property. The church, which here held no significant amount of land, provided the organic intellectuals of this feudal formation in the form of country curates. The Girondist commercial and maritime bourgeoisie was oriented toward the sea (in connection with mercantilism and Antilles slavery); it moved into the countryside less than elsewhere in France.

Under these circumstances the bourgeoisie, which in France as a whole succeeded in joining with the peasants against feudalism, was stopped in Brittany by the combination of peasant revolt and aristocratic counterrevolution. The restoration that followed 1793 brought about a compromise: the rural bloc (aristocracy and peasants) was allowed to remain hegemonic in Brittany provided that it accept the hegemony of the big bourgeoisie over France as a whole.

For a century such an alliance operated in this way. Within Brittany the rural bloc (the whites) was dominant, isolating the urban bloc composed of blues (the local bourgeoisie) and of reds (the small local bourgeoisie). The hegemony of the industrial bourgeoisie over France as a whole both helped and hindered rural aristocratic proprietors in modernizing (producing for the market, buying equipment, etc.). The latter were able to do so without losing their leadership of the countryside, leadership which functioned on the ideological plane through the Concordat and through paternalistic formulae (e.g., Christian Democracy).

The capitalist development resulting from this compromise accelerated beginning in 1914 and especially in 1945, and finally broke up the alliances on which it had been based. Industry and the appearance of a working-class proletariat gradually undermined the traditional dependence of the descendants of the reds on the blues. On their side the blues, faced with the threat of socialism, made peace with the whites (by abandoning anticlericalism). In the countryside the process of modernization accelerated the disintegration of the rural world (massive emigration) and substituted for the old peasantry, which was relatively closed (self-subsistence polyculture) small, modernized, and specialized proprietors strongly dominated by agroindustrial capital (formal domination). The great capitalist proprietors had lost their political importance as a means of controlling the peasants. Electoral power shifted to the urban zones. A white-blue alliance replaced the blue-red one. Industrial capital intervened directly in the peasant economy without the mediation of the aristocrats. Out of this disintegration of the old alliances emerged the autonomous movement of the small peasantry subject to formal domination.

Breton ideology, which served in the nineteenth century to unify the rural bloc (wherein the aristocrats presented themselves, in a verbal defense of regionalism, as the defenders of the rural world against the misery of industrial capitalism), changed its content. It became the ideological expression of the peasant revolt, with the ambiguities that this revolt of small producers necessarily comported. Due to this, it met with a favorable response in the petty bourgeoisie (students) that wavered between capital and labor. The regionalization it proposed matched the strategy desired by the big bourgeoisie.

10. Although I believe that Yannick Guin's analysis of class struggles and of the interrelation with national struggles is correct, I am not always convinced by his conclusions. Did not the counterrevolutionary resistance of the Chouans (the failure of the bourgeoisie to separate the peasants from the aristocracy) result from the concern of the ruling elements of the bourgeoisie (before Thermidor and particularly afterward) not to foster a radical peasant revolution, the seed of which existed? In this case, is it not onesided to characterize the Chouannerie as counterrevolutionary? Is there no analogy between Czechs and Croats, who expected nothing from the timid bourgeois revolution of 1848, and the peasants of northern Portugal who expected nothing more from the socialists and communists in the Lisbon government?

Finally, so be it: the French revolution was not to be remade. We can only note the absence of an embryonic proletariat, an absence which resulted from the objective immaturity of capitalist relations at the time. This proletariat, despite its courage, was crushed by the bourgeoisie and did not succeed in allying with the poor Breton peasants.

And so? Why is it that from 1914 to the present the reds have not succeeded in allying with the peasants and cutting them off from the embourgeoisified aristocracy? Should this not have been the strategy of the workers' movement? Why did the latter leave the initiative to the bourgeoisie, and find itself in no better position when the blues abandoned it to re-ally with the whites?

And when the peasants, abandoned in their turn by the whites, brought into capitalism and subjected to its formal domination, began to revolt, was it not the task of the workers' movement to ally with them because theirs was a struggle against capital? Is it correct to consider this struggle lost in advance because it contravenes the "development of the productive forces"? Does not the struggle of the working class itself, by reducing profits, also prevent maximum accumulation? Is the role of the exploited to make it easier, by their silence, for the exploiters to bring about the development of the productive forces?

Should we not also take a different position with regard to the support of the petty bourgeoisie for this peasant revolt? Which petty bourgeoisie are we talking about? Small producers (artisans, shop-keepers) threatened by capital, or the new petty bourgeoisie composed of nonmanual workers and proletarianized employees already exploited by capital? In the latter case would not an alliance with the peasants, equally exploited by capital, be correct? And why would the working class hesitate to join it?

Should priority be given to the development of the productive forces or to the class struggle? Is the task of the proletariat to do nothing which objectively impedes the development of the productive forces? Is this not a social-democratic way of understanding this task? Should not the proletariat reject this goal, which is that of the exploiting classes, to concentrate exclusively on fostering the contradictions of this development in order to build an effective revolutionary bloc?

Is it not onesided to consider the demand for regionalization as the new strategy of the big bourgeoisie? Like many others, is this demand not ambivalent? Of course it can be coopted by the bourgeoisie, at least if it is part of an overall social-democratic strategy. But could it not also serve as a lever of anticapitalist mobilization?

Even if it served the agrarian bloc in the past, can Breton ideology be unilaterally characterized as reactionary, given the anticapitalist struggles that have attended its rebirth? Why? Because it goes against the development of the productive forces and the steamroller of cultural homogenization, which is only the generalization of the bourgeois ideology of *homo consumens universalis?* Are we talking about reviving a corpse or a dying entity (the Breton language)? Or are we talking about a protest against bourgeois ideology hiding behind the smokescreen of universality?

The Irish case

11. The case of Ireland resulted from a process engendered by the same family of historical conditions as that of Brittany. However, Ireland's fate was very different (62-3). Invoking the religious factor as an explanation is unconvincing: in Germany, Catholics and Protestants are not killing each other. In fact, if the outcome of the Irish problem has been different from that of the Breton problem this occurred independently of a different relation of power. During a long period Ireland was as populated as England— because in England the bourgeoisie made a compromise with the feudal aristocracy, one which was much more favorable to the latter than in France. The English bourgeoisie never considered siding with the Irish rebellion against the English proprietors. Perhaps it was even the power that the English aristocracy gained from its domination over Ireland which forced the English bourgeoisie to conclude the compromise begun in 1688.

Following this, the bourgeoisie passed to the English proletariat its contempt, to put it mildly, for the fate of the exploited Irish peasants. This total lack of solidarity corrupted the English workers' movement very early on, as Marx observed, and prepared it to accept the imperialist ideology, so aptly formulated by Cecil Rhodes, about the export of the social question.

The case of Catalonia and the Basque country

12. This case is interesting because it inverts the terms of the current problem of unequal development. Here the oppressed nationalities are those of the regions where capitalist development is furthest advanced (62-4, 62-5).

We cannot understand a phenomenon of this type if we disregard the formation of unequal development in Spain during the feudal and mercantilist periods. No one knows how the Spanish nation would have evolved if the development of the peninsula had not been blocked at this stage, the country being corrupted by the wealth too easily taken from America. Thus Spain played the role of an intermediary *rentier*, collecting its tithe between America and northwestern Europe until it lost its position and thus became useless. If internal accumulation had taken place, a Spanish nation would doubtless have resulted. We cannot know if this would have happened by the Castellanization of Catalonia, the Catalanization of Castille, or a synthesis of the two. At any rate, the Languedoc was Gallicized, and Spain would have been able to evolve toward the formation of a capitalist nation, complete both on the economic level and on that of linguistic homogenization.

Spain stagnated at this stage for two or three centuries during which the central power constantly oppressed the Catalan and Basque minorities. When beginning in the 1950s, sudden industrial growth led to Spain's overcoming its backwardness, it was again confronted with the national problem. But in the meantime this had become the problem of an advanced, multinational center.

The case of advanced multinational centers:
Belgium, Switzerland, Canada

13. Which is more important, the nation (the question of the relations between different peoples of one country) or the state as

the framework within which the regulation of capital accumulation occurs? In fact, the establishment of class blocs occurs within the framework of the state, because state policy—both internal (credit, conjuncture, control of the workforce, national economic policy) and external (place in the international division of labor and methods of external economic policy)—brings this establishment about. This state may be national or multinational.

It is not impossible for a multinational bourgeois state to function. The Swiss confederation functions well despite real national conflicts which the federal system contains within the cantonal framework. It is true that Switzerland is an exception due to its position in the world system and that it has created this *chef d'oeuvre* of bourgeois policy, cantonalizing politics while at the same time having an integrated economic policy for the confederation. In fact, Switzerland, like the United States, proves that regionalization can be a means of lowering the level of political consciousness.

It is true that in a multinational state the balance is rarely equal among the constituent nations. The Walloon bourgeoisie dominated Belgium for a long time and oppressed the Flemish (peasants). Recently, the process of accumulation has led to the preferential development of industry in Flanders and the new Flemish working class has become significant. It is this new working class, which is social-democratic (in its more backward political forms, particularly Christian-Democratic ones) that has raised the language question.

The same can be said about Canada, whose exclusively English bourgeoisie has ruled over the peasant, conquered people of Quebec. The emergence of the demand for Quebec nationality stems from the industrialization of the province. This demand takes particular forms because it is confronted by the domination of the United States, which encountered no such resistance in English Canada, where it brought the local bourgeoisie under its sway like any North American provincial bourgeoisie.

The case of the United States

14. Let us remind ourselves of several questions: Do blacks and

whites belong to the same nation? What does a (bourgeois) nation mean if it has within it real (for a long time legal and now *de facto*) discrimination other than that based strictly and solely on class? Is this analogous to the problem of the Jews in the capitalist countries where they are discriminated against? Marx told the Jews to renounce their Jewishness. The American Communist Party during the 1930s developed the thesis of a black nation within its territory, the South, its foreign occupiers, the whites, its emigrants, the blacks of the northern cities (62-6, 62-7, 62-8). What is the situation today, now that the majority of blacks have broken all ties with the South and hence lost their status as a minority of oppressed peasants?

Beyond this, does the American nation exist? The state certainly does. The federated states are not nation-states, and despite their size they are no more than Swiss cantons, that is, means to reduce political questions to the level of local quarrels. Beyond this, two theses are possible and perhaps complementary. Either the American nation really exists because all origins have been transcended not ethnically (the melting pot is a myth) but culturally. Or this transcendence occurred through a reduction to the lowest common denominator, the culture perfectly suited to capitalism, that of *homo consumens*.

Furthermore, the case of the United States poses a more general question, that of recognition of organized social minority groups. The cultural-ethnic groups (blacks, Italians, Polish, WASPS, etc.) may constitute groups of this type, which obviously do not enjoy equal status (WASP domination is evident). The Zionist position claims that there are Jewish communities.

The regional question and the problem of "underdevelopment"

15. Based on this overview, several general observations can be made. First, we should not confuse inequalities of development in the centers with national inequalities. The latter can interact with the former but the two can also exist separately, not interact, or reverse positions. Moreover, we should not *a fortiori* equate the

problem of these inequalities in the centers with that of the center-periphery opposition in the imperialist system. The analogy has its limits. In one case—that of Italy—the problem is very similar. But this is an exception. Inequality is not a problem of the use of space. This contemporary technocratic division has as its goal the mystification of the nature of the process of unequal development, which is inherent in capitalism: the operation of blocs on the state level both globally and locally.

The struggles and controversies over regional problems raise all the questions of the universality of culture in relation to the development of the productive forces. Doubtless regional inequalities in development express the unequal development of the productive forces. But the relation is not one of unilateral cause and effect by one on the other. It is dialectical: the original unequal maturity of the productive forces explains the different modalities of the hegemonic blocs, modalities which in turn widen the gap in the development of the productive forces. In this general sense, the different regional and national inequalities in development during the capitalist era are analogous and must be studied in the same way, i.e., by analyzing the dialectic of class struggle–relations and forces of production.

Nevertheless, one important difference makes it wrong to transpose to regional problems the general analysis of the center-periphery interrelation on the world scale of the imperialist system: regional inequalities exist within the framework of a unified capitalist state. As we have seen, the social reproduction of the capitalist system takes place by means of state policies directed both toward the internal conditions of this reproduction (internal state policies) and toward external conditions (external policy). Neither the supra-state instance nor supereconomic autonomous imperialism exists with regard to national states. The interrelation of internal class blocs and the interrelation of international alliances are not of the same type. Local internal blocs line up in relation to a hegemonic national bloc, which expresses itself in and through the state.

Chapter 6

Center and Periphery
in the Capitalist System:
The National Question Today

The theme of this chapter relates to the whole of my work, which has been concerned primarily with analyzing the material base for the reproduction of the contemporary capitalist system as a world system (70, 71, 72). I will not return to this analysis here but will restate the conclusions relating to the unequal international division of labor (section I) in order to use it as a basis for describing and analyzing the class structure of the contemporary imperialist system and for placing contemporary national questions within this context (section III).

I. The unequal international division of labor,
the material base of the contemporary imperialist system

Analysis reveals a fundamental difference between the auto-centered model of accumulation and that which characterizes the peripheral capitalist system, thereby disproving all linear theories of stages of development. Complete, autonomous capitalism is impossible in the periphery. The socialist break is objectively necessary there. In this very specific sense, the national liberation movement is a moment in the socialist transformation of the world and not a stage in the development of capitalism on a world scale. This is a perpetual question, although one which is constantly posed in new terms. It is these new terms which I will examine here.

It is worth noting that the concepts of center and periphery, basic to my analysis but rejected by all proimperialist currents within Marxism, were introduced by Lenin in direct relation to his analysis of the imperialist system (82-10).

1. The determining relation in an autocentered capitalist system is between the sector producing mass consumer goods and the sector producing capital goods. This relation effectively characterized the historical development of capitalism in the center of the system (in Europe, North America, and Japan). It thus abstractly defines the pure capitalist mode of production and was so analyzed in *Capital*. Marx in fact showed that in the capitalist mode of production there is an objective, i.e., a necessary, relation between the rate of surplus value and the level of development of the productive forces. The rate of surplus value essentially determines the structure of the social distribution of national income, its division between wages and profits, and thereby that of demand: wages correspond essentially to the demand for mass consumer goods, while profits are totally or partially saved with a view to investment. The level of development of the productive forces expresses itself in the social division of labor: the distribution of labor power in appropriate proportions to each of the two sectors.

2. Although this model is schematic, it is faithful to the essence of the system. By abstracting external relations I do not mean to suggest that capitalist development takes place in an autarchic, national framework but that the basic relations of the system can be understood by abstracting these relations. More precisely, external relations are subject to the logic and the needs of autocentered internal accumulation. Furthermore, the historically relative character of the distinction between mass and luxury consumption also clearly comes in here. Strictly speaking, luxury products are those the demand for which derives from the consumed portion of profit, while the demand that derives from wages grows with the development of the productive forces. However, this historical progression in the type of mass products has decisive importance for an understanding of the problem at hand. When the system began the

demand structure fostered the agricultural revolution by offering an outlet for food products on the internal market. Agrarian capitalism thus preceded the origin and achievement of the capitalist mode in industry.

3. We can draw three important conclusions from this model. First, the appearance of the capitalist mode of production in the regions destined to become the centers of the world capitalist system flowed from an internal process of disintegration of pre-capitalist (here feudal) modes. The disintegration of the feudal relations of production in the rural European world constituted the social framework for the agricultural revolution, which preceded and made possible the industrial one. A prior rise in agricultural productivity made possible the expulsion from the rural world of a surplus, proletarianized population and at the same time created the marketable food surplus necessary for the production of this proletariat.

Second, the articulation in time and space of the class alliances that enabled the new capitalist relations to spread in industry took different forms but always expressed the same basic condition: the alliance of the new dominant class (the industrial bourgeoisie) with landed property (either peasant, after a French-style revolution, or latifundiary when old feudal property was transformed and integrated into the market, as in England or Germany) within the framework of a complete and powerful national state.

Finally, the subjection of external (economic and political) relations to the needs of internal accumulation thus gradually created the world capitalist system. This system emerged as a group of autocentered and interdependent (although unequally advanced) central formations and of peripheral formations subject to the logic of accumulation in the centers that dominated them.

I conclude from this that the view of stages of development (with simply a certain historical lag from one to the other) is generally valid for the gradual establishment of the centers but is not so for the peripheries. This conclusion is the underlying cause of all the implicit and explicit disagreements about the future of the third world. The counter thesis holds, explicitly or implicitly, that despite their extraverted origin, underdeveloped economies are progressing through specific stages in their evolution toward the establishment of autocentered, complete economies. These will be capitalist or socialist depending on the case, for reasons outside the domain defined by this analysis.

4. Let us consider the stages in the evolution of the peripheries of the capitalist system, at least since the middle of the last century. In this model of accumulation in the periphery of the world system an export sector was created, on the initiative of the center, that would play the determining role in creating and shaping the market. To understand the underlying reason why it was possible to create this export sector, we must look to the conditions which made it profitable. National central capital was not forced to emigrate by a lack of possible outlets in the center: it emigrated toward the periphery in search of higher returns. The equalization of the rate of profit redistributed the benefits accruing from these higher returns and made the export of capital appear to be a means of combating the tendency of the rate of profit to fall. The real reason for the creation of the export sector was to obtain from the periphery products that formed the basis of constant capital (raw materials) or variable capital (food products) at prices of production below those for analogous products, or substitutes for specific products produced in the center.

5. Here is where the theory of unequal exchange comes in. The products exported by the periphery are attractive to the extent to which the gap between the returns to labor is greater than the gap in productivity. And it may be so from the moment the society is subject by all economic and extraeconomic means to this new function of furnishing cheap labor power for the export sector. From then on, the principal articulation that characterizes the accumulation process in the center—which is translated by the existence of an objective relation between the returns to labor and the level of development of the productive forces—completely disappears. The returns to labor in the export sector will be as low

as the economic, social, and political conditions allow. As to the level of development of the productive forces, it will be heterogeneous (while in the autocentered model it was homogeneous), advanced in the export sector and backward in the rest of the economy. This backwardness, maintained by the system, is the condition that enables the export sector to avail itself of cheap labor power.

6. Under these circumstances the internal market created by the development of the export sector will be limited and biased. The limited nature of the internal market accounts for the fact that the periphery attracts only a limited amount of capital from the center, although it offers a higher return on it. The contradiction between the capacity to consume and the capacity to produce is resolved on the level of the system on the world scale (center and periphery) through the growth of the market in the center, with the periphery playing a subordinate and limited role. This dynamic leads to a growing polarization in wealth to the benefit of the center.

Nevertheless, once the export sector reaches a certain size, an internal market appears. Compared to the market created in the central process, this market is biased against the demand for mass consumer goods in favor of luxury goods. If all the capital invested in the export sector were foreign and if all its projects were reexported to the center, the internal market would in fact be limited to the demand for mass consumer goods, a demand in itself limited by the low level of returns to labor. But in fact, part of this capital is local. Moreover, the methods used to assure a low return to labor are based on strengthening diverse local social strata which keep the system going: latifundiaries here, kulaks there, commercial comprador bourgeoisie, state bureaucracy, and so on. The internal market is thus primarily based on the luxury demand of these social strata.

This schema effectively corresponds to historial reality in the first phase of the imperialist system. This phase probably had its golden age between 1880 and 1914, although it began earlier in

Latin America and lasted in other places, notably in tropical Africa, until the 1950s. This was the age of the colonial pact, the colonial and semicolonial form of dominance over the peripheries.

7. This model is qualitatively different in three respects from the central model. First, the capitalist model was introduced from the outside by political domination. Here precapitalist rural relations did not disintegrate but rather were deformed by being subjected to the laws of accumulation of the central capitalist mode that dominated them. We can see this in the absence of a prior agricultural revolution, that is, in the stagnation of agricultural productivity.

Second, the class alliances that provided the political framework for the reproduction of the system were not primarily internal class alliances but rather an international alliance between dominant monopoly capital and its (subordinate) allies. Broadly, the latter were feudal elements (read: the range of varied dominant classes in precapitalist rural systems) and the comprador bourgeoisie. There was no complete and independent national state which really served these local classes but only an administration in the service of monopoly capital, either directly (colonial case) or indirectly (semicolonial case). Third, external relations were here not subject to the logic of internal development but rather were the driving force and the determinant of the direction and pace of development.

8. Today this first phase of imperialism is over. What forces brought this about and what kind of evolution ensued? The anti-imperialist national liberation movement was the motive force of the transformation. This movement united in effect three social forces: (a) the nascent, superexploited proletariat, (b) the peasant mass, doubly exploited by the dominant local classes and by monopoly capital to whose advantage the feudal elements had entered into the world market, and (c) the national bourgeoisie, at this stage more a potential than an actual class, which wanted to modify the terms of the international division of labor in order to gain an economic base for itself. In fact, the internal division of labor under the colonial pact was simple: the periphery exported

only primary products, with which it had to import all the manufactured goods necessary to meet its needs, primarily the needs
of luxury consumption; it could not develop industry. The national bourgeoisie and the proletariat vied for the leadership of
the national liberation movement, that is, the leadership of the
peasant revolt.

Overall, this first phase ended in the victory of the national
liberation movement under bourgeois leadership. The victory
forced imperialism to accept a change in the terms of the division
of labor and made possible the beginnings of industrialization in
the third world. We can date this victory. In some places it came
early: in Mexico with the 1910 revolution; in Turkey under Kemal
Ataturk; in Egypt with the Wafd; in Brazil and Argentina in a
populist form. In other places it came late: in southern Asia after the
Second World War; in Africa with the independence of the 1960s.
Except in East Asia and Cuba, where the national liberation
movement opted out of the world capitalist system, everywhere the
triumphant national bourgeoisie followed a strategy of industrialization that now has a name: the strategy of import substitution.

9. Because of the specific articulation expressed in the link
between the export sector and luxury consumption that characterizes the peripheral model, industrialization through import
substitution begins at the end. That is, with products corresponding to the most advanced stages of development in the center, with
durable goods. These products are big consumers of capital and
scarce resources (skilled labor, etc.). This results in a basic distortion in the process of resource allocation in favor of these products
and to the detriment of the production of mass consumer goods.
The latter sector is systematically neglected: there is no demand for
its products and it does not attract the financial or human resources
necessary for it to modernize. This is how we can explain the
stagnation of subsistence agriculture, the potential products of
which are in low demand and which has no serious means of trans-
forming the allocation of scarce resources. Given the structure of
income distribution, the structures of relative prices, and the

structures of demand, the choice of any development strategy based on profitability necessarily brings about this systematic distortion.

Seen from the social perspective, this model leads to a specific phenomenon, i.e., the marginalization of the masses. By that we mean an array of mechanisms which impoverish the masses and which take a variety of forms: proletarianization, semiproletarianization, impoverishment without proletarianization of the peasants, urbanization, and massive growth in urban unemployment and underemployment, to name a few. The function of unemployment and underdevelopment here is thus different from that in the central model: the weight of unemployment keeps the returns to labor at a relatively rigid minimum and blocks both the export and the luxury production sector. Wages are not at once a cost and an income that creates a demand essential to the model but are only a cost, with demand originating from outside or from the income of privileged social groups.

The extraverted origin of development, which continues despite the growing diversification of the economy and its industrialization, is not a sort of original sin external to the model of peripheral, dependent accumulation. For this is a model of the reproduction of the social and economic conditions for its operation. The marginalization of the masses is the very condition for the integration of the minority into the world system, the guarantee of a growing income for this minority, which encourages it to adopt Europe-type models of consumption. The extension of this model of consumption guarantees the profitability of the luxury production sector and strengthens the social, cultural, ideological, and political integration of the privileged classes.

10. At this stage of diversification and deepening of underdevelopment, new mechanisms of domination and dependence appear, cultural and political as well as economic. The latter include technological dependence and the domination of transnational firms. The luxury production sector calls for capital intensive investments which only the great transnational, oligopolistic firms can mobilize and which are the material underpinning of tech-

nological dependence. But also at this stage more complex forms of property structure and of economic management appear.

Historical experience shows that the participation of local private or public capital, even in a subordinate role, in the process of industrialization through import substitution is common. It also shows that at least in the bigger countries the development of export and luxury production sectors may be sufficient to enable the creation of a capital goods sector. The state is often the impetus for this. The development of basic industry and of a public sector does not mean, however, that the system is evolving toward an autocentered, complete form. For this capital goods sector serves not the development of mass consumption but the growth of export and luxury production.

11. This second phase of imperialism is in no way a stage toward the establishment of an autocentered economy. It is not the reproduction of an earlier phase of central development but, on the contrary, an extension of the first extraverted phase. In fact, three points can be made.

a. The agricultural revolution has still not taken place. Probably we need to introduce certain qualifications. The national bourgeoisie in power has often moved to eliminate old imperialist allies and particularly to carry out agrarian reforms that lay the basis for the beginning of capitalist agriculture (the "green revolution"). Can this development erase the original backwardness of agriculture and bring the peripheral model close to the central model? This question must be answered not only in theory but also in fact. Paradoxically, the relative backwardness of agriculture is such that third world countries where the majority of the population is rural, have become importers of food products. The reason for this is political: in our era the bourgeoisie must depend on those classes, however broad (kulaks instead of big proprietors), that are capable of dominating the peasants. It cannot depend on the peasant mass, whose interests conflict with its own. Although the central bourgeoisies have sufficient time for gradual primitive accumulation based on the peasant alliance, the bourgeoisies of the periphery are doubly constrained by the external pressure of the monopolies and the internal pressure of socialism among the peasants.

b. The dominant class alliances are still international: the bourgeoisie replaced old feudal and comprador elements as the subordinate ally of imperialism. Due to this, the bourgeoisie, beginning in this second phase, loses its former national character: it becomes "compradorized." The national state that it dominates therefore remains weak and only partially integrated.

c. The development process continues to depend on exports, which consist of raw materials. This primary means of financing necessary imports of equipment in the last instance determines the pace of growth, which in this sense remains extraverted.

12. The demand for a "new international economic order" brings about the crisis of this second phase. Reduced to its essentials, this demand seems to be the following: to force a rise in the price of raw materials exported by third world countries in order to create additional means, with the import of advanced technology, of financing a new stage of industrialization. This stage would be characterized by massive exports of manufactured products to the centers from the peripheries, which have the advantages of natural resources and a cheap, plentiful workforce (thus the demand for access to the markets of developed countries for these industrial products).

This demand has been the apparent common goal of the entire third world since 1973. It is presented as the necessary and sufficient condition for the achievement of political independence through the acquisition of an economic base. It is also presented as a possible common demand of all the states of the third world, independent of their social options and their international sympathies.

13. This new situation raises several essential questions which must be discussed quite openly. The first is whether the local bourgeoisie—which generally controls these states—can struggle against imperialism and impose its point of view. Certain authors in fact claim that this new international division of labor is the strategic objective of imperialism itself; that this demand is being manipulated by the monopolies, particularly North American ones;

and that it is thus not a proper goal for third world states which are in conflict with imperialist strategy. These authors usually give preeminence to interimperialist conflicts (United States, Europe, Japan) rather than to this apparent north-south conflict. We know that this theory was widely discussed at the time when the oil-exporting countries raised oil prices in 1973 and it had rightwing, leftwing and even ultra-leftwing versions. The facts do not support this interpretation. Indeed, it is nothing more than the naive view of the ultra-left which, taking its desires for reality, would like the bloc of bourgeoisies to be totally unified throughout the world so as to simplify on paper the tasks of the proletariat (70a, b).

In the past, the peripheral bourgeoisie clashed with imperialism. The monopolies did not plan the transition from the first to the second phase of imperialism: it was imposed by the national liberation movements when the peripheral bourgeoisies won from imperialism the right to industrialize. But I have argued that the strategy of industrialization followed during this second phase transformed the relations between the peripheral bourgeoisie and the monopolies. The peripheral bourgeoisie ceased to be national and became the junior partner of imperialism by integrating itself into the new division of labor. Today this partner is rebelling and demanding new modalities in the division of labor. This does not make it national, since its demand is contained within the system; but still it is rebelling. Should this rebellion succeed, it would simply inaugurate a new phase of imperialism, characterized by a new division of labor. For there is no doubt in theory that this rebellion can be coopted. But in theory only; for what counts in history are the accidents along the way, and some serious ones can occur in the peripheries and the centers during the contradiction-filled transition from the second to the theoretical third phase of imperialism.

14. The second question is whether this eventual third phase would or would not be a stage toward the autonomy of the peripheries. The third world bourgeoisies claim so, as they stated during the second phase. But the facts have shattered these illusions, which were shared by an important sector of the third world Left.

Indeed this demand, if it were met, would in no way be a stage in a process of development leading gradually to the creation of complete capitalist formations similar to those of the developed centers. The reason for this is that the new division of labor would be based on export of cheap manufactures by the periphery—that is, products which, given comparative productivity, would permit the rate of profit to rise on the scale of the world system. The worldwide equalization of profit would then modify relative prices and because of this would mask the supplementary transfer of value from the periphery to the center. In other words, the new division of labor would perpetuate and aggravate unequal exchange. It would also perpetuate in the peripheries the distortion of the demand structure to the detriment of mass consumption, just as in the preceding phases. The development of the world system would thus remain basically unequal. From then on, external demand would continue to be the principal driving force behind this type of still dependent development.

Let me add that in the framework of renewed dependence, the backwardness of agriculture would also be perpetuated. No doubt one could introduce certain qualifications here because, despite everything, capitalism would continue to progress in agriculture as it began to do during the second phase of imperialism. But here its pace would be much slower than in traditional and new export sectors and in luxury production for the internal market, all of which benefit from the massive import of the most advanced technology.

15. Within this general framework, we should question the real meaning of the slogans about autocentered development and collective autonomy, slogans that accompany the demand for this new international division of labor. The first slogan really has no content. It is nothing more than the ideological justification for the unfounded claim that development by progressive stages within the world system of unequal division of labor would lead to economic independence.

16. On the other hand, the second slogan has a meaning in this perspective, but a very specific meaning. The first phases of im-

perialism implied no cooperation between countries and regions of the periphery. Exclusively extraverted and limited in their industrialization by the needs of their internal markets, the peripheral economies had nothing to exchange with one another. In principle, the third phase in the unequal division of labor would not create more positive cooperation among third world countries, except to join them in struggle for a rise in the prices of their primary exports (through producers' associations), since this second wave of peripheral industrialization would be impelled by export to the centers.

Yet the countries of the third world are very unequally placed to take advantage of this new division of labor. Those which are best placed by virtue of their economic potential (abundant natural resources, most advanced proletarianization, etc.) and their political stability (legitimation of the power of the weak local bourgeoisie, military power, etc.) could move faster down the road of new dependency if they also had at their disposal the markets of less developed countries and if they had direct access to their providers of cheap raw materials and food products. The problem of so-called subimperialism becomes relevant here.

One example will illustrate this division in the interrelation of the third and fourth worlds within the new global perspective. Taken together, the Persian Gulf states, Egypt, and the Sudan—if the political conditions existed, which is far from the case today—would be a good candidate. The Persian Gulf states would furnish the capital, export industries would be concentrated in Egypt, the Sudan would export food products to the latter. But let us take a closer look at the mechanisms of this interrelationship. Even if Sudanese agriculture could be modernized to furnish the necessary exportable surplus, its productivity would long remain below that of the advanced countries. But Sudanese food products would have to be competitive with those of North America on the Egyptian market in order to keep Egyptian salaries as low as possible. This would be possible only if superexploitation of the Sudanese peasants continued (rewards to labor more unequal than the distribution of productivity). The Egyptian proletariat would also be superexploited; its low wages combined with its relatively high productivity would allow export of its products to the centers. A double and articulated unequal exchange would take place to the benefit of the center. The Sudan would cease to be directly dependent on the center and become the partner of the first-rank periphery, where export industry would be concentrated.

17. If this is the content of the organization of the new phase of imperialism, can the triple demand for national autonomy, collective autonomy, and a new world order also have a completely different meaning with different goals? If so, under what conditions?

The neoimperialist interpretation of this program is that of a new international division of labor to which internal strategies such as the objectives of intra–third world cooperation are subjected. But the same program takes on another meaning entirely when the procedure is reversed, i.e., when we first define the internal goals of real, autocentered and popular development and then examine the ways in which the world order would have to be changed to make the realization of these goals possible (cf. 74c).

True autocentered development is necessarily popular development. For extroverted development in all the phases of evolution of the imperialist system effectively benefits the dominant privileged classes which are allied with the monopolies. Inversely and complementarily, popular development can only be national and autocentered. To serve the great masses of the peasantry, industrialization must first be used to increase rural productivity. In the same way, those wishing to serve the urban popular masses must stop luxury production for the local market and exportation, both of which are based on the reproduction of a cheap labor force. Let us look more closely at this two-pronged strategy of national independence and social progress.

Up to now, industrialization in the third world has not been conceived of as a means to agricultural progress. In reverse order from the countries of the center, where the agricultural revolution preceded the industrial one, the countries of the periphery imported the second without having begun the first stage. This explains the distortions characterizing these countries and the renewed dependence in which they are trapped. Thus it is necessary to turn the tide. Third world industry continues to be parasitic in the sense that it gets its accumulation by levies from the rural world in real terms (it obtains its labor power from the rural exodus) and in financial terms (fiscal levies, internal terms of exchange unfavorable to the peasants, etc.) without in turn supporting agricultural development. How can this be changed? Clearly, all criteria of profitability, which are necessarily based on the reproduction of price structures and structures of income distribution, must be totally rejected and replaced by other criteria for the allocation of resources. Two essential questions arise here: (1) how to join a modern industrial sector, with a changed basic orientation, with that of small, rural industries, making possible the direct mobilization of latent forces of progress; and (2) why the social form necessary here is rural collectivization, even at a low level of development of the productive forces, and not private agriculture, however reshaped by radical agrarian reform. It is only under these conditions that progress in agriculture, which must first overcome its historic backwardness, can finance healthy industrialization and create a food surplus to guarantee national independence.

In the same way, industry must be put in the service of the poor urban masses and cease to be run according to criteria of profitability, which favor the privileged local market and export toward the developed centers. In no case can industry so transformed adopt ready-made technological models from the developed countries. Nor can it find them in the older technology of the centers by borrowing yesterday's production techniques, as the theme of intermediary technology suggests. The problem here is different, since industrialization must bring about the agricultural revolution, while in the center the former was built on the latter. The real question revolves not around the conditions for the transfer of technology but the creation of conditions favoring creativity in this area, not for reasons of cultural nationalism but for objective reasons. Another problem should be pointed out, that is, borrowed technology necessarily carries with it capitalist relations of production, while the social framework needed for the agricultural revolution and urban mobilization must be socialist. This question is essential. It translates the necessary character of socialism in the periphery, which is the indispensable condition for progress and independence and not merely the result of an ideological or moral decision. For this reason, I will continue to argue that the movement for national liberation in the periphery constitutes first a moment in the socialist transformation of the world and only later a phase in capitalist development.

18. Although a model for autocentered development is not synonymous with autarchy, internal and external political factors may lead to the latter, whether it is desired or not. This may be the case not only for large countries such as the USSR or China but also for small countries such as Korea, Vietnam, Cambodia, Cuba, or Albania. Although autarchy in itself is not synonymous with autocentered development, it does provide the condition for it in certain historical circumstances, such as, for example, Burma.

But if autarchy is too abruptly imposed it can impede autocentered development by creating additional costs, which may be very heavy in certain cases. For we cannot reject totally the theory of comparative advantage; we must note only that if the international division of labor is unequal the theory loses its validity. A country that chooses the autocentered and popular road may find that importing certain inputs needed to accelerate development (notably, in some cases, energy or certain raw materials or types of equipment) may be cheaper than doing without them.

19. To deal with this type of problem, the liberated states of the third world could act collectively in two ways. First, they could practice mutual aid. Since they are rich in natural resources, which are most often exploited exclusively to the profit of the developed countries, they could exchange among themselves raw materials useful to their national projects for autonomous development. Currently, these imports almost always go via the developed

centers, which control the raw material markets and centralized payment facilities. Through mutual-aid agreements (commercial and multilateral payment agreements) the liberated countries of the third world could by-pass these intermediaries. Furthermore, exchange of technology could accelerate the introduction of appropriate production techniques, since the problems which these countries have to resolve are often similar.

This type of intra–third world cooperation is very different from what takes place within the neoimperialist framework. It is no longer a question of common markets that can only produce and aggravate inequalities in development. I am proposing the general outlines of an overall agreement (package deal) in the spirit of cooperation in the service of national, autonomous development.

20. The second type of collective action is designed to modify the international division of labor between the developed countries and the countries of the third world. This means the reduction of inequality and no longer simple change. Already at the present time a good number of third world countries subscribe to the idea of countering consumer monopolies with associations of raw materials' producers and of strengthening these associations by establishing a collective support fund. In fact, this would necessitate, to start with, national, state control over the exploitation of natural resources. By this I mean not only formal nationalization of this exploitation but also and especially the regulation of the export flow and its reduction to the level of imports set by the internal strategy of autocentered development. For currently the extraverted strategy is based on exactly the opposite relation: exports are first pushed to the maximum, solely to service the demand from the centers, and then the question is raised as to how to utilize the returns from these exports. The unequal international division of labor rests on this strategy. To reduce the inequality in the division of labor certainly means to reduce the flow of raw materials exports.

The formidable resistance of the developed world to this reduction is evidence that the center cannot do without the pillage of the third world. If this pillage were stopped, the centers would as a consequence have to modify their structures in order to adapt to a new and less unequal international division of labor. Then and only then could we begin to speak of a real new world order and not only of new terms in the unequal international division of labor.

21. These two general lines, that of a new imperialist order and that of an order that would initiate real progress in the liberation of third world peoples, are not two abstract themes. They are already colliding in the real world, and are the source of daily conflicts.

The reason for this is above all the contradictory nature of the national liberation movement, which is at once the expression of capitalist development and of the crisis of capitalism. Capitalist and socialist tendencies thus are constantly at odds within the movement itself, precisely because the forces of capitalism are ever those of a weak, peripheral, dependent capitalism which objectively cannot realize the goals of a complete capitalism. These forces are in conflict in all third world regimes. In those countries which have broken with capitalism, these bourgeois tendencies persist, as we well know. But conversely, the capitalist states of the third world do not have the complete and unequivocal character of central capitalist states. This explains the volatile nature of their regimes and the wide range of situations, from triumphant neo-colonialism to nationalism in conflict with imperialism, by way of shameful or crisis-ridden neocolonialism.

For the conflict with imperialism has certainly begun. The themes of the new international order have up until now been totally rejected, as the failure of the fourth UN Conference on Trade and Development (UNCTAD) and the north-south negotiations indicate. On the ideological level, the Club of Rome is trying to counter with an alternative construction. This is because the themes of the new order convey the aspiration to control natural resources and to strengthen national states, an aspiration that imperialism does not accept.

Theoretically, the new unequal division of labor would satisfy everyone, the peripheral bourgeoisies and the monopolies in the center. For the transfer of industries would bring about the recreation of an unemployed reserve army, which a quarter century of growth has reduced to the point where the system has lost its normal flexibility. And this unemployment would allow the rate of surplus value to rise in the center itself. In the longer run, the center would develop new activities for the overall control of the system— the quartenary industries (software, research and development activities, etc.), new growth industries, the military sector—thereby renewing and deepening the conditions for social-democratic hegemony in the center.

But as we know, in the long run we are all dead. Today resistance to the transfer of industries still overwhelmingly prevails. This pushes up against the wall the bourgeoisies of the third world who as the weaker partners must carry all the weight of the crisis. Thus it becomes impossible to attenuate the violent social contradictions in the third world: the food deficit is growing, the establishment of export industries has been put off *sine die,* and so on. Because of this, political conditions can evolve in a direction favorable to the initiation of autocentered development. Such is reality: the struggle of the third world against the dominant imperialist hegemony. For many reasons, this struggle is still today the primary force for the transformation of the world.

II. The class structure of the contemporary imperialist system

The unequal international division of labor accounts for the class structure of the contemporary imperialist system.

In 1976 world population passed the 4 billion mark. Of this total 750 million are in the developed capitalist centers (Europe: 370 million; North America: 250 million; Japan: 110 million), 2 billion are in the dominated peripheries (Asia: 1300 million; Africa: 400 million; Latin America: 350 million), 1,350 million are in noncapitalist countries (the USSR and Eastern Europe: 360 million; China, Vietnam, Laos, Cambodia, Korea, Cuba: almost 1 billion).

The capitalist centers' active population, which consists overwhelmingly of urban wage workers, is divided into three basically equal parts: the working class; the old petty bourgeoisie and the new proletarianized one; the middle (basically salaried) and capitalist layers and classes. Among the 240 million wage workers exploited by capital there are today, with the crisis, almost 25 million unemployed (about 7 percent of the active population).

The population of the periphery is still about four-fifths rural (only Latin America and the Arab world are as yet highly urbanized) and it is estimated that 75 percent of the peasants are poor and/or exploited. But the urban population of the periphery (400 million) is almost two-thirds as large as that of the centers (600 million) and is growing much faster. The unemployment figure for third world cities is at least 50 million, according to the most conservative estimates, that is, twice the unemployment figure in the center in a time of crisis and six or seven times this figure in prosperous times—which are prosperous only in the system's center.

The income distribution of these classes on a world scale is set out in Table 1. It is important to keep these figures in mind. The basic question of our era is precisely whether the center-periphery combination constitutes a single world, a single system, or two relatively autonomous realities. If one believes, as I do, that the imperialist system is the prime dominant reality, one must draw several conclusions.

1. The bourgeoisie and the privileged social layers attached to it, which form about one-tenth of the system's population, monopolize almost half the income. This is in gross terms equal to a rate of surplus labor extorted in relation to labor paid on the order of 100 percent (see below for the meaning of the calculation).

The categories "middle and bourgeois layers" include the bourgeoisie in the strict sense of the term—the class that owns and controls the means of production—and the technical and social managers of this control who, despite the fact that they are wage earners, share in varying degrees the lifestyle and ideology of the bourgeoisie. The income of these layers includes the nondistributed profits of enterprise.

Table 1
World Income Distribution by Class (1975)

	(1) Millions of persons	(2) Percentage of (1)	(3) Average income per person ($)	(4) Total income (billions of $)	(5) Percentage of (4)
A. Centers					
Peasantry	35	3	4,300	150	6
Working class					
"inferior" category	50	4	3,000	150	6
"superior" category	60	4	4,500	270	10
Proletarianized petty bourgeoisie	110	8	5,200	570	21
Middle and bourgeois layers	90	7	12,000	1,080	40
Unemployed	25	2	—	—	—
Total of A	370	27	6,000	2,220	83
B. Peripheries					
Peasantry					
poor and exploited	600	44	200	120	4
middle	150	11	400	60	2
owners and capitalists	50	4	1,000	50	2
Working class	50	4	600	30	1
Proletarianized petty bourgeoisie	80	6	800	65	2
Middle and bourgeois layers	20	1	6,800	135	5
Urban unemployed	50	4	—	—	—
Total of B	1,000	73	460	460	17
Grand Total	1,370	100	1,950	2,680	100

Discrepancies in percentages result from rounding.

The concentration of the bourgeoisie in the center of the system obviously results from its imperialist character. The peripheral bourgeoisie is still largely rural. In the periphery, only the urban bourgeoisie has a European type lifestyle and this class makes up scarcely 1 percent of the population of the system. The middle layers and the urban bourgeoisie of the periphery (the rural element of the bourgeoisie is included in the peasantry) are still very small numerically, the more so as half its members and its incomes derive from Latin America.

2. All the other social classes furnish surplus labor in various forms to the ultimate benefit of capital, which dominates the whole of the system and exploits all its parts. This is true not only for the working class but also for the proletarianized petty bourgeoisie (salaried workers who are less and less skilled), the pauperized petty bourgeoisie (small producers chained to market mechanisms), and the great mass of peasants. Islands outside the system—ethnographic reservations—are insignificant in our day.

3. Today we cannot confuse the proletariat with the working class, still less with the working class of the imperialist centers alone. The employed working class is composed of at least four parts. One-third is today exploited by capital on the periphery of the system, where an at least equal mass of unemployed persons exists. Although it produces under technical conditions which are often comparable, it is deprived of the most elementary rights. This part of the working class receives no more than one-sixth of the wages of the working class exploited in the center of the system (the rate of surplus value here is probably on the order of 400–500 percent on the average).

In the center the working class is more and more divided into two parts, the more exploited of which is growing in relative proportion and is gradually being dispossessed of the rights it had won. This type of division of the working class is doubtless not entirely new but has taken on greater proportions and become more systematic as a result of the global strategies introduced by capital during the Second World War in the United States (when the black population largely took the place of the old working class in the northern metropolises), and extended to postwar Europe with the massive immigration of the 1960s. In its wake have followed characteristic political and ideological effects: the opposition of old union and partisan organizations, spontaneous movements, instability of unemployment (marginalization of the youth), conjunction with the women's movement (with its working class element), and so on.

I have drawn a line between the "inferior" and "superior" categories of the working class in the centers, corresponding grossly to a numerical division. This enables me to distinguish between the relatively stable part of the working class and that which labors under more difficult, more unstable, and more poorly paid working conditions. Based on divisions that are national (immigrants in Europe), racial (blacks in the United States), regional (southerners in Italy), sexual (temporary female employees), this division has already radically altered the conditions of the class struggle from what they were only half a century ago. Immigrants, minorities, women, and young people today make up almost half the working class in the centers.

The absolute number of the working class (salaried manual workers) of the periphery is no longer negligible. But the majority of these workers are employed in small firms: employment in big mining, transportation firms, and in manufacturing industries is limited. This is not due primarily to the fact of lesser productivity (corresponding to a lesser concentration of capital, especially indigenous capital), for these small enterprises are often modern. It is due above all to the structure of the international division of industrial labor, which is unequal and weighs on the side of light and subcontracting and maintenance industries in the periphery. Correcting for the differences in the style and cost of living from city to country, the average wages of the working class are often as low as the incomes of the peasantry.

For the peripheries, I tried to give an indication of urban unemployment only, without taking account of rural underemployment, whether overt (peasants without land who can sell their labor power only for part of the year) or hidden. The estimate of 25 percent of the active population is conservative in the extreme.

The superior part of the working class in the centers is not growing in number (and thus is decreasing proportionately). It is still highly organized, but it also includes a large proportion of foremen, supervisors, and the like, whose jobs are in between direct production and the organization of work. The "labor aristocracy," which believes it should support the capitalist social and ideological system, is recruited from this category.

The active industrial reserve army has never been small, contrary to ideological rhetoric. It has never been less than 25–33 percent of the working class. But the mass of it, which is structurally stable, is becoming more and more localized in the periphery. Once again this is a new phenomenon, one which appeared after 1945. The conjunctural fluctuations in unemployment in the center remain important but small in relation to the continued growth of the reserve army in the periphery, even in a period of prosperity. This fact obviously has an impact on the comparative conditions of the class struggle and also has ideological and political consequences. The new tendencies in the international division of labor (redeployment) articulate with this structure.

4. The categories grouped under the rubric of "proletarianized petty bourgeoisie" are heterogenous in appearance. I have drawn a line here at an income level that is not significantly higher than that of the upper categories of the working class. Probably the term "petty bourgeoisie" is not really appropriate. It defines quite well the status of petty producers (artisans and small merchants), certain categories of which are gradually being destroyed by competition from modern capitalist enterprises. But it is misleading when applied to the new and numerically expanding petty bourgeoisie, which consists primarily of wage workers who, having nothing to sell but their labor power, are in fact proletarians (as their salary level indicates). Furthermore, the process of progressively taking the skill out of these nonmanual jobs is very rapid. The over-

whelming majority of this category (80 percent) already consists of wage workers, notably of this type. It is true that there exist at the same time new categories of petty producers, car mechanics, for instance, but, unlike the old producers, the latter are frequently in a situation of formal submission to dominant capital. Doubtless, social stratification empirically based on income data has the drawback of this heterogeneity.

The numerical mass of the proletarianized petty bourgeoisie, wage workers in the main, is already greater than that of the working class on the scale of the system as a whole. The living standard of this new proletarian stratum—it has only its labor power to sell—is not significantly different from that of the working class. Its concentration in the center of the system results in large measure from the unequal international division of labor between the center and the periphery. The ideological effects of the formation of this new proletarian layer are already visible: examples include radical movements in America based on a different problematic than that of the traditional working class (gay liberation, the feminist movement, etc.), linked perhaps with the nature of the integration of this category into the work process. It remains to be seen what form this category will take: an autonomous class, a part of the proletariat, or a wavering petty bourgeoisie.

The category "proletarianized petty bourgeoisie" of the periphery is defined so as to group together all the occupations of the petty urban world whose incomes are scarcely higher—this means these workers cannot have a Western mode of consumption. But this category of wage workers in the modern sector (the analogue of the new petty bourgeoisie) is in the minority here (30 million?), while the subcategory of artisans, small merchants, and domestics is in the majority.

5. The mass of the poor peasantry (microfundiaries, small peasants without modern technical means of production) and the exploited peasantry (agricultural workers, sharecroppers, etc.) in the periphery makes up the great bulk of the producers of the imperialist system: 44 percent alone, 55 percent if we include

middle peasants. The income of this enormous mass is tiny: 4 percent of the total product of the imperialist system.

Is it possible to use a table of the equivalents, expressed in incomes, of production within the capitalist system, to analyze the contradictions within this system (without reducing it to a simple and abstract capitalist mode) and pinpoint the tendencies in the accumulation which they control?

For the vulgar economist there is no problem. Prices are the only economic reality: there is nothing other than the immediate phenomenal appearance; value in the Marxist sense is a "metaphysical" category and a pointless detour; capital and labor are two distinct factors of production. The income of each class thus corresponds to its contribution to production, the productivity of each factor being measured by its reward, with allowance made for imperfect competition. But all this is merely a vulgar tautology.

For the vulgar Marxist this table poses no problem either. The reasoning would be along the following lines: if group A were a single country, the value produced would be $2,220 billion (thus $8,700 for each of the 225 million productive workers). The value of labor power would be measured by the value paid to the producers (here $1,040 billion). Surplus value—the form of surplus labor in the capitalist mode—would be $1,080 billion and the rate of surplus value would be about 100 percent.

For group B we cannot speak of the capitalist mode in the strict sense but can speak of surplus labor, since we are talking about a class society ("half feudal, half capitalist"). The value produced is $460 billion; this is $520 per productive worker (880 million in number). Labor productivity is on the average 6 percent of that in A. The volume of surplus labor extorted by the exploiters—landed proprietors and capitalists—is $185 billion (50 + 135); and the rate of surplus labor in relation to necessary labor is 185/275, or 67 percent. Although workers in B are poorer than those in A, they are less exploited.

Of course, this version does not preclude the possibility of transfers of value from B to A, but only under three conditions:

(1) as the ownership of the exploiting capital in B comes from A, the visible profits are transferred from B to A; (2) if there is equalization of profit on the scale of the group A + B, a systematic distortion in the organic compositions (higher in A) brings about a value/price of production distortion unfavorable to B; or (3) we take account of imperfect competition. But all this remains quantitatively small.

I do not accept this view, which derives from a systematic obfuscation of the fact of imperialism, expressing a bourgeois point of view within distorted Marxism, whether social-democratic or revisionist. In fact, the very nature of this table is problematic. The prices in which incomes are accounted constitute an immediate empirical category resulting from the summation of the real remuneration of labor set by the conditions of its exploitation and of profit calculated around a certain rate (or several). We cannot deduct comparative productivities from the comparison of incomes (salaries plus profits). We must do the reverse, that is, begin with a comparative analysis of working conditions which define the comparative productivities and the rates of extraction of surplus labor. For the tendencies for the equalization of profit are superimposed on combinations of returns to labor and labor productivity which vary with the conditions of exploitation.

Moreover, capital does not really dominate the whole of the work process systemwide: the great mass of agricultural production and a good part of petty artisanal production are only subject to the formal domination of capital over the process of production without its always being involved in the direct work process. Thus the existing social classes cannot be reduced to two, the bourgeoisie and the proletariat, nor can the system be reduced to a capitalist mode of production functioning on a world scale.

The peasants of the periphery are integrated into precapitalist modes of production by the type of social relations of production and the level of development of the productive forces, which are class modes. This is why the hypothesis of self-subsistence agrarian societies corresponding to earlier communal modes, to the division of society into classes (or the transition to the formation of classes) is only partially applicable and ultimately incorrect: it discounts the integration of the agrarian societies of the periphery into the imperialist system. For in their turn these precapitalist class societies are certainly integrated into the imperialist system. The surplus labor furnished by the exploited peasants and extorted by their traditional exploiters takes the form of commodities circulating throughout the system. Inside underdeveloped countries, it constitutes a material element of the value of the labor power of the local proletariat; and on the outside it constitutes the elements of the value of constant capital and of the labor power of the exploited proletariat in the center.

Furthermore, this integration takes a number of forms. It may be exclusively market integration, with capital intervening not at all in the immediate labor process. More and more this intervention is taking place, the producers remaining free in appearance but in appearance only: they are forced to buy fertilizer, insecticide, agricultural instruments and machinery, to produce a given product under the supervision of the buyers, agrobusiness firms, or the extension services that oblige producers to adopt given production techniques. Due to this, subjection to capital is gradually becoming a reality.

Thus more than two classes exist because there is not a single mode of production, the capitalist mode, but rather several interrelated modes within the capitalist system. It is this global domination of capital over the system that allows us to speak of value as the dominant, general category of the form of the product. Of course, the category of surplus value is more limited in its applicability and cannot, like that of surplus labor, be extended to precapitalist modes. But the domination of capital brings about the transformation of the surplus labor of the exploited producers outside the capitalist mode into surplus value and finally into profit for capital in general and for its monopoly sectors in particular. Because of this it is appropriate to reduce the mass of surplus labor monopolized by capital (a mass created within the capitalist mode and in the integrated and subject precapitalist modes) to the value paid to the labor power directly and indirectly exploited by capital. This gives an overall rate of surplus value for the system, one that controls the level of the rate or rates of profit.

I can illustrate this line of reasoning with regard to the transfer of value (the terms of transfer are debatable; I am really talking about the distribution of value among the existing classes) based on the figures in Table 1 and on hypotheses, as realistic as possible, related to the different levels of development of the productive forces in the different modes of production articulated, as well as the forms and rates of the exploitation of labor. In fact, production figures as taken from national accounts are not estimates of value but of estimated quantities at prices of production, with abstraction made of imperfect competition. Thus we are looking at transfers in relation to prices of production, that is, systematic distortions in actual prices as compared with production prices due to different conditions of the class struggle and the extraction of surplus labor. I will take the precaution of recalling that in Marxism labor productivity is the productivity of labor in a given branch producing a commodity having a given use value and that there is no sense comparing productivity from one branch to another, as vulgar economies does in its confusion between productivity and profitability.

Thus one could reason as follows. Suppose that the direct producers in the center (working class, peasants, proletarianized petty bourgeoisie: 255 million workers) are exploited under technical conditions which maximize the productivity of their labor in each of the branches of production concerned; and take 100 as an index of this productivity for each of these branches. The return to labor here is about $4,300 per worker and the value created about $8,700, the rate of surplus value being about 100 percent.

In the periphery there are 50 million workers, 80 million proletarianized petty bourgeois, and 750 million peasants who work in conditions of productivity and exploitation which are not the same as those in analogous branches of production in the center. Productivity is comparable in industry because the capitalist mode has been established there. Nevertheless, it can be stated that average productivity in the periphery is comparatively at an index of 50 (it is probably higher). Taking this difference in productivity into account, the value produced by these 50 million workers at the average rate of exploitation of the center (100 percent of surplus value) would be .50 × 50 × $8,700, or $220 billion. If the value of the industrial production of the periphery given empirically, i.e., in going prices, is less than this it is because the rate of exploitation of the workers is much higher than in the center (their salaries are not even half of those in the center but are seven times less), and because the resulting extra surplus labor is not necessarily made up for by a volume of profits that would presuppose a considerably higher rate than in the center. As a result, effective prices differ from prices of production.

As to what the proletarianized petty bourgeoisie produces, I hypothesize an average comparative productivity index of only 30, to take account of the fact that the portion of noncapitalist artisans is relatively larger here and that wage workers in the modern tertiary sector of a capitalist structure analogous to that of the center are smaller in number. The value produced is, still according to these hypotheses, .30 × 80 × $8,700, or $210 million. Here also, we can see that the returns to labor are in a 1 to 6.5 relation, while productivity is only in a 1 to 3 relation.

Agricultural productivity in B is one-tenth that of A, according to figures from the UN Food and Agricultural Organization. The physical product per agricultural worker, measured in comparable physical terms (quintals of grain, with all production being reduced to this equivalent) is in fact in a relation of 1 to 10. Even assuming that the value produced by the peasants of the periphery is reduced to that of its living labor component, with the contribution of dead labor (capital) being zero, if the peasant mass in fact did not furnish extra surplus labor compared to that extorted from the peasants in the center, the return per peasant would here be .10 × $4,300, or $430, while it is in fact only $240. The extra surplus labor is (430 − 240) ×750, or $140 billion and the value of the product is underestimated by that amount (it is in appearance 120 + 60 or $180 billion).

In all, according to these hypotheses, the extra surplus labor extorted from the producers of the periphery due to the harsher conditions of exploitation is on the order of $290 billion, the value produced by these producers being on the order of $220 billion for the workers, $210 billion for the proletarianized petty bourgeoisie and 180 + 140, or $320 billion for the peasantry, for a total of $750 billion, while the apparent value in current prices is only $460 billion.

Where does this extra surplus labor of almost $300 billion go? If we accept that the income of the peripheral bourgeoisie ($135 billion) results from a normal rate of return on the capital it controls (the same as that in the nonmonopoly sectors elsewhere), this surplus labor must be transferred to the center, where it swells the income of the capitalist class (which, without this, would have $780 billion instead of $1,080 billion) and perhaps even (in part) that of the workers who are otherwise exploited. Of course, if the rate of profit is higher in the periphery than in the center, a part of this $300 billion would be in the global income of $185 billion, from which the bourgeoisie and the landed proprietors of the periphery benefit.

In any event, the existence of this mass of extra surplus labor, wherever it goes, allows the average rate of exploitation and profit to rise on the scale of the system. Without this, income distribution, instead of being $1,415 billion for the workers and $1,265 for the bourgeoisie (rate of extraction of surplus labor: 90 percent) would be $1,715 billion against $965 billion (corresponding to a rate of exploitation of 57 percent).

This statistical illustration of the nature of the imperialist problem is not arbitrary. On the contrary, the basic statistics and hypotheses are conservative and tend to underestimate the magnitude of the surplus labor extracted on the periphery of the system. This calculation rests in fact on a systematic comparison of real productivity and real return to labor which reveals that the disparity always operates in the same direction: the return to labor in the periphery is always much less than the comparative productivity and this disparity is always considerable.

This means simply that the misery of the peripheral workers does not stem only from the backwardness in the development of the productive forces. The peripheral workers are also superexploited. How and to whose profit?

The superexploitation of the peripheral workers—the surplus labor which they furnish—could benefit, in principle: (1) the local classes which exploit them (landed proprietors and local capitalists); (2) capital dominant on the scale of the system, that of the monopolies; and (3) the workers (or some of them, at least) of the imperialist centers. We cannot *a priori* reject any of these three possibilities. We must first analyze concrete reality and then try to understand theoretically and politically the meaning of this reality in terms of the class struggle.

The volume of surplus labor extracted from the workers, employees, and peasants of the periphery is obviously much too great for me to believe that it is retained completely by the local exploiting classes in the form of rent and profit. The total income of these exploiting classes ($185 billion) is in fact less than the extra surplus labor extracted ($300 billion). Admitting that ground rents are excessive (we know that there is no normal rent level determined by an economic law, but that this level is determined by a power relation among the three partners in the class struggle) and that the rate of profit for indigenous capital is higher than in the center (which no serious empirical study confirms: the highest rates of profit go not to indigenous capital but to monopoly capital), nevertheless, as a decisive proportion of this surplus labor does not appear in the income distributed in the periphery, it can only be undergoing a transfer to the center. This is an invisible transfer because it is included in the price structures.

If, moreover, this surplus labor were retained by the local exploiting classes, we would see a prodigious development of capitalism, which could then resolve the problem of underdevelopment. For, however antipathetic these classes are, they are not overall any more parasitical than their counterparts in the center. But up to the present time there has been no development of this magnitude. Contrary to the bourgeois theory of underdevelopment, the periphery is not poor but impoverished because it is superexploited, and it is this superexploitation that both reproduces its poverty and retards its development.

How and why is this superexploitation possible? An analysis of the concrete conditions of class struggle is necessary here. The survival—the reproduction even—of precapitalist relations of exploitation is the means of this superexploitation. The distortion in the structure of development based on the unequal international division of labor imposed by imperialism brings about a continuous reproduction of an industrial reserve army of massive unemployment (while this same division of labor reduces this reserve in the center, that is, transfers the inherent contradiction of the capitalist mode to the periphery of the system it dominates). This creates for the young proletariat, deprived of all rights (which is no accident), conditions unfavorable to its struggles.

We must push the analysis of class struggle beyond this point. For since transfer takes place, this system of superexploitation works to the benefit of monopoly capital. The local exploiting classes are only the intermediaries, the junior partners, in this exploitation. This is precisely where their responsibility lies: in their collusion with imperialism. And it is precisely because imperialism benefits from this superexploitation that it operates via international class alliances.

In turn, these alliances have brought about, on the one hand, the reproduction of precapitalist relations and on the other, distortion in the development of capitalism based on the unequal international division of labor. This is why historical development has generally not destroyed precapitalist modes (while development in the center has by and large broken them up) but on the contrary has reproduced them by subjecting them. This essential point escapes those superficial analysts who equate capitalist development in the periphery with capitalist development *per se*.

Does the transfer of surplus labor benefit dominant capital, the proletariat in the centers, or both? It would be very surprising if most of this transfer of surplus labor failed to benefit monopoly capital. For after all, in the class struggle monopoly capital has the last word (as long as we remain within the imperialist system) and thus defines the strategies for the international division of labor in accordance with its own interest, which is to raise the global rate of exploitation.

This said, the transfer nevertheless affects society as a whole and in all its aspects and determines simultaneously the conditions of asymmetrical reproduction, accelerating the capacity for accumulation in the center and reducing and deforming it in the periphery. The transfer thus reproduces the conditions for the unequal international division of labor. It is this asymmetrical structure that gives the workers in the center the possibility of carrying on their economic class struggles under more favorable conditions. It allows salaries and productivity to grow in tandem over a long period, bringing about a relative loss which capital makes up for by continually raising the rate of extraction of surplus labor in the periphery.

But at the same time these conditions create a fertile soil for the political illusions of reformism, which has thereby achieved hegemony among the workers of the center. It is these ideologies—interclass national solidarity based on the recognition of the decisive importance of sources of supply of raw materials to assure regular growth in the center, old and new nationalism (panoccidentalism with racist overtones)—more than the material corruption of the labor aristocracy (which also exists but is impossible to measure) that reproduce imperialist ideological hegemony.

The reader can see that this way of formulating and answering questions begins with the analysis of class struggle and of exploitation. The point of departure is, in fact, a survey of the modes of production (type of relations of production and level of development of the productive forces). Based on that, labor productivity was evaluated in the different areas of activity on the one hand and on the other hand the rates of extraction of surplus labor that characterize these areas in the conditions of fundamental, immediate (exploited against direct exploiters) struggles. The only condition for the validity of the method is the recognition that the imperialist system is the basic reality, that is, that the product of the labor of all the direct producers of the system is commodified and therefore has measurable value. I am not unaware that a part of this product is directly consumed by the producers. But the peasants are no longer self-subsisting and except for several unimportant islands, are all also forced to produce for the market.

I began with the analysis of the concrete conditions of the exploitation of labor and of the class struggle rather than with immediate economic quantities (production estimated by current prices, distribution of their equivalent in incomes), because the latter are, in the final analysis, derived from the class struggle and do not express primary economic laws. A few points should be born in mind in relation to this.

a. The method does not suppose a reasoning in value terms in the Marxist sense but only in prices of production. The analysis in value terms is indispensable and is the only one which can answer the questions that leave Sraffan analysis speechless, as I argued in *The Law of Value and Historical Materialism*.

b. The world system is dominated by the commodity (and by value) and all the precapitalist modes subjected to capital's domination therefore produce commodities. The terms of exchange between them can thus be such that the surplus labor created in one place is appropriated in another: value can be transferred. But this cannot result from the mechanical working of the law of value of the same type as the equalization of profit (73b-1). Is this a pure power relation, or rather, does it result from the real workings of the class struggle? I opt for the second, richer, line of thought.

c. I am not concerned with calculating the value or values of labor power in discussing what the workers objectively need to reproduce it. In listing the incomes attributed here and there in nominal terms I am not concerned about their real purchasing power. For if real salaries are by chance not as bad as the comparison of nominal salaries might indicate, this is because, as Rey concludes, "behind each exploited worker stand ten equally exploited peasants" (73b-1).

On the contrary, any method which begins with prices leaves out the class struggle and leads to an economistic reduction of Marxism. It gives preeminence to the law of value (which would directly determine price) over historical materialism (the class struggle). All theories that deny that surplus labor is transferred from the periphery to the center presume, implicitly if not explicitly, that price is the starting point. To say that productivity in the periphery is 6 percent of that in the center because the product per worker (at stated prices) is 6 percent is to ignore the relations of production, the labor process, and the extortion of surplus labor and thus to descend to vulgar economy. It is of little importance that these theories are accompanied by declarations about the preeminence of the relations of production over circulation, and so on. These are additions that contradict the essence of the method of analysis.

Elsewhere I have expressed my views about this proimperialist current within Marxism, which obviously is not itself exempt from the effects of the class struggle. This brand of Marxism, limited to 4 percent of the exploited workers of the capitalist world, can no longer act as a subversive force. It no longer even convinces the 4 percent whom it claims to lead. They are gradually abandoning all references, even verbal ones, to Marxism, which has taken refuge in academic rhetoric (90-4). On the other hand, my analysis corresponds to the interests of 90 percent of the men and women of the capitalist world. It lays the basis for a worker-peasant alliance, an alliance of all exploited workers, on the basis of internationalism, that is, the conditions necessary to change the world.

The method which I reject is based in a West-centered and linear conception of history. It leads directly to seeing current struggles in terms of the development rather than the overthrow of capitalism. If underdevelopment is backwardness and not superexploitation, capitalist accumulation will gradually overcome it; the national liberation movement is an integral part of the still rising bourgeois revolution; the possible resistance of the peasants to this development is useless and reactionary. On the contrary, our thesis is that national liberation is part of the crisis of capitalism, of the socialist revolution; and the resistance of the peasants today, that is during the imperialist era, is revolutionary because it lays the foundation for the worker-peasant alliance.

It is important to be aware of the political origin of the gradual development of this line of thought. It developed within the national liberation movements in Asia, Africa, and Latin America. The question raised was whether the peasantry of the periphery was exploited not only directly by local feudal elements but beyond that by dominant capital, and whether due to this, its resistance to so-called development was not evidence of anticapitalist potential. This involved the question of whether it was not incorrect to consider these struggles as necessarily—as vulgar Marxism claims—part of capitalist development, rather than as part of the struggle against all class society. I will not here give the history of the rich and multifarious controversies generated by these questions (cf. 73).

In my own case, critical study of the Nassarian and then the Malian experience in the beginning of the 1960s made it easier to begin criticizing revisionism, culminating with the Chinese cultural revolution. That led me to work out for Africa a typology of modes of extortion of surplus labor from the peasants based on the distinction between the "trade economy" (where I rejected the idea of self-subsistence economy and where the contribution of P.-P. Rey should be noted), the concession economy (where the contribution of Catherine Coquery-Vidrovitch was important), and the reserve economy of South Africa (this analysis was taken up in English several years later by H. Wolpe and thus could finally reach southern Africa).

At the same time, the critique of the traditional analysis of the Latin America communist parties led to questioning the nature—

feudal or capitalist—of the rural relations of production in the mercantilist and imperialist periods in Latin America. Although incisive—and debatable—formulations were used in the beginning, the question raised about the effects of asymmetrical integration into the world capitalist system yielded remarkable results. Here the contributions of Andre Gunder Frank, of Fernando Henrique Cardoso, and of many others should be recalled. The return to a critical view of oriental feudalism also belongs here, including the analysis of Kostas Vergopoulos about modern Ottoman Greece, my own about the Arab world, and that of the activists of the Indian subcontinent.

It goes without saying that these criticisms and self-criticisms were motivated by the success of the worker-peasant alliance in China, in Vietnam, and later in Cambodia. Progressively, there emerged analyses that were systematically consistent and formulated the question of the genesis and division of value and of surplus labor on a world scale. The high point of this formulation was the debate about unequal exchange, out of which two camps—anti-imperialist and proimperialist—clearly emerged.

Need I note that this line of thought had to start from the recognition that the imperialist system is the fundamental basis within the framework of which the class struggle operates during our times? The historical preoccupation with the emergence of social classes (in the communal modes) was completely subordinated to that concerning the integration of these classes into the imperialist system. This is why, as rich as their contribution has been on this level (for instance, Meillassoux' insight with regard to the role of the circulation of wives and of prestige goods) anthropologists who are more concerned with the past, by insisting on the model of self-subsistence, were in danger of developing a line of research which would prove incorrect in the long run because it neglected the effects of the extortion of surplus labor in the imperialist system.

In the course of these controversies, different theses were proposed: the exploitation of the small peasants within a simple petty commodity mode by the exclusive means of the market, the interference of capital in the process of production and the emergence of its "formal" domination, and so on. Different answers were given to the question about the formation and the destination of peasant surplus labor. It would be pretentious to offer a definitive answer to this question, and I am sufficiently conscious of the ultimate importance of the test of praxis to refrain from doing so. In any case, these questions are important and the very fact of asking them while vulgar Marxism obscures them is a sign of the importance attributed to them. But I will observe in passing that these questions are not as new as it sometimes seems: I have found in Kautsky a first example, embryonic but clear, of this type of analysis, which was effectively buried later with the triumph of the reformist *ouvriérisme* of the movement.

Critical synthesis of these controversies now permits the following five propositions:

1. The apparent international relations between centers and peripheries must be analyzed in terms of relations between the capitalist mode and precapitalist, subject mode(s).

2. Subjection–formal domination implies a relation of extortion of surplus labor which is not only based on commodity exchange but also presumes the interference of capital in the process of production, which must be carefully distinguished from the labor process.

3. The surplus labor transferred does not come from the mechanical workings of the law of value. The price of the transferred surplus thus depends only on a power relation between bourgeoisies (or exploiting classes in general). My analysis of mining rent in the contemporary imperialist system in *The Law of Value and Historical Imperialism* confirmed this. This power relation rests on underlying relations of exploitation.

4. As a consequence, "at the same time as each one of its workers, capital simultaneously exploits ten peasants who furnish the agricultural surplus necessary for the reproduction of this worker's labor power" (73b-1). This quantitative estimate is not

arbitrary: it corresponds almost exactly to the real proportions of Table 1.

5. This superexploitation impedes the development of the productive forces in the periphery. As a result, the necessary peasant revolution is not bourgeois but is part of the struggle to overthrow capitalism. For it can no longer be carried out under bourgeois leadership. It will be carried out under the leadership of proletarian ideology or not at all.

Different attempts have been made to measure the transfer of value from the periphery to the center: my own, that of Hosea Jaffe, and that of Andre Gunder Frank (90-4, 72c-5, 72c-6). It may seem odd that since Lenin's *Imperialism* so few researchers have dealt with the question of the mechanisms of exploitation in the periphery. Doubtless, it is difficult to isolate these problems from others and the analysis of accumulation on a world scale cannot replace that of the operating mechanisms of capitalism in the center. But this argument does not justify the absence of analyses dealing with particular aspects of exploitation in the periphery, including partial factual analyses, quantitative insofar as possible. In this area, the complicit silence of bourgeois literature and of the dominant current in Marxist literature simply reflects the power of the imperialist–social-democratic alliance.

Andre Gunder Frank's study of the "disequilibria of multinational commodity exchanges and unequal economic development" provided precious quantitative information about the contribution of the periphery to the financing of accumulation in the center. This study, the first of its kind, tried to evaluate the surplus in the balance of trade of the periphery; in other words, the tribute paid by the periphery to the accumulation of capital in the center. For 1928, this surplus was $1,490 million, which represented 18 percent of the exports from the periphery, and this jumps to 28 percent if we exclude China and North Africa. To this tribute we must add transportation payments related to center-periphery trade (or $1,320 million). In addition, Frank reminds us that these sums, evaluated in current prices, made up only the visible part of the transfer of value: the structure of prices, based on unequal exchange, hides the submerged part of the iceberg.

This surplus allowed Great Britain and Europe to cover their deficit ($2,900 million, half to the advantage of Great Britain and half to the advantage of continental Europe), taking account of the surplus from the United States and the Dominions ($1,410 million). Frank is adamant on this new and essential point: surplus from the periphery enabled Europe to finance its investments in the young centers (the United States and the Dominions). Such an insight is an answer to the argument that investments from the imperialist countries went to the young centers rather than to the dominated countries.

Frank showed that this same structure characterized world trade during the entire imperialist phase. Thus, for the period 1881–1885, the average annual deficit of Great Britain was $507 million, that of continental Europe was $381 million, while the surplus of the United States was $108 million and that of the underdeveloped countries was $780 million. For the period 1911–1913, the figures were $652, $1142, $536, and $1,258 million (current dollars) respectively. Finally, Frank states that the same was doubtless true for the first part of the nineteenth century, world trade having gone from $500 million in 1820 to $5,000 million in 1870 and $20,000 million in 1913, while the British deficit went from £10 million to £100 million and then to £140 million.

There remains an important question that Frank does not address. If this same structure characterized the preimperialist period (1820–1870) as well as the imperialist period, what is the meaning of the imperialist break? There is a strong tendency to underplay the importance of this break, and much confusion has been introduced into this question by all those who want to equate center-periphery conflict within the capitalist system through the different stages of its evolution (mercantilist, preimperialist, imperialist phase) with the conflict between imperialist countries and countries dominated by imperialism. I believe it is necessary to make this distinction very clearly. The fact that the same commercial structure characterized all phases of capitalism with regard to center-periphery trade simply means that the periphery paid tribute to the accumulation of the center during each phase of its evolution.

The nature of the imperialist break is on another level. First on the quantitative level, the export of capital which monopoly had made possible allowed the capitalist mode of production to be directly implanted in the periphery and exploitation to be intensified as a result. To the forms of formal domination and diverse levies on the level of circulation were juxtaposed new forms of real domination which in turn strengthened the original forms by extending their scope. But over and above this quantitative leap, the essential nature of the break is on a decisive and entirely new qualitative plane. From then on, the hegemonic sector of capital, that of the monopolies, acquired the capacity to balance concessions in one place by superprofits in another, through the simultaneous exploitation of labor power in the center and in the periphery of the system. This is the foundation of social-democratic policy, which is thus always social-imperialist. It is at the same time the basis of unequal exchange. The decisive importance of this break, particularly on the level of strategy for the socialist transformation, should be stressed.

Another study by Frank, "Limits of the extent of the internal market by the international division of labor and by relations of production," recalls the intimate connection that exists between the unequal international division of labor and internal social structure. Frank notes that the unequal division of labor and the disequilibrium of exchange operated during the entire last two centuries to the detriment of the periphery. This occurred independently of the terms of exchange, whether they got better (in the nineteenth century) or worse (in the twentieth century). Unequal exchange in the strict sense in which we are using it belongs to the imperialist phase alone and thus caps a long history of asymmetrical relations. This asymmetry does not relate to the nature of the products exchanged. Frank reminds us of the reasons. The absence of pull effects capable of generating autonomous capitalist development in the periphery is due to the latter's social structure. Here, too, it is the class alliance of imperialism with the local bourgeoisie that creates the social conditions permitting the reproduction of the conditions for imperialist exploitation, with the modalities which evolved in tandem with those defining the terms of the unequal international division of labor, in conjunction with the phases of imperialism controlled by the development of national liberation struggles.

III. The national question in the periphery of the imperialist system

1. The national question, which in the nineteenth century was primarily that of oppressed European nations, was transferred in the twentieth century to Asia and Africa, where it became the colonial question.

This was not only a geographical transfer. As a correlate of the formation of the imperialist system, it implied a change in the very nature of the national question. The old national question, that of European nationalities oppressed by absolutist feudal regimes, was part of the incomplete bourgeois revolution. The new national question, that of the peoples oppressed by capitalist imperialism, is part of the rising socialist revolution. It is, more precisely, one of those "bourgeois democratic" demands (like the peasant demand for agrarian reform) which can only be satisfied during the bourgeois stage of an uninterrupted revolution under proletarian leadership (70c).

The principal axis of the new national question is thus defined by its anti-imperialist character. The goal of what follows is not to take up those general controversies concerning the nature of imperialism, the meaning and perspectives of the national liberation movement, and so on, and to restate theses I have already put forward in these areas. I am only going to define the nature of the nations oppressed by imperialism, their particular characteristics today in contrast with those which yesterday defined the oppressed nations of Europe.

2. It does not suffice to proclaim that capitalist development necessarily engenders the transformation of ethnic groups into nations (this development moreover has not been the only path for the establishment of nations). We must also note that only the constitution of central capitalism allows the national formation to take shape. On the other hand, capitalist development in its peripheral forms destroys society and hinders its possible constitution into a nation. The reason is that capitalism is not based on the systematic strengthening of the local commodity, capital, and labor market as the axis of its development, of autocentered development.

Integration into the international system on the basis of the unequal international division of labor and the extraverted character of the economy, with modernization beginning in the new export sectors, does not create a decisive internal market. Insofar as one is created at all, it becomes the basis for an import substitution industry exclusively geared to the demand of the exploiting classes. Production for the satisfaction of the needs of the large masses basically continues to be organized within the rural, self-subsistence framework, following the modalities of predominant formal domination.

The crushing domination of foreign capital removes all meaning from the expression "capital market." Local capital, fragmented and subordinate, does not reach the critical mass needed to constitute a capital market. The monetary and financial systems also remain extraverted, partial, and limited in their functions. The predominance of formal domination also prevents one from speaking of a generalized labor market, despite the relative importance of the reserve army of urban unemployed.

All these familiar phenomena of the disarticulation of the economy and of underdeveloped society impeded the formation of a nation. They also modify, in the same way, the meaning and content of the state. The most extreme position related to this problem claims that the peripheral state is nothing more than an administration, an excrescence of the dominant imperialist state, to which one cannot transfer the classic Marxist analysis that defines the state as the hegemonic bloc of local exploiting classes (77d-10). But this onesided and simplifying thesis does not allow us to understand the differences among the feudal-comprador state (imperial China, for instance), the dependent bourgeois state (modern Egypt), the neocolonial state (government by a comprador bureaucracy close to the colonial administration), or the populist, nationalist state, among others. It substitutes for an analysis in terms of variable alliances (yesterday the feudal-comprador alliance, today the dependent bourgeois alliance; imperialist capital dominant with local, subordinate exploiting classes as transmitters) an analysis in terms of "foreign agents." But, as extreme as this thesis is, it does draw attention to the submission of the exploiting classes in the international alliance and the direct representation of the interests of foreign classes.

The correct thesis about the peripheral capitalist state of our period must be based on a concrete analysis of the local hegemonic bloc—transmitter of imperialist domination. Because this bloc is weak and subordinate, the countries of the periphery are the weak links in the imperialist chain. Thus the revolutionary bloc can form more easily and in the framework of a general strategy of uninterrupted revolution by stages, create effective tactical alliances likely to erode the hegemonic bloc.

3. One of the characteristics in which we can see the absence of a national construct is the fundamentally foreign nature of the culture of the local bourgeoisie. Denationalized, acculturated, these dominant classes progressively take on the look of strangers in their own country due to their daily lifestyle, modeled on that of *homo consumens universalis*. In extreme cases, a caricature of bilingualism obtains: the ruling class uses the language of the old colonial masters while the people continue to speak the vernacular. How can we speak of nation and national culture under such conditions?

4. The peoples of the periphery, separated by boundaries that are for the most part arbitrary and artificial, constitute neither one nor

several nations, in the framework of the majority of the states that define their international existence. They are formed of one or more ethnic groups, sometimes close (linguistically, for instance) sometimes far apart; sometimes clearly separate geographically, sometimes intermingled and living in symbiosis (farmers and herders of different ethnic groups coexisting in the same area, for example). They may also be very unequal numerically. These ethnic groups have sometimes retained, for all or some of their members, more or less ancient forms of social organization (clans, tribes). Sometimes they have been constituted into precapitalist, advanced tributary ethnic groups ("quasi nations").

Different modalities of oppression, of ancient or recent origin, characterize the relations between these ethnic groups. There are conquered peoples and conquering peoples of past epochs, majorities and minorities, those whom peripheral capitalist development has favored and those it has disfavored, and those which predominate among the urban elite and those which are excluded from it, among others. As a whole, these realities create conditions unfavorable to the maturation of class consciousness. Class struggles frequently manifest themselves as ethnic struggles; thus they can be manipulated internally and externally by reactionary classes and imperialist forces.

5. Under these conditions, the national liberation movement is often "a national movement without a nation" (77). At a given moment, the unity of the anti-imperialist classes can provide the means to overcome these divisions. Nkrumah's pan-Africanism, from which developed the Organization of African Unity (OAU), pan-Indian unity, and even the artificial unity of Pakistan show that this is possible. But this kind of national or pseudonational unity survives only with difficulty the circumstances which made it possible for the moment. Once independence is acquired, internal contradictions come to the fore. A sytematic study of these contradictions would merit more attention than it has heretofore received; the break-up of Pakistan, the permanent threat which weighs on India, the civil wars of the former Congo during the

1960s, the civil war in Nigeria, current events in the eastern horn of Africa and in the western Sahara, tribal uprisings (for instance in the southern Sudan) show the instability of these nonnational state units.

6. Under these circumstances, what attitude should the popular vanguard take with regard to the problem of nationalities? It certainly cannot deny their existence, as is often the official position. It cannot be content with the goal of the abolition of class exploitation; it must explicitly put into its program the immediate and real struggle against all forms of discrimination, inequality, and oppression based on ethnicity, language, religion, or custom. But should it go so far as to uphold the right to national self-determination to the point of secession? We cannot avoid this question.

Two principles must be kept in mind. The first is that the right to self-determination up to secession must be recognized in principle. The second is that secession should only be accepted as a last resort when all else has failed, when the vanguard has failed to get the exploited masses to accept a struggle for real local autonomy within the framework of as large a unified state as possible. For the anti-imperialist struggle has nothing to gain from the weakening of the states of the periphery by balkanization, which moreover could go on *ad infinitum*.

7. The states of the third world are still unstable. But they are so to different degrees, depending on the character of their precapitalist antecedents and the nature of the hegemonic bloc in power. These antecedents are indeed sometimes nations, tributary quasinations, close ethnic groups, and sometimes fragmented tribes without historic or linguistic unity. The bloc in power sometimes consists of latifundiary classes with roots going back to national precolonial history, sometimes of a clearly constituted though new industrial bourgeoisie, and sometimes, by contrast, almost exclusively of a light comprador bureaucratic layer fabricated by the colonizer and without local roots.

The conjunction of ethnic fragmentation and comprador bureaucratic power defines a type of state that is particularly unstable. It is no accident that this conjunction, which prevails in sub-Saharan Africa, is accompanied by the absence of national languages and by cultural alienation in its most violent form. The sad past of whole regions of the continent fashioned during the slave trade exacerbates the weakness of these societies. The slave trade not only bled white entire peoples; it also engendered the establishment of slave-trading coastal military states and produced a local ideology of the corrupt despotism involved in this trade. The subsequent Christianization of these societies has perpetuated cultural dependence on Europe, while the comprador bureaucratic power was able to reproduce the despotic and corrupt ideological models of the trade.

Will the new state, resting on these bases, be able to create a nation and civil society? Cornered between dominant imperialism, which can intervene effectively with modest means (coups d'état, military operations involving a few hundred mercenaries, etc.), and tribal divisions, the state cannot stabilize itself. The peasant struggles, which always take on tribal dimensions, can threaten it, can be manipulated from the outside and inside, leading to the break-up of the comprador bureaucracy. These conjunctions explain in large measure the regressions occurring with accelerating frequency on the continent. Doubtless the formation of civil society, separate from the state, as a concomitant of complete capitalist development, is embryonic everywhere in the third world. But it has more or less begun and it can scarcely do so in the most unstable situations.

Few political thinkers who are conscious of these problems have dared to tackle them. Nkrumah's greatness lay in his attempt to overcome this problem through pan-Africanism. It was probably utopian, but it had its moment of strong and real impact, without which the establishment of contemporary states would perhaps have been even more uncertain.

8. The national liberation movement has nevertheless sometimes operated within a different situation, in real precapitalist nations (complete tributary ones) or in strong and homogeneous

quasinations of this type (China, Korea, Vietnam, Cambodia among the liberated countries; Egypt, Morocco, Iran, Madagascar, Sri Lanka, Burma, Thailand, and even Indonesia among countries still in the imperialist network). Specific problems relative to the national question are sometimes added to those of the local nation, like the problematic of the Arab nation or that of Latin American pan-Hispanicism.

It goes without saying that these conditions have generally been a factor favorable to the radicalization of the class struggle. In East Asia, we have seen a particularly favorable conjuncture consisting of three elements: first, the marked differentiation of the rural classes on the basis of harsh feudalism, which was the basis for the revolutionary uprising of the peasantry; second, the existence of a proletarian core and of an intelligentsia with cultural roots deep in national history, confronted with the social, political, and ideological reality of imperialist exploitation; and third, the marked character of the national existence of homogeneous peoples (Chinese, Vietnamese, Cambodian, Korean). It is no accident that in this region national liberation paved the way for the establishment of powerful national and popular states whose involvement in the long socialist transition has the best chance of success. It is no accident that in the Congo in 1960–1963 or in Ethiopia at present anti-imperialist and social struggles of great magnitude either failed or succeeded only with much greater difficulty in becoming radicalized and developing a correct strategy. Elsewhere, then, we must think about a strategy which takes account of very different conjunctures from those of East Asia.

9. Marxist discussion of the colonial and national questions is as yet little developed. The viewpoints expressed by Marx and Engels do not suffice as a basis from which to draw general conclusions useful for today. The viewpoints subsequently developed in the congresses of the Second and Third Internationals, and those of Rosa Luxemburg, Lenin, Trotsky, and Stalin treat essentially two series of questions: those about precapitalist modes of production (especially controversies about the asiatic, slave, and

feudal modes), and those about the nature of the imperialist system and national liberation in general (70). The first of these controversies has been the most often disappointing because the most important interested parties, the peoples of Asia and Africa, have been almost totally excluded. Infinite exegesis of several elliptical texts of Marx and Engels (the *Grundrisse*, journal articles, letters), for which Marxology has a predeliction, is completely inadequate. The second series of controversies furnished for the Third International a global Leninist framework which is basically correct. But it cannot make up for the lack of concrete analysis.

10. Today the situation calls for concrete and systematic thought about the interrelationship of class and national struggles. This thought must be based on the following five principles.

First, the struggle for socialism in the periphery of the imperialist system cannot be separated from, and even less opposed to, the struggle for national liberation. The fact of imperialism obliges us to envisage the transition to socialism as resulting from the historical fusion of the goals of social and national liberation.

Second, this double-edged struggle cannot really be carried through—in terms of either national or social liberation—except by the popular bloc under the ideological leadership of the proletariat. The autonomy of the popular strategy must be affirmed in theory and in practice. This autonomy guarantees the possible success of a strategy of uninterrupted revolution by stages. Its absence reduces the popular forces to a supporting role for bourgeois strategies, which are so many dead ends.

Third, the popular bloc must try to overcome national contradictions among the people and preserve the largest possible state framework.

Fourth, the popular bloc must adopt a flexible tactic, based on a correct analysis of the nature of the hegemonic bloc of the local state and the weaknesses and contradictions that characterize it. It must also know how to take advantage of opportunities to weaken this hegemonic bloc.

Fifth, the popular bloc must be extremely vigilant with regard to foreign powers and especially superpowers who try to bend all confused forces to the ends of their overall planetary strategy. Each time these principles are forgotten in theory and in practice, movements, even popular ones, objectively become playthings in the hands of the superpowers.

In light of these principles, we could undertake a critical examination of the strategy and tactics adopted during recent times: those with positive outcomes, as in East Asia, and those with less positive or even quite negative ones, including Chile, Argentina, Brazil, Peru, and Latin America in general, wavering between revisionism and Guevaraism; Palestine and Nasserism; communist movements in India, Bangladesh, and Southeast Asia; popular movements of Lumumbaism and of Black Africa and Madagascar in general, and liberation movements in South Africa.

Chapter 7

National Liberation
and the Socialist Transition:
Is the Bourgeoisie Still a Rising Class?

The fundamental question of our time, to which all other major and minor questions are related, is whether the bourgeoisie is still a rising class. If so, what would be the determining manifestations of this? Continued development of the productive forces in the hegemonic imperialist centers and its leading role on the world scale in shaping societies in all their aspects? Or the extraordinary development of capitalism in the regions of Latin America, Asia, and Africa that up to the present have only barely been touched by it? Or the emergence (or reemergence) of neocapitalist (or simply capitalist) forms in regions which had broken with capitalism to begin a socialist transition: the USSR and, also, perhaps, countries such as Cuba, China, and Vietnam.

If, on the other hand, one maintains that the bourgeoisie is no longer a rising class, what would be the determining manifestations of the crisis of capitalism? The reevaluation, however purely intellectual and marginal, of the civilization of the advanced centers, together with a crisis of values and the emergence of a new consciousness of self-management? Or the blocking of capitalist development in Latin America, Asia, and Africa and thus the possibility—the necessity—of radicalization based on the national liberation struggle leading to the socialist transition? Or, finally, the blocking of a restoration of capitalism after the socialist break and the progress, despite everything, of the experiences in the socialist transition through successive and unequal advances?

In addition, there is still the question of whether capitalism can be transcended only by communism reached via the socialist transition. Could capitalism be followed by a new and still necessary (or at least possible) mode of class production, which would assure a development of the productive forces sufficient to make the abolition of classes an inescapable precondition for further progress?

The elements of immediate reality are sufficiently contradictory to support, if one wishes to, polemical responses on either side. The great classic texts of Marxism—Marx, Engels, Lenin, and Mao—are sufficiently rich so that such responses could be based on Marxology. I have chosen instead to base my argument on a two-pronged systematic way of thinking: on one side, on the history of capitalist development on a world scale, and on the other, on the conceptual tool of Marxism used to understand this history. Once our purpose is to understand in order to act, we can no longer claim, as bourgeois theoreticians do, to separate science from ideology.

I have already started this argument in the preceding section, by proposing (1) an historical and theoretical explanation of the reasons for the appearance and development of capitalism in opposition to the theoretical propositions inspired by West-centered and linear philosophy, and (2) a more developed analysis of the contradictions of the contemporary era, which manifest themselves in the center-periphery conflict within the world capitalist system in the different phases of imperialism. This is the basis on which a correct evaluation of the liberation movement and of its prospects may perhaps be developed.

I will now try to go further, shifting from historical to more general levels: on the one hand, to the ambivalent and contradictory nature of the national liberation movement, and on the other hand, to the ambivalent and contradictory nature of the socialist transition.

I. The contradictory nature of national liberation

1. All West-centered studies put the analysis of the functions of the periphery of the capitalist system in a marginal, decorative place. The West-centered analysis of the transition to capitalism leaves out the decisive role played by the periphery from the beginning, claiming that the internal contradictions of feudalism alone explain the transition. It even makes this position into a Marxist principle. The discussion of the European transition to capitalism is a good example of this. The revisionists of our day, inspired by Tökei's schemas, use this principle as a basis for their conclusion that only Europe could have invented capitalism, Asia being condemned to stagnate indefinitely in the prior stage.

In reality, internal contradictions are primary and decisive. They are the same for all tributary systems and imply the necessary transition to capitalism in every case. By themselves and without any external impact, they were capable of generating capitalism in Europe and elsewhere. But we must not confuse this general proposition with the concrete explanation of the transition as it really took place. If it began more quickly and sooner in Europe, this is not because Europe alone was capable of inventing capitalism but because of the primitive character of feudalism. In the concrete, historical formation of capitalism, Europe created and subjected a periphery as early as the mercantilist period, the exploitation of which both quickened the pace of its own development and arrested and then distorted that of the subject regions. What the ideologues of imperialism do, even when they pretend to be Marxists, is to confuse fundamental methodological propositions with the real, concrete development of history, thus reducing facts to a mere schema.

If an epidemic had wiped out the entire population of Asia, Africa, and America, European capitalism would still have been established, but without a periphery. Similarly, if an epidemic had wiped out the entire world population except that of China, capitalism would have been created in China. But such an epidemic did not take place. And capitalism was in fact established through the exploitation of the periphery. Thus we must deal with this fact and not invoke supposedly theoretical discussions in order to avoid this disturbing fact.

A parallel exists in the debate about imperialism. Rosa Luxemburg believed she could show that the mechanism of accumulation could not work, even theoretically, without a periphery. She was wrong. Lenin recalled that the schemas of Volume II of *Capital* established the possibility of accumulation without an external milieu. But Lenin did not draw the conclusion from this that the periphery did not exist. On the contrary.

2. Moreover, are the "external effects" being denied really external? External to what? If we consider the world capitalist system, center-periphery relations are not external but are certainly internal to the system. The contradictions of capitalism must be apprehended at this level, on the plane of concrete capitalist reality. In order to eliminate the most troubling contradictions, some *a priori* reduce the capitalist system to a mode of production (in its abstract purity). The innumerable "readings of *Capital*" are thus substitutes for readings of capitalism; and dogmatic rigidity becomes a basic principle.

The logic of this line leads directly to abandoning Marxism. If we push this separation between internal and external effects to its logical conclusion and disregard any dialectic we must conclude that contradictions cannot be understood even on the level of the national formation but only on the level of the basic unit wherein capitalist exploitation arises, the firm. Is circulation not effectively excluded from this supposedly Marxist, impoverished analysis in favor of unending preoccupation with the genesis of exploitation in the relations of production? Under the pretext that production governs circulation in Marxism, any discussion of circulation is dubbed "circulation" and thus reality is disregarded, thought is sterilized, action is precluded. If the redistribution of surplus value via the circulation of capital (Volume III of *Capital*), the analysis of the relation between productive and unproductive work, the correct definition of the collective worker, and the analysis of the class alliances of a given formation are all put outside the purview of the study, the political position arrived at can be called anarcho-syndicalism. This encourages workers to take no interest in politics. This theoretical reduction fosters a self-management mode in its naive version.

We must keep a vision of the totality. The latter—the world capitalist system in this case—can be reduced neither to the pure capitalist mode nor even to a constellation of unequal national formations. We must detail the content of this inequality, which takes shape in relation to the totality and not in relation to each of its parts. Inequality, whatever its origins, generates an organized hierarchy which it not only statically reproduces but also dynamically re-creates.

The capitalist system has always been a world system. We cannot understand anything about it if we exclude the interaction between the internal effect of one of its parts and the effects external to this part. For this reason, the contribution of those who have emphasized the role of the periphery in the establishment of capitalism from its beginnings is neither small nor even supplementary. They reestablished history in its true dimension. Thus we cannot criticize them for having "neglected" internal effects: others had already studied this fully and our authors made use of this contribution in a perspective which, by linking internal to so-called external effects, gave to capitalism its full shape. Based on these works, it is necessary to reformulate the questions fundamental to our understanding of capitalism, among others: the interaction between production and circulation (and the problematic of long-distance trade in the precapitalist systems and in the transition to capitalism); the international division of labor and unequal exchange, that is, the organization of the production process on a world scale; and the workings of the political and ideological superstructure—in other words, all the questions the dogmatic reduction of capitalism to the pure capitalist mode attempts to eliminate.

3. Within this framework, the question of the failure of the transition to capitalism of the most evolved tributary societies and the success of Europe can be scientifically investigated. Historically a hundred attempts precede the decisive breakthrough that leads to a point of no return. I have shown the concrete reasons for which Arab mercantilism was so abortive. The Egyptian mercantilism of Mohammed Ali had begun a capitalist development which was perhaps stopped only by European aggression (76b-6). Even in the West, if we look closely, we discover that before the English breakthrough there were the failures of Italy and Spain. Are we going to confine the European miracle to the area of northern Europe? Start with Marx and end with Max Weber?

There is nothing surprising about this series of failures on the part of non-European societies. In the same way we see that attempts to build socialism fail more frequently than any general theory would suggest. Should we draw the conclusion from the failure of the Paris Commune that the French formation will never be able to create socialism? And what should we say about the failure of English Chartism in the nineteenth century and the radicalization of the workers' movement in the United States during the twentieth? It is true that some still claim socialism was impossible in Russia (unless a German revolution came to its aid) and is condemned in advance in China, Vietnam, and everywhere else except in Europe and the United States.

4. If it has always been a world system, the capitalist system has nonetheless gone through several stages. In this progression, the imperialist break was fundamental. In fact, this break marked the end of the rising progression of capitalism on a world scale and the beginning of its crisis. In this sense, it was certainly the "highest stage" of capitalism. Naturally, capitalism continued to develop after 1880 and even more quickly than it had in the past. But this development no longer brought about the emergence of new centers: from that time on, the development of capitalism was simultaneously the development of imperialism and of underdevelopment. It is possible to periodize in turn the imperialist period

and even to highlight the controlling lines of a possible new stage of the imperialist system.

The thesis of "absolute limits," which can be attributed to Rosa Luxemburg, ignores this decisive point, that the development of capitalism in the periphery remains the development of a dependent and incomplete capitalism. And the error of certain attempts at periodization also comes from underestimating the importance of the nature of the imperialist break (cf. 72a).

5. This break inaugurated the period of socialist transition on a world scale in the framework of a model of unequal development. This is the essence of the position I support. For imperialism transferred the center of gravity of the contradictions of capitalism and relegated the major contradictions of yesterday to the rank of secondary contradictions, modified by new contradictions. The class struggle in the centers has ceased to be the prime motive force of history. Cecil Rhodes understood that civil war could be avoided in Europe by transferring the contradictions of capitalism through external expansion. Social-democratic hegemony has no other meaning.

But at the same time, imperialism pushed to center stage a new anticapitalist force, that of the peripheral nations, whose struggle has become the motive force of history. A gigantic struggle has begun, pitting the bourgeoisie against the proletariat of these nations, and the outcome will be decisive for socialism. As national liberation cannot be achieved under the leadership of the bourgeoisie, it must be carried out through the stages of development of the imperialist system, until the moment when the proletariat succeeds in taking over the leadership and when the achievement of national liberation creates the new problems of the socialist transition. It is thus that socialism makes its way, a way which cannot be predicted in advance.

The result of this situation is that the analysis of the contradictions of contemporary capitalism must from the first take the entire world system as its field of inquiry. Nothing will come out of the hundred-thousandth reading of *Capital* that can help us understand these contradictions. Indefinite dwelling on the preeminence of the analysis of capitalist exploitation at its sources, in the relations of capitalist production, will help us fill elementary texts and a few academic Marxological theses, but will not move us forward at all. Any Marxist who believes that analyzing the contradictions on a world scale is a decorative exercise, any Marxist who, as a consequence, considers the anti-imperialist struggle as a supplement, not to say an act of charity, lacks the means to act to transform reality. In that case, is he or she really a Marxist?

But to state that the analysis of accumulation on a world scale should be made on the world scale and not on the basis of the periphery alone is to express a wish that will remain unfulfilled so long as there is no radical shift away from the nondialectical, West-centered view that sees transformations in the periphery as deriving from those in the center. Given that 99 percent of the analyses of accumulation ignore the world picture and focus exclusively on the centers—as 99 percent of the analyses of the transition to capitalism ignore the mercantilist periphery—and given that these analyses are not only incomplete but based on a fundamental error, we must start from the other end to create the conditions for a correct overall analysis.

National liberation and socialism

1. I will now deal with the problem from the broadest perspective, that of the Marxist debate about imperialism, and try to define the strategy for the socialist transformation on a world scale and the relations between the different political and social forces at work to different degrees and within different contexts in this direction. On this point there are two fundamentally different views. Each claims to be Marxist and claims that the other is not.

2. The first sees imperialism as constituting an absolutely essential, qualitative break in the history of capitalism. This resulted at the end of the nineteenth century from the establishment of imperialism through the transition from classic competitive capi-

talism (to give it a name but without illusion as to the nature of this competition) to imperialist capitalism. Before and *after* imperialism, all problems are different.

Imperialism is not only, nor even primarily, an economic type of transformation inside the imperialist centers, a transition from the quantitative to the qualitative in the centralization and the concentration of capital and recognized as such by the social democrats even before revolutionaries like Lenin. Certainly, there now exist centralization, concentration, monopolies, and interpenetration of finance and industrial capital, and, concomitantly, subjection of the whole of noncapitalist societies to imperialism. But the roots of this subjection are in the past and capitalism did not await the end of the nineteenth century to take on world dimensions. Primitive accumulation itself already had a kind of world dimension before the Industrial Revolution. The manifestation of important political phenomena, and even of the colonial phenomenon, preceded imperialism in certain regions and in certain respects.

If imperialism nonetheless constituted a qualitative break, this is because the centralization-concentration of monopoly capital created the possibility of the export of the capitalist mode of production through the investment of this capital outside the centers of origin. The implantation of segments of the production process outside of and distant from the nation of origin and under different social conditions became possible. The process of the integration and the subjection of societies originally having precapitalist modes of production thus took on completely new proportions. Even if this implantation was quantitatively still sporadic, it was determining.

Later this expansion of capitalism to the world scale in the imperialist phase brought about basic transformations. This is the crucial point of the debate, that of fundamental transformations, of the place of different social classes in the center and in the periphery. We cannot understand these transformations in the relations between social classes within the center, in the periphery, and on a world scale, and the place of different social classes in the class struggle if we treat the countries separately, whether they are imperialist or dominated by imperialism. We can only understand them in the context of their world relations, in a global strategy.

Certainly the fundamental contradiction of the capitalist mode of production and thus of the world capitalist system is that between the bourgeoisie and the proletariat. But, once we have pronounced this banality, we still have to decide on a strategy. That is, on the relations between the different proletariats, the different bourgeoisies, and the other classes subjected to imperialism—especially, in the periphery, in relation to precapitalist modes of production—and how they stand in relation to one another in an overall revolutionary strategy.

With the entrance of capitalism into the imperialist phase, transformations occurred. These may be summarized as follows: The center of gravity of capitalist exploitation shifted in relation to the fact that the relative mass of surplus value centralized to the profit of the monopolies of the imperialist countries grew both in relative and absolute terms. It came more and more from the exploitation of the peoples of the periphery. It was surplus value directly created by the proletariat of the periphery. Or, and this was greater in volume, it was a surplus generated in various modes of production coming from exploiting classes, circulation via local intermediaries under particular forms, transformed into surplus value for the benefit of the monopolies by the formal subjection of these precapitalist peasant or feudal modes of production and the exploitation of large peasant masses.

This shift in the center of gravity did not result from the quantitative measure of the mass of surplus value generated in various places within the whole of the system. On the quantitative plane, the mass of surplus value continued to be generated mainly in the center. But the center of gravity, the sensitive point, shifted toward the exploitation of the periphery. Monopoly capitalism thus gave an objective basis to the social-democratic hegemony among the working classes of the West. This hegemony, visible and indisputable in the Second International, was denounced by Lenin precisely for its relation to the phenomenon of imperialism. Furthermore, the extension of capitalist imperialism to the scale of the planet closed the road to the expansion of capitalism through bourgeois revolutions in backward countries.

The bourgeoisie in the periphery thereafter developed only in the imperialist track and was no longer capable of leading a more or less radical bourgeois revolution, which obviously does not mean that capitalism is no longer developing. It is developing, but within the imperialist framework. By contrast, the peasant movement, which in the center had historically been an integral part of the bourgeois revolution, became part of the socialist revolution. Peasant demands cannot then lead to bourgeois revolutions but must objectively become a part of the socialist revolution on a world scale. This does not mean that they automatically lead to it: for that there must exist proletarian leadership and outlook. In other words, the development of capitalism in the periphery within the imperialist track and the rise of the national liberation movement are not part of capitalist and bourgeois development but part of their crisis.

To define the major camps of social forces and then to determine which are primary and which are secondary according to this thesis, it is not sufficient to recall that on the side of the socialist forces there are the proletarians of the center (even if there is social-democratic hegemony) and of the periphery and, to simplify, the exploited peasantry of the periphery; and that on the other side, in the camp of the capitalist forces, there are monopoly capital and all the dependent bourgeoisie and allied exploiting classes of the periphery. For in this class alliance on a world scale the spearhead of the forces of socialism has shifted from the Western proletariat toward the proletarian nuclei of the periphery in relation to the imperialist phenomenon. From this results the hegemony of social democracy among the Western proletariat and the possibility of a revolutionary worker-peasant alliance in the periphery.

The argument of those who constantly invoke the fundamental

contradiction between the bourgeosie and the proletariat scarcely moves the discussion forward. The proletariat exists on the world scale in various places. And at any given moment of history certain sectors of the proletariat are more advanced than others.

Quotations from Marx cannot help us to explain this phenomenon because the phenomenon of imperialism came after Marx. Quotations from Lenin are perhaps a bit more helpful, since it was Lenin who first analyzed imperialism in a decisive manner. But he died in 1924; the system has continued, struggles have developed, things have changed. Lenin was above all preoccupied with the struggle in the Second International against revisionism and with the preparation of the Russian revolution. He correctly situated this in the framework of imperialism but he did not give an answer to everything that happened during his lifetime and certainly not *a fortiori* to everything which happened after it.

In fact, it appears that socialist revolutions have taken place only in the periphery of the system (China, Vietnam, Korea, Cambodia, Laos, Cuba). Despite the development of capitalism in the periphery and the absence of immediate prospects, it appears that the popular working and peasant masses have rarely placed themselves under the ideological domination of the bourgeoisie and of imperialism and that their revolutionary potential is therefore enormous. Thus it is highly likely that the movement will continue in the same direction. On the other hand, the working classes of the West have, up to the present, been under the sway of social-democratic or revisionist hegemony (which are more and more clearly coming to be the same ideology). This does not rule out class struggle on their part, nor battles, including political ones, which sometimes become violent. But it does deprive the latter of a socialist perspective.

However, these facts can always be disputed, because what is true one day is not necessarily true the next. And from the other side, revolutions in the name of socialism in the periphery raise a series of problems after their accomplishment. I am not talking about a peaceful, problem-free transition to communism, that is, to the abolition of social classes, commodity relations, and the division of labor. The final goal is far away, still extremely far away.

Thus these arguments, whether they consist of quotations from Marx or Lenin or of facts themselves, still leave the discussion open. We must observe real struggles and analyze how they articulate and what their meaning is. Here let me forestall an additional misunderstanding: no prophecy is possible about the course of history. I can simply emphasize the dialectical relationship between the struggles in the center and those in the periphery. In such a situation, which are primary struggles? Which are secondary? In other words, which struggles have a qualitative impact on others?

To the extent that imperialism can transfer exploitation to the periphery and can deepen this exploitation, it acquires the objective means to strengthen social-democratic ideology in the center. As a consequence, imperialism is successful in dividing the working class, in depriving it of an autonomous political perspective, and of integrating its struggles into projects that it continues to control.

To the extent that the periphery offers different degrees of resistance—the highest being liberation, that is, the exit from the imperialist system—to the extent that the movement for national liberation under proletarian leadership spreads, really engaging the great mass of exploited peasants, there exists the possibility of a qualitative break. This is not socialism but only a break toward socialism, the end of imperialist exploitation but not necessarily of the development of indigenous capitalist forces. This is the meaning of the maximum level of resistance to imperialist exploitation. The minimum level is that of the dependent bourgeoisies which at a given conjuncture lead the national liberation movement and through these struggles attain *de facto* a new division more favorable to themselves and thereby limit the profits of monopoly capital.

To the extent that the periphery offers different degrees of resistance, then, imperialist capital is forced to transfer the contradiction to the metropoles, thus reducing the objective basis for social democracy and strengthening the tendencies toward renewed revolution. Up to the present (that is, between 1870 and 1978) the primary tendency has been for national liberation struggles—from the strongest, led by the proletariat which breaks with imperialism, to the weakest, led by the bourgeoisie which extracts concessions compensated for by readjustments in the imperialist system—to be the motive force of contemporary history. Thus, the enlarging or shrinking of the objective basis for social democracy in the center has depended, in the main, on liberation struggles for over a century now. Of course there have been ups and downs, since this resistance and these struggles have developed not in a linear fashion but through a process of victories and defeats, whether led by the proletariat or the bourgeoisie.

3. Is the national liberation movement what I claim, the motive force of history and the primary force for the creation of socialism? When, through gross oversimplification, this movement is reduced to the struggle for the national political independence of Asia and of Africa, it is tempting to conclude that this movement was in reality only a relatively brief phase of contemporary history: from 1945 to 1965–1970, perhaps.

Let us return then to the course of contemporary history. Since 1880 the fact of imperialism has controlled all important events, weighed all confrontations, and determined their outcome. Simultaneously, since 1880 the national liberation struggle has emerged and progressively grown.

In the first phase, from 1880 to 1914, the national liberation struggle was not yet the immediate motive force of history, although the revolt of the working classes in the center of the system had ceased to be so. This is why this phase was the golden age of imperialism. The working classes had already been subordinated by their imperialist bourgeoisies and, although only 1914 would indicate the catastrophic dimensions of this, the Second International appears in retrospect to have been the instrument of this subordination. The liberation movements were only beginning to establish themselves but they were not yet out of the precapitalist age. Their task was more to resist aggression than to liberate anything. This is why during this phase interimperialist contradictions held center stage: this was the Belle Epoque, when great-power diplomacy was the immediate motive force of history. This phase ended with the First World War, the Russian revolution, the May Fourth Movement in China, Kemal Ataturk, the Egyptian Wafd, and Indian Congress Party.

From 1918 to 1945 center stage was no longer held exclusively by interimperialist contradictions, although these still existed and caused conflict between the conquerors and conquered of 1918. At the same time, this era saw the rise of the Russian revolution, its stagnation, and its reverses; the rise of the Chinese revolution; the rise of liberation movements on three continents: Latin American populism, modern independence revolts, and repressed revolutions in Asia and Africa. This complex of rising forces once again indicates the internal contradictions of the centers. The crises of the era following the First World War and of 1930 highlight these social contradictions. The period closed with the Second World War, which marked the end of the rise of the Western workers' movement, while other forces, those of the Soviet Union and those of national liberation, continued to develop.

Beginning in 1945 a third period opened, during which the predominance of national liberation was achieved. Interimperialist contradictions were attenuated by American hegemony to the point where the notion of superimperialism seemed to be confirmed. Only "seemed" because this view, anticipated by Kautsky and very much in vogue in the United States, arises from an economist reduction: the state is the passive instrument of the multinationals, which shape the world in their image (71-6). I do not share this point of view, but that is not the question. For in any event, the Western workers' movement did not recover from the defeat of the 1930s and 1940s. As time passed, it seemed to be just as subordinated as it was before 1914. The Soviet Union, confined within the borders of its zone of influence, acted on the world scene only in relation to liberation movements. It was through the alliances it made with these movements that it acquired a world dimension. During this quarter century, national liberation was achieved in east Asia and Cuba, which undertook possible socialist transitions, while elsewhere the movement attained its first objective, political independence, without having begun such transitions.

Will the completion of this phase put an end to the national liberation movement and to its potential for socialist transformation? This is Gérard Chaliand's position (77e-1). It seems to have been confirmed by the immediate facts over these last years, which makes it temporarily popular. And yet it is incorrect because it reduces the goal of national liberation to independence. But the latter does not resolve the contradictions of peripheral capitalism. Doubtless it creates new conditions, from which the pause arises. The transcendence of the phase of embryonic peripheral capitalism imposed by political domination ("the colonial mode of production," as Rey calls it) by the spontaneous reproduction of dependent capitalism (the neocolonial mode of production) through the hegemony of the local bourgeoisie, via the economic mechanism of the capitalist system, modifies the nature of the objective, the methods of struggle, and the positions of the camps (10-6, 73b-1).

For these reasons Chaliand proposes that we consider the era of liberation movements to be over and that we call by its name, the internal class struggle, the era which is beginning in the third world. His error is in failing to see that this class struggle continues to operate in the framework of still incomplete national liberation. The bourgeoisies of the third world try to carry through this struggle and to retain the leadership of it, as I have argued in my analysis of the strategy they adopt to attain economic independence. The popular classes must not ignore this struggle any more than they previously ignored the goal of independence. But they must use the autonomy of their movement to take over the leadership and by means of this begin the socialist transition. This is why national liberation continues to hold center stage. History and history only—not theory and even less Marxology—will tell if this will coincide with the reemergence of a workers' movement in the West.

4. Set within this framework, which is that of uninterrupted

revolution by stages, debates over the strategy of the new phase of
national liberation take on practical importance. These are real
debates within the movement and the struggle, debates whose real
importance cuts through the unimportance of theories that insist
on the primacy of the class struggle and conceal beneath their
triviality the fact that they erase the conditions for class struggle on
a world scale.

The contradictory nature of national liberation is expressed in
this twofold reality. On the one hand, each partial victory for
national liberation creates the conditions for the deepening of
capitalist development. On the other hand, it does not mitigate the
contradictions between the popular masses and imperialism and its
allies but on the contrary aggravates them.

Is it possible that this movement will go on indefinitely, passing
through successive stages without ever bringing about the qualitative break which will inaugurate the socialist transition? In this
case, will the process of capitalist development become complete
and the center-periphery contradiction disappear? Marx had considered the possibility that Europe, ripe for socialist revolution,
might have to deal with rising capitalism from this "little corner of
the world." But he wrote this before imperialism, and thus made
the twofold assumption that the European workers' movement
would continue to become radicalized and that capitalist development in Asia would be nondependent.

Since that time the hypothesis of the complete development
of capitalism in the peripheries subject to imperialism has not
come true. Marxism does not reason on "ifs" that are contrary to
reality understood in its real movement. The new phase of imperialism which is taking shape based on the real social forces
of contemporary capitalism is not going in the direction of the
completion of capitalism (the goal of economic independence
proclaimed by the bourgeoisies of the third world cannot be attained with the strategies they propose) but is prolonging the line of
dependent, incomplete development.

Of course, *if* the popular forces do not act in the periphery and *if* the process is thus pursued beyond this new phase, that is, *if* capitalism continues to survive let us say a thousand years, it will finally find the means to resolve its contradictions. In this science-fiction hypothesis, imperialism will have disappeared, having played its historic role of spreading capitalism from this "little corner of Europe" to the whole world. Imperialism would not have been the highest stage of capitalism but only a transitory modality of its deployment. But even following this hypothesis, which is without political importance, the question of communism would still exist. In a totally homogenized world where capitalism would already have suppressed nations and national inequalities, the class struggle would finally acquire that purity dreamed of by certain people—unless in this science-fiction world it was too late, unless the regime of "one-dimensional man" had nullified the laws discovered by historical materialism. If we begin a chain of reasoning like this, we must follow it to the end, leave the solid ground of real struggles between real forces operating in a no less real world for the free play of all hypotheses.

5. The current crisis provides additional evidence that the center-periphery contradiction continues to be the prime means by which the range of fundamental and secondary contradictions of the system are manifesting themselves. In fact, we see that a series of victories for national liberation movements has characterized the last phase. The most important have been those of the peoples of East Asia; the least important have been those of the oil bourgeoisies, who have obtained a new division of profits by utilizing the interimperialist contradictions of a given moment. All that has played a decisive role in the current crisis of imperialism, that is, in its need to readjust itself to this resistance by the periphery.

The consequence is obviously a resurgence of struggles in the center, whether on the ideological or the economic level, since the link between the two remains very strong. Without the Chinese cultural revolution, we would be hard pressed to understand certain things that have happened in the West. The critique of revisionism in the West began in small groups linked to anti-imperialist struggles (Algeria, Vietnam, Palestine). Even on this level the effect is decisive.

On another level, the victorious resistance of the periphery has led to an accelerated falling rate of profit in the center, partially obscured by the mechanisms of stagflation; the transfer of the contradiction to the working classes of the center; and the attempt to implement an economic policy designed to recreate a reserve army there, at least partially. At the same time, imperialism has chosen to close ranks. The imperialist bourgeoisies of the subordinate metropoles once again are lining up under the leadership of the dominant American fraction in order to form a common front to limit as much as possible the victories of national liberation movements in the periphery and thus to mitigate the contradictions in the center. The failure of both the fourth UNCTAD conference and of the "north-south dialogue" testify to this refusal on the part of imperialism to grant concessions to the bourgeoisies of the periphery (74c, 78).

Let me restate that this analysis does not claim to be a prophecy and that weak spots can shift at any given moment. Nonetheless, I must emphasize this reality: for a century the primary tendency has been for the national liberation struggle to be the motive force of history. This means that all struggles, including those in the center, are determined in relation and in accord with this principal struggle in the capitalist system. Of course, a class struggle on this scale must not be understood as a juxtaposition of class struggles in different countries, of different modes of production, which only maintain episodic and random relations. They are organized in relation to a class alliance on a world scale and in relation to the position of different fractions of classes in this world alliance, which determines which are the vanguard elements, the bulk of the troops, the primary enemy, and so on.

6. This is one point of view, generally not accepted in the West. But there is a second, diametrically opposed vision. This is that the contradiction between the proletariat and the bourgeoisie in the center of the system continues to be the principal contradiction of

the entire system. This position also holds that the national liberation movement is an integral part of the worldwide bourgeois revolution. It is openly predominant in the social-democratic workers' currents as well as in those of revisionist communism and even—implicitly not to say explicitly—in the Left opposition in the West, and testifies to the ideological hegemony of social democracy. This position was taken by the Second International, and justified it in embracing imperialist ideology. One might have thought that Lenin would have eliminated it from the movement to the left of social democracy. Not at all.

The supporters of this second position will continue to be mystified about the development of capitalism in the periphery. But they do not see—since they must negate imperialism—that it is a question of dependent capitalism, which is incapable of realizing the goal of national liberation, and thus leaves intact all the potential for a socialist revolution. On the other hand, when it comes to social democratic hegemony in the West, they persist in attributing this to subjective and circumstantial factors. This is why we hold that this second view is one variant of imperialist ideology, which can take the naive form of social democracy or revisionism as well as leftwing forms.

7. The conflict between these two visions, whether open or hidden, exists everywhere and at all times. In this regard, the debate about unequal exchange has been revealing. We have seen positions gradually take shape in service of the ideological loyalties of each of the two camps. We have seen the Trotskyists chime in with the revisionists and even seen some erratic Maoists in the West join this camp.

Another example of the conflict between these two views is in the debates concerning the current crisis (74a, b). On the one side, the Maoists identify this crisis in the first instance as a crisis of imperialism, that is, of the international division of labor and of the world class alliances that control it. In this view, the origin of the crisis is first located in the defeats of imperialism in the East, defeats which have modified the objective conditions of the class struggle in the centers as they have modified the objective framework of interimperialist contradictions. Others refuse to call the crisis a crisis of imperialism. They claim that class struggles in the center are the fundamental cause and that these struggles determine the objective framework for accumulation on a world scale.

On West-centeredness once again

1. West-centeredness is the product of capitalism and particularly of its imperialist phase; it penetrates the workers' movement and even thought that claims to be Marxist. Its immediate manifestation is the absence of interest in non-Western societies, which inevitably leads to a serious distortion of the history of the West itself. For the West cannot be understood without the East, neither in the past during the mercantilist epoch nor today during the imperialist epoch. The benefits that Western peoples within the imperialist framework derive from the exploitation of the periphery constitute the objective basis for the penetration of West-centeredness into the workers' movement. This enables bourgeois ideology to become that of the whole society, while it was only partially so before imperialism. These benefits are not illusory, as certain people have claimed, because the real interest of the proletariat of the centers is to free itself from capitalist exploitation. They are, within the framework of the operation of capitalism, completely real: it is imperialist exploitation on a world scale that creates full employment and the growth of real salaries in the center.

This situation will have an important impact relative to the socialist transition in the developed centers. Will the peoples of the West, if they are not forced to it by the liberation of the periphery, be disposed to renounce imperialism and face the long transition that will be necessary before the advantages of their liberation from capitalism balance the difficulties of reconversion? The least we can say is that the effect of West-centeredness is to hide this cruel reality from the peoples of the West. A moment's thought would seem to lead to the conclusion that it is precisely there that the imperialist bourgeoisies are awaiting the Left. It is on these difficulties that eventual breakthroughs in the West are likely to founder (81).

For example, Western nations are more and more petty bourgeois nations, in that there is a concentration of middle layers whose functions can only be understood on the scale of operation of the world system, as Poulantzas has shown (81a-1). The overdevelopment of the tertiary sector, which has become unproductive, and the possible subsequent concentration of the quartenary sector under the hypothesis of a new international division of labor relegating certain industries to the periphery, have for counterpart the concentration of the generation of surplus value in the periphery through the direct exploitation at higher rates of surplus value, formal domination over precapitalist sectors, the pillage of natural resources, and so on. Under these conditions, the reconversion that the socialist transition implies for the central societies will create considerable difficulties.

The ambiguities of popular and working-class movements in the West reveal the opportunist withdrawal in the face of these problems. We see it clearly today in relation to the battle for economic independence and a rise in the price of raw materials which third world countries are engaged in. The question is: Who will definitively maintain the superprofits of the monopolies: the working classes of the centers or the peoples (including the bourgeoisies) of the peripheries? I find it disturbing that the Western Left lines up without hesitation on the side of imperialism: their excuse for escaping their responsibility is that this battle is being led by the states and thus by the bourgeoisies of the third world. The bourgeoisie has understood perfectly well how to exploit this weakness. It has succeeded in explaining without difficulty that Western nations have a right to the natural wealth of the third world, that Western peoples should not have to finance the appetites of the sheiks and bureaucrats of the third world. In the short term, this imperialist theme has put the Right several lengths ahead, as recent revolutions in Europe have shown. And an important part of the far left shares the attitudes of the social-democratic and dominant revisionist currents, as do the economic planners in the East European countries.

2. West-centeredness systematically distorts Marxism. Through dogmatic rigidity, it has virtually turned an instrument of revolutionary action into an academic discipline. The debate over unequal exchange has convinced me that insistence on the "preeminence of production over circulation" is nothing but an ideological excuse. For ultimately this debate has led to formulating problems in terms of relations of production, generation of surplus on a world scale, and world circulation of the surplus controlled by the capitalist relations of production on a world scale. It is in these terms that it has been established that the higher rates of surplus value in the periphery, the absolute surplus value obtained through formal domination, reduced or suppressed rents are all concealed beneath the appearance of "relative prices." It is a case of generation of the surplus and at the same time of the distribution that flows from the very process of its generation. The latter in its turn controls the forms of accumulation: unproductive overdevelopment at one end, the absolute law of pauperization at the other.

The anticirculationist argument thus conceals the intent to refuse to analyze the generation of surplus on a world scale and to confine this analysis to the centers. This is because it has been *a priori* decreed that surplus value is produced only in the centers and it would be inconvenient to find it increasingly generated in the periphery. It is not surprising to find this argument in Trotskyist writing. This is the case for Geoffrey Kay (72c-4), who is not only ignorant of the arguments in the debate but moreover naively declares his intention to prove that the misery of the third world is due not to its overexploitation by capital but to the fact that it is not exploited *enough*. The capitalist law of accumulation enables the rise in the living standard of the masses, and the proof is the history of the West. Additional proof is the misery of the periphery. Kay never asks himself whether the misery of the third world and the wealth of the West are related. The relative stability of salaries in the national income of the West means that at least the rate of surplus value is constant there. Moreover, the overdevelopment of unproductive functions that do not generate surplus value but redistribute it suggests that this rate is declining there. In the periphery, on the other hand, the rate and mass of surplus value are still growing: the growth of productivity is much more rapid there than that of the returns to labor. This enormous, staggeringly clear fact, which would seem since Lenin to have become obvious, totally escapes our Marxist, whose thesis—which recalls Rostow's in its denial that underdevelopment and development are two sides of the same coin—would be well received by the Ford Foundation.

On the other side, Charles Michalet, whose problematic is the same as mine (the world system envisaged in its totality as a framework for the generation of surplus value), writes that multi-nationalization "permits expanded reproduction through the shift in the site of exploitation toward zones having a higher rate of surplus value with an identical organic composition," "is accompanied by an integrated structure of spheres of production and circulation on a world base," or "does not mean the disappearance of the inherent laws of capitalism but rather their extension to a world scale" (71a-3).

Certainly there is much more to say about the question of how the law of value operates on the scale of the world economic system. But it seems obvious that we will not progress if we continue to repeat the abc's: the law of value in the pure capitalist mode of production.

3. Having once and for all given up any interest in the real field of operation of capitalism, the world system, West-centered Marxists are forced to take refuge in Marxology. Theoreticism and readings of *Capital* take the place of analyzing reality. As Michel Beaud has pointed out, the tendency is to "derive theory from theory" (82-15). Superspecialization is contrary to Marxism but is in accord with academic tendencies. Politically, it is still revisionism, whether of the Left or Right; it is still indifferent to the problem of imperialism, viewed as the speciality of other researchers, or as an attack of third worldist fever, or as the

attraction of ethnographic exoticism, or as the overflowing of a charitable spirit. Historians of this type are preoccupied with illustrating the marvelous history of the West and with proving "scientifically" that only Europe could have brought about the progress of humanity. What better proof that the ideology of the dominant class has become the ideology of society?

4. Nothing in Marx's thought lends itself to such misuse. Marx never wanted to be taken for a prophet. Happily, he was only a man, who lived neither outside space nor outside time. But the religious spirit of others has freed his legacy from this modesty. It has been forgotten that he only laid the basis for historical materialism and discovered the essential laws of capitalism. It has been forgotten that he had no other ambition, especially not that of depriving his successors of advancing the struggle under new conditions which he scarcely tried to predict. The best of his successors, Lenin and Mao, did not so deprive themselves: for a rigid dogmatist, what could be more heterodox than the contributions of Leninism and Maoism to Marxism?

In my view, the contribution of Leninism consists above all in having applied the Marxist method to the conditions of the new imperialist epoch. This framework enabled Lenin correctly to analyze the revisionism of the Second International by relating it to its objective bases and from there to formulate the strategy for the socialist revolution in the new conditions of unequal development within the imperialist system. As to the contribution of Maoism, it consists above all in the application of the Marxist method to an analysis of the conditions of class struggle in the transitional period.

Marx was at work between 1840 and 1880, that is, at the moment when the bourgeois revolution was emerging from its original little corner of England and spreading throughout Europe. Its rise was putting an end to initial primitive accumulation and to the role the old periphery had played in it. This initial subjection by that time had already blocked and even brought about regression in Latin America, Asia, and Africa—through the genocide of the Amerindians, the slave trade, the destruction of Indian and

Egyptian industry, the opium trade imposed on China, and so on—and these continents had not yet begun to take off again under the impact of their integration as a periphery in the imperialist era. To voluntarily disregard this context, to transform phrases, often taken from drafts which Marx did not think worthy of publication, into so many "revelations" is, in reality, to betray him in the worst way: by embalming him.

II. *The contradictory nature of the socialist transition*

1. Soviet experience has taught us that the socialist transition does not necessarily lead to communism. The debate over the nature and laws of Soviet society is still open. I have maintained that this class society was of a new type because state centralization of capital constituted a qualitative leap. It suppressed certain basic laws of capitalism, flowing from the fragmentation of control, and particularly the dominance of the economic instance which is related to it.

Thus it established new relations between the economic base and the superstructure, which became dominant again. This is why some have thought it useful to give a name to this new class mode. The Chinese Maoists call it "state monopoly capitalism" and its ruling class the "state monopoly bourgeoisie," reserving the term "monopoly capitalism" pure and simple for the West. On this basis, they speak of the "restoration of capitalism." I will return to the differences implied by these two terms.

But the Soviet experience is not the only one at issue. The political demands put forward by the tendencies that dominate the Western working class are similar: gradual movement toward the state mode or toward state monopoly capitalism (in the real sense, not in that used by the revisionist parties). Serious social democrats (in Sweden, for instance) do not try to hide this—state property must take the place of fragmented capital—nor do the Western communist parties. The Trotskyists lead objectively to the same position since as the others they make a cult of the unilateral determination by the productive forces. The self-management tendency has not yet responded to the series of fundamental questions which a socialist transition would pose in the West; it is afloat in contradictions and at times in naivetes. Finally, the experience of the third world countries seems also to show that when the bourgeoisie appears as a rising class there, it is always in the form of a state bourgeoisie.

Should we draw the conclusion from these similarities that the state mode is a possible successor to capitalism? In this case, the class struggles between exploited and exploiters would once again work in favor of a third party, a new class in formation, emerging in part from within the exploited class (party and organizational bureaucrats, technical cadres of the labor aristocracy, etc.) and in part parallel to it (new layers of technocrats).

2. Powerful objective forces are effectively at work in this way during the socialist transition. The specific contribution of Maoism to Marxism-Leninism is precisely in having developed the theory of the contradictions of the transition. This contribution has been developed within the concrete and specific conditions of China. But it also has been based on a reassessment of Soviet history. It has gotten out of the rut of the false theory of the degeneration attributed by Trotskyism to the peasant character of Russia by positively defining the conditions necessary for the worker-peasant alliance. In this way Maoism has universal applicability.

Its applicability certainly goes beyond the future experiences of transition from peripheral capitalism. For there is no doubt that the problems of the eventual transition from central capitalism will be no less serious nor fundamentally different. The same forces that work toward restoration or the emergence of the statist mode within peripheral situations will be at work within central situations: these forces originate in the continued existence of commodity relations, of the infrastructure of technical organization, and of the division of labor during the transition. Not to speak of the specific difficulties of the central transition as outlined above in relation to the destruction of imperialism. But there does not yet exist a social praxis of this transition, since the Paris Commune did not have the time to create it. Therefore, my observations will be limited to the contradictions of the peripheral transition.

Here I refer the reader to other writings and earlier discussion in this volume, notably the discussion about the meaning of independent and popular autocentered development, the strategy of putting industry in the service of agricultural development, and the "three revolutions" in the relations of production, technology, and culture. Vital questions remain to be explored, doubtless through practice first, but without putting off theoretical consideration of those problems that are maturing. Among others, the questions of autarky for small socialist countries and cooperation between socialist countries, and the question of the initiation of this cooperation between countries already advanced in their national liberation.

These questions have given rise to the expression of contradictory opinions and of equally contradictory practice, as well as to positive debates which have lead to subtler formulations. This has been the case, for example, with the discussion that put an end to the myth of the suicide of the petty bourgeoisie; discussions concerning the social organization of the rural world (cooperatives vs. the strengthening of petty commodity production) and the modalities of articulation between big and small industry in the direct service of collectivities, especially rural ones; and controversies concerning the advantages and difficulties of autarky and the "neutrality" of imported technology.

But the two essential questions which express the contradictions of the transition are the state and national questions, already discussed. The continued existence of the state during the transition testifies to the continued existence of classes, based on the continued existence of commodity relations. Of course, here we are dealing not with vestiges of old classes but above all with the new, rising class—whether we call it a bourgeoisie or something else. The anarchist tendencies of the Western Left have obviously distorted the debate over this question.

In the same way, since socialism takes form in the disintegration of the imperialist system, the national phenomenon retains all its importance during the transition. For this same reason, I have rejected the naive West-centered position which, in putting to the fore the "necessary disappearance of nations," objectively becomes an excuse for disregarding the effects of imperialism.

3. The contradiction of the socialist transition thus lies in the alternatives of a classless society or a new class society, either of which can emerge during the transition. A new class society or simply the restoration of capitalism? If we are talking about a new mode of production, the statist class society is highly likely to become stabilized over a long historical period, all the more so as this mode would be a progressive one since it would give a fillip to the development of the productive forces. The dominant class of this mode would thus be a rising class. If we are talking about a simple restoration, the state mode would be a transitory mode, unstable, unprogressive, and the hegemony of the dominant class would constitute the last gasp of a decadent bourgeoisie.

This fundamental debate has begun. Which of the two positions do the facts support? We know little about Soviet society, the analysis of its fundamental laws having so far been distorted by the desire to find in it *a priori* the expression of either of the laws of socialism (even if it is degenerate, which means little beyond the short transition), or of the laws of capitalism. For instance, the expression of the law of the tendency of the rate of profit to fall is sought. But this society seems relatively stable despite its difficulties: the impossibility of liberation, the continued backwardness of agriculture, national conflicts, and so on. Similarly, in Eastern Europe, Rumania seems to have stabilized in a state mode. But on the other hand, appearances at least do not indicate that Poland, Hungary, Czechoslovakia, or Cuba have reached a stable equilibrium. In Egypt, a third world country which has created an organizational form inspired by the same model although in a weak and dependent version, experience seems to show that the state mode—which it is true never reached its complete form here—is only a stage in the development of capitalism.

Analysis of these problems, which is necessary, will involve not only a close examination of the working of economic laws characterizing these systems but also the integration of this into a global understanding of the relations between the economic base and the superstructural, political, and ideological instances.

The social nature of Soviet society

1. In the analysis of the relations between relations and forces of production some have maintained that as the development of technology in the USSR is in all respects similar to that in the West, by the type of division of labor and of the organization which it controls, we must consider the mode of production prevailing in Soviet society to be capitalist. Theirs is a solid argument in support of this view.

Nonetheless, we need to ask two further questions. The first concerns the effects of the centralization of capital on the operation of the system. Does such centralization not erase the fragmentation characteristic of capital, along with its effects (economistic ideology)? Does it not explain the functional dominance of ideology in the USSR, as I have expressed it? The second concerns the possibility of a higher development of the productive forces on the basis of this centralization. Is the Soviet mode not new and superior in that it permits the transcendence of the limits imposed by the competition of capitals?

It is dangerous to underestimate the formidable attraction of revisionism for the western working classes and the possibility of a revisionist alliance which they would support. Is the goal of the Swedish social democrats fundamentally different?

Bukharin had envisaged this type of state monopoly capitalism (70b-5). That the Soviet Union, still very backward, has not actually tested this potential does not seem necessarily convincing to me. A new mode starts on a lower level and procedes to a higher one. If this mode permits the resolution of the center-periphery contradiction, which is inherent in capitalism, would this alone not make it a superior mode? Once again, to avoid dishonest exploitation of this hypothesis, it must be repeated that the Soviet mode is one means of partially transcending capitalism, the other being communism.

2. Analysis of the debates about Soviet planning must be carried out within this framework. They must be related to the social nature of the USSR and the analysis of the class struggle in the USSR (80a, b).

The results of Soviet economic growth have been unequal, slower than predicted, and not in conformity with the plans. Can this be attributed to the bureaucratic deformation of a state that remains fundamentally a workers' state, as a certain Trotskyist thesis has it? Or does it reflect the resistance of the exploited classes? I suggest that in the USSR as elsewhere it is the class struggle that determines the pace and direction of economic development. The hypothesis is that because the state bourgeoisie is not subject to the competition of capitals over which it has collective control, prices are determined by costs instead of by the laws of the market. Under these circumstances, the resistance of the workers to the intensification of work as a basis for the extortion of rising relative surplus value is easier than in the West.

The right to work, won in October, is a weapon in the class struggle, a weapon which the regime has only been partially able to circumvent through the multiplication of administrative constraints. But will it be able to go further, to suppress this right and to reestablish, by control over the unemployment rate, normal conditions for the sale of labor power? Although Yugoslavia has overcome this obstacle, it has largely nullified the effects of it by simultaneously recognizing workers' control.

3. This thesis concerning the transparency of relations of exploitation in the Soviet system of generalized state capital and its effects on the relations between economic base and ideological superstructure calls for more systematic thought about the func-

tions of nationalist ideology. I am proposing that nationalism is primarily what holds this society together. In the West economic dominance reduced ideology to consumerism and science and technology to ideology. The effects of this reduction have become apparent: social crises, crises of values, crises of youth, and the like. In the USSR will nationalism forestall this crisis?

It still remains to specify what kind of nationalism we are talking about. At first, an attempt was made to create a Soviet nationalism transcending that of the Russian, Slavic, and Asiatic nationalities. Although disguised as a liberating mission on the scale of all humanity, this nationalism coincided with the slavophile aspect of traditional ideology. Nicolas Berdiaev and Alexander Koyré had anticipated its function (80d). Gradually, this nationalism became Russified. It thus more and more conflicted with the resurgence of Turko-Muslim nationalism in Central Asia, of that of the Caucasus and of the Ukraine. The Great Russian population, no longer in the majority, was condemned demographically to become increasingly a minority. The considerable state centralization of the Soviet Union, despite its federal form, has up to now prevented the most bloody nationalist conflicts. But for how long? And how will the Russian state react to these contradictions? By granting concessions, not to say by giving up Asia and encouraging neocolonial independence there, as West-centered ideologues wish to see it? Or on the contrary, by expanding and moving outward, by external aggression, especially against China and the slavic nations of the west? We need better knowledge of the currents which cut across contemporary Soviet life.

Technocracy and labor aristocracy in the USSR and the West

1. The evolution of the USSR prompts reflection on the question of state capitalism and the objective forces at work toward a nonsocialist resolution of the contradictions of contemporary capitalism. The question is whether the state mode must necessarily take the Soviet form and thus be practically the outcome of a

socialist revolution undermined by the inadequacy of the class struggle which follows it. Or state capitalism could also progressively grow out of monopoly capitalism under the impact of the gradual concentration of capital and of its fusion with the state. The thesis of superimperialism explicitly raised this possibility and even called it a necessary stage on the peaceful road of socialist development. B. Rizzi, followed by J. Burnham, has taken this thesis from Kautsky and Hilferding and combined it with the "rise of the technocrats" (80e).

2. An answer to this question needs a much more systematic analysis than that which we currently have about the relations between technocracy and the labor aristocracy of the developed capitalist countries. The social-democratic tendency in the Western workers' movement continues in fact to be ambivalent as to the class interests it represents. There is little doubt that in the beginning this tendency reflected the gradual establishment of a labor aristocracy grafted onto imperialist exploitation and in effective control of the workers' movement. The history of English labor and of German social democracy testifies to this. However, as the new petty bourgeoisie became established, social democracy tended to represent the alienated form of the interests of the new technocracy, the upper layer of this comfortable proletariat of white collar workers and technical cadres. The attempt of monopoly capital to make this new layer play the role which the peasants played in the previous stage, that of antiworker troops, has not always brought the expected results, especially in southern Europe and Scandinavia, in contrast to England and West Germany.

Thus a gap has formed between rightwing social democracy on the one hand, domesticated by the monopolies and subjecting the working class to the joint leadership of the technocracy and the labor aristocracy (between whom the contradictions have lessened), and on the other hand a more ambivalent movement that maintains some distance from the monopolies. At times this movement takes a social democratic form, as in Sweden, where the labor aristocracy seems to prevail and to pull the technocracy along; at times it takes a conflicted form, the movement being divided between communist parties dominated by the labor aristocracy and new style socialist parties with a technocratic membership, as in southern Europe.

3. On this basis, can we propose a distinction between Eurocommunism, which proposes state capitalism independent of Moscow and based on the hegemony of the labor aristocracy within a bloc including national technocracy, and the more traditional social democracy, based on the compromise between monopoly capital and the technocracy and the labor aristocracy?

In other words, should we make a distinction between the new revisionism of Eurocommunism and the old revisionism inherited by social democracy from the Second International? Is Eurocommunism, still in formation and as yet poorly defined, a sign of this new tendency, or is it nothing more than a mask concealing a shift toward social democracy that is still difficult to acknowledge (81a)?

Whether we like it or not, the question of the socialist future of the developed world raises these questions. The mechanical application of the lessons of October, rejected by Luxemburg and Gramsci in their day, can less than ever satisfy those who wish to work for a socialist Europe and leave sectarian ghettoes behind. In particular, the analysis of the weak links that the countries of southern Europe could eventually be involves answering these questions. This analysis, of course, must systematically reexamine the question of the common market and of European unification.

4. An important stage in the analysis of the system's tendencies seems to have been reached with Robert Fossaert's proposition of the concept of "development value" (82-1). Exchange value characterizes the stage of capitalist development based on the fragmentation of capital and the autonomy of production units. It implies that this unit, with its definite boundaries, defines the collective worker whose work is the source of the value created, as it implies that socially necessary labor time is what capital pays this collective worker. The development of the productive forces brings about the emergence of a new form of value because the productivity of labor

depends from then on largely on nonmortgageable global social expenses, expenses for research and development which determine the level of science and technology developed. Socially necessary labor is, then, that which is expended in the whole of the social body and the boundaries of the area defining the collective worker are pushed outward to coincide with those of the nation and even of the world system.

Fossaert uses this concept of development value to analyze the articulation of value transfers at each of the stages of capitalist development: on the one hand in the tax–public expenditure system (where he notes that when the transfers produced by this system attain a very high level, 40 percent of the national product, taxation becomes a method of economic control and therefore control through exchange value becomes control through development value); and on the other hand in the money and credit system (where he notes that this passage is marked by the interconnection and nationalization of the credit system).

The emergence of development value reflects the contradiction between the level attained by the productive forces and the continued existence of relations of production that have become inadequate. This contradiction, already apparent, is overcome at least in part by the new mode developing in the West that Fossaert calls capitalist-statist. But development value also exists in the socialist-statist mode, which constitutes a second road (historically, the Soviet road) for the resolution of the contradiction without the abolition of classes.

This analysis seems quite fruitful. The concept of development value gives a precise response to the question of the collective worker in the sense outlined in *The Law of Value and Historical Materialism*: the opening up of the boundaries of the production unit. This analysis also complements that relating to expanded reproduction under advanced capitalism. I had situated in this framework the necessary introduction of a "department III" for the absorption of the surplus to correspond to the development of the productive forces without the abolition of relations of exploitation, through the effects of monopolistic competition (cost of sale, etc.) and through state expenditures, both unproductive and productive, in relation to the needs of the development of science and technology.

But we must go further. Doesn't the value form necessarily continue to exist, although in new guises, along with the division of labor and the state, the foundations of and the arenas for the expression of class antagonisms? Will not the new form of value that accompanies the abolition not of capital itself but of its fragmentation make the relations of exploitation transparent? If this is the case, state capitalist and state socialist modes should tend to reestablish the dominance of ideology in reproduction. The separation between state and civil society, political and economic power, characterizes the true capitalist mode alone, based as it is on the fragmentation of economic power and the economistic ideology of the generalized market.

It is no accident that democracy in the West is a concomitant of capitalism, although its extension to the working classes became possible only with imperialism—but that is no accident either. Transcendence of the fragmentation of capital through development value eliminates the separation between state and civil society, political power and economic power. That is, it eliminates democracy and reestablishes ideological absolutism, whether in the form of "one-dimensional man" in the West or that of nationalist pseudosocialist ideology in the East. This analysis, originating with the Frankfurt school, was inspired not only by Hitlerian totalitarianism and Stalinism but also by the internalized totalitarianism of advanced Western society. It is a salient reminder that the other alternative—the elimination of value, the division of labor, the state, and thus of classes—works in the opposite direction to extend and deepen civil society and thus democracy, which becomes anarchy in the etymological sense. Here we must identify the backward step taken within the Frankfurt school itself, notably by Hannah Arendt. This reduces the rich analysis of the emergence of ideological absolutism in conjunction with the evolution of the economic base down to a political schema of totalitarianism, separate from the base-superstructure dialectic. This reduction, which nullifies the problem of ideological absolutism in the advanced West, ultimately sank through successive degradations to the level of the most threadbare bourgeois ideology, as formulated in polemical discussion or by Raymond Aron and his students in France (Alain Besançon, the "new philosophers," etc.), who adopt the most banal American politocology.

III. The "three worlds" concept and the reinstatement of the national phenomenon

1. The three worlds concept divides the countries of the world system into three groups: the first world (the two superpowers—the United States and the USSR); the second world (middle rank powers—the secondary imperialisms of Western Europe and Japan and the countries of Eastern Europe); and the third world (countries of Asia, Africa, and Latin America). This classification is intended to replace the old Soviet division into two camps: capitalist and socialist, which itself had evolved with the appearance of the nonaligned group.

The latter classification claimed to distinguish between countries in accord with both their social nature (capitalist or socialist) and their foreign policy (American or Soviet alignment). It claimed that these two aspects were indissolubly linked. Later, when the nonaligned group was created through the initiative of Tito, Nasser, and Nehru, the same logic was extended to these countries. The attempt was made to link their neutral foreign policy to the specific features of their social regimes, characterized as national democratic, the "noncapitalist road." The growth of the nonaligned group to include virtually all the countries of Asia and Africa (when the OAU joined as a bloc) has shown this attempt at analysis to be devoid of content.

These Soviet distinctions are incorrect. Instead, I submit that (a) so-called socialist societies are not socialist but constitute a new group of class societies based on the state mode of production; the Chinese maintain that these are state monopoly capitalist societies, while Western societies are monopoly capitalist; (b) the relations between the USSR and the popular democracies are unequal relations; the nature and modalities of their operation remain to be clarified; (c) the societies called national democracies are peripheral capitalist societies; (d) if there is a relationship between a country's social structure considered in all its subtlety and its external policies, this relation cannot be reduced to a simple linear determination wherein a pro- or anti-Soviet attitude corresponds to a certain degree of socialism; (e) these distinctions serve to mask Soviet superpower policy and the strategies of this policy through successive periods of the cold war and detente; and (f) the alignments proffered (total or partial alignment, nonalignment considered as transitional) have constituted and continue to constitute a blocking factor in the dynamic of internal class struggles and of the anti-imperialist struggle. By forcing all social and political forces to choose one camp or the other, and thus to choose between American and Soviet leadership whether they wish to or not, supporters of this position have subordinated social struggles to the imperatives of external alignments. In this sense, they have been a distorting factor in the development of struggles, reducing their potential anticapitalist scope.

2. The reclassification proposed by the Chinese, however, bends the stick too far in the other direction (75-2, 75-3). This concept is based exclusively on the national factor, reduced in this case to the shape and place of nations in the system. There are two superpowers, which alone are capable of direct and indirect action everywhere in the world. There are developed societies which are economically independent (with unequal interdependence) because they were historically created as autocentered societies (capitalist or state capitalist) but which are incapable of politically intervening on the world scale. There are underdeveloped societies, which are economically dependent, because they were historically created as subjected and extraverted peripheries and are politically

and militarily weak and unstable. The classification has nothing to say about the precise social nature of these regimes, except that they are not socialist. An exception is made for China (unclassifiable or third world?), the Asian socialist countries (Korea, Vietnam, Cambodia, Laos), and possibly Cuba, which are seen as third world and socialist at the same time.

This position reinstates the national factor which the other ignored, a reinstatement both timely and amply justified everywhere by the facts. The national factor endures even during socialist construction (think of the relations between China, Vietnam, and Cambodia, for instance, or between Yugoslavia and Albania). Finally, the reclassification helps to rid us of remaining illusions about socialist states and the noncapitalist road. The reinstatement of the national factor brings precision to the formula, "the states want independence, the nations liberation, and the peoples revolution" (75-1) at the same time as this very formula establishes the limits of the national factor (the peoples want revolution).

If we perceive that states and nations are realities, not of course independent of class but not reducible to classes in a unilateral way, we can better understand the formulation. Peoples are defined as anticapitalist class blocs, these blocs being different in the center and in the periphery of the imperialist system. Nations are the historical units of antagonistic classes; they exist. Given this, what is called the national interest is nothing other than the reflection of the modalities which the world character of capitalism imposes on local hegemonic blocs, which must become integrated into the system of class opposition and alliance on a world scale. These nations operate by means of states which are more or less national and implement policy, that is, internal and international alliances.

3. But the three worlds concept does not explain reality if it is taken literally and if one reduces all reality to the national factor as reinstated by it. This would amount to substituting nations for classes, a substitution that would encourage us to forego a concrete analysis of the internal and external class conflicts and

alliances by means of which the system operates, reproduces itself, and is transformed.

The USSR and the United States are indeed both superpowers and both class societies. But they do not have the same history and do not occupy symmetrical positions in the world system. The United States is an imperialist superpower which grew out of the gradual establishment of imperialism during the last century and out of the partial eclipse of secondary imperialists as world powers. It operates throughout the nonsocialist and non-Soviet world in accordance with the economic laws of imperialism (capital investment, extraction of surplus labor, etc.). The USSR was established as a new class society on the basis of a socialist revolution, after having been confined within its boundaries and then within those of its specific area of influence. Its internal mode of organization leads it to intervene elsewhere in a different way. Besides, since the internal social structures of the two superpowers are different, the reciprocal relations between these internal structures and the external interventions in which each of the superpowers is engaged are different.

Western Europe and Japan on the one hand and Eastern Europe on the other are not in analogous positions either. They differ as to internal structure (hegemonic blocs, ideologies, etc.) as well as international position (secondary imperialist heirs, small countries). And the social structures of the peripheral countries are different enough to make the nature of their states different (except if one accepts the extremist thesis that grants no autonomy to peripheral states).

The different states of the second and third worlds are not struggling for independence in the same way, nor for the same type of independence. The different nations of the third world are not struggling for liberation in the same way. As to the popular blocs of revolutionary classes, they are obviously different from one country to another. The enemies of independence, of these different types of liberation, and of different revolutions on the order of the day are not the same everywhere, nor are they organized into blocs in the same way. Thus one will be wrong nine times out of ten in asserting that the primary enemy is the same everywhere and for everyone: clearly it is not the same in Angola as in Czechoslovakia.

Thus we can see that external policy is in no way a privileged domain which is in perfect conformity with the class nature of different nations. Moreover, it is sufficient to examine how alliances are made and unmade (for example, Ethiopia and Somalia) to understand this. This said, a general principle may be formulated here. An autonomous popular bloc that leads a struggle according to its own interests can profitably make very broad internal and external alliances (e.g., Vietnam). But if these alliances are used to fill in gaps in the popular bloc, they turn the popular forces into the plaything of both internal and external reaction.

4. The analysis of how the economic, political, and ideological network of the capitalist world operates is doubtless fairly advanced today. Unfortunately, we cannot say the same of the Soviet network. Works concerning the economic function of the division of labor within COMECON are still superficial and generally inspired by revisionist ideologues (80b). As to the critics, they are still too eager to transfer to this new reality the results of the analysis of the Western system.

5. The Chinese thesis of social imperialism and Soviet expansionism has the advantage of proposing an integration of Soviet policy into an overall frame of reference that gives concrete definition to the new (starting in the mid 1960s) international situation. According to this, after the Second World War a new stage of imperialism arose, characterized by American hegemony over the whole of the imperialist system, the confinement of the Soviet world, and Chinese isolation. This period supposedly ended and a new phase began, in which American hegemony was challenged, primarily and fundamentally by national liberation struggles (the most important fact for the United States was the failure of its policy in Asia, in China, and in Vietnam), and secondarily by the modification of interimperialist relations between the American hegemonic element and European and Japanese subordinate elements. Within this framework, the resurgence of struggles in the

weak centers (southern Europe) interacted with the rise of the national liberation movement, just as the bourgeoisies of the periphery tried to gain a second wind by extracting a new and less unfavorable division of world surplus value.

These changes in hegemony and world balance have supposedly led the Soviet Union to plan to exploit the American decline with the goal of establishing a new empire over a bigger area. In the past, the USSR was locked within the area of its direct dependencies, beyond which it had no bases, and the revisionist parties were themselves confined to their own local political lives. American imperialism exercised hegemony over a vast, organized system, thanks to the twofold support of the European and Japanese subordinate bourgeoisies (the countries of the second world) and the exploiting classes of the third world in diverse alliances.

This analysis presupposes that the Soviet Union evolved from a revolution which was socialist to begin with but which degenerated from the construction of socialism toward a class society, one which does not yet have an empire equal to its appetite. The countries of Eastern Europe, which can be classified as part of the second world due to their level of development, remain small countries. But the major problem is that the USSR does not have bases in the third world. There is no system in the third world which is solidly connected to a class alliance with the Soviet system.

The USSR has taken advantage of occasional alliances with the bourgeoisies at the head of national liberation movements at one moment or the other, intending thereby to wrest them from American hegemony and temporarily succeeding. But the case of Egypt indicated the fragility of these alliances. Thus the USSR would now try to exploit the American decline and to establish its empire by seeking more serious positions in the second and third worlds. It would seek in particular to use the possible transformation of old subordinate imperialisms into subordinate social imperialisms.

Within this framework, social imperialism pursues goals more or less analogous to those of classical imperialism: the search for external sources of exploitation to strengthen the revisionist alliance (subjection of the working class to its dominant class within the framework of the hegemony of nationalist ideology) which would supplant the social-democratic alliance. Of course, this search must take specific forms adapted to the concrete situation. For instance, the search for raw materials is perhaps secondary given the autarchic development of these within a huge country originally created by a socialist revolution. The attempt to subordinate more advanced industrialized countries capable of furnishing more effective technology would perhaps better suit the concrete Soviet situation.

In this perspective, we must also disentangle strategic goals from tactical means. The search for foreign bases may be only a tactical means in the struggle against the major competing imperialism to bring about a new and more satisfying division elsewhere. The Arab, Indian, and African worlds, "the soft underbelly" of the periphery—in contrast to Latin America, infinitely more subjected to North American hegemony, where there is conflict between the national liberation movements, the interests of hegemonic imperialism, the interests of the secondary imperialisms which exercise their domination there, and important local conflicts—can become the main arenas for the "conflict of the century" without necessarily being their real final or primary objective.

It remains to be seen if this analysis is correct, that is, if it corresponds not to plausible objectives of what the Chinese call the "new tsars" but to their real intentions. Writings like those of A. Amalrik (80d-3) even if they lack scientific value, at least serve to remind us that there are ideological currents in the USSR that see the promotion of anti-Chinese belligerency as a means to overcome the internal crisis and particularly the revolt of the oppressed Asiatic peoples of the Soviet Union. The leaders in Peking pay close attention to these facts, which are poorly understood in the West. They cannot at any price tolerate the creation of a Moscow-Washington axis against them. But experience has shown that such fears, as justified as they may be, often hinder more than they promote a cool and correct analysis of the enemy's strategy.

Chapter 8

The Theory of Imperialism
and the Contemporary Crisis

From the foregoing analysis, I can draw eight conclusions.

First conclusion: the theory of imperialism is synonymous with the theory of capital accumulation on a world scale, the articulation of various modes of extortion of surplus labor based on the specific modalities of unequal development in our era. The fundamental law that governs accumulation on a world scale is thus the expression of the law of value operating on the scale of the imperialist system as a whole. So to get to the root of the problem of imperialism, we must go back to the law of value. Indeed, in *Capital,* the theory of the capitalist mode of production is constructed on the basis of a precise elaboration of the law of value, which constitutes its infrastructure.

1. The law of value not only accounts for the character of the social product in the capitalist mode, that is, its commodity nature. It not only reveals the origin of profit, that is, surplus value. It also enables us to understand the laws of accumulation that control the reproduction and expansion of the capitalist mode. These laws, expressed in the equilibria and disequilibria between the two departments of capitalist production (production of means of production and production of means of consumption), place the value of labor power on an objective basis. In fact, the laws of accumulation establish the objective connection between the value of labor power and the level of development of the productive forces (90-3, 90-4).

The unity of the commodity, capital, and labor markets, that is, the coexistence of a bourgeois state, a national bourgeoisie, and a national working class implicitly and explicitly constitutes the framework necessary to give meaning to the law of value.

2. The underlying spatial hypothesis corresponding to the analysis of *Capital* is that the law of value effectively operates within the framework of each of the national capitalist spaces (England, France, Germany, the United States, etc.). Actually, this hypothesis corresponds to the reality of the middle of the last century, which is what Marx analyzed. It no longer corresponds to reality. With imperialism, capital circulates and is reproduced on a world scale. Commodities are tending to become globalized, as is the working class itself. There is no longer a single national space, not even the United States, which has a framework adequate for the reproduction of the conditions of accumulation. The globalization of the productive process implies the globalization of the space within which the law of value operates.

3. The theory of imperialism must therefore be constructed on the infrastructural basis of the theory of value operating on a world scale. In these conditions, the law of value must account for the different levels in the selling price of labor in the different segments of the imperialist system.

My argument here is (a) that commodities, because they are global, have a single world value; (b) that capital, because it is global, tends toward an average rate of return, or toward a specific range of rates structured in terms of this latter rate; (c) that the labor market remains segmented and that because of this local conditions of the class struggle allow for unequal rates of surplus value.

There are no possible alternative explanations for differences in the price of labor power. Those who deny the objective relation between the value of labor power and the development of the productive forces are forced to make of real wages an empirical category. This is either biologically determined ("subsistence"), as the Ricardians believe, and thus replaces the law of accumulation with a law of population; or it is indeterminate ("the historical and moral elements") and thus loses all rigor, becoming a synonym for anything at all.

Therefore, if we are to establish a relationship between the value of labor power and the development of the productive forces, we must specify which productive forces we mean: sectoral, national, or global. Within any national space, the productive forces are unequally developed from one branch to the other, but labor power has the same value. Any discussion that links wages with sectoral productivity is necessarily marginalist and tautological, for one cannot compare productivity from one branch to the other. The unity of the commodity, capital, and labor markets on the one hand, and the determination of the equilibria of accumulation within this market on the other, forces us to conclude that the value of labor power is objectively related to the national (average) level of the development of the productive forces.

But given the globalization of the commodity and capital markets, as well as that of the space within which the equilibria of accumulation are realized, the value of labor power on the scale of the world system is connected to the "average" world level of development of the productive forces. National differences in the price of labor power are no longer due to different average levels of national development but to the segmentation of the working class. Thus the state–politics–class struggle elements must be introduced into the theory of imperialism.

Even on the empirical level, it does not make sense to speak of "differences in productivity." In the same branch of production, producing identical commodities, sold on the same market at the same price, obtained by the same technology, labor has the same productivity, although wages may differ. Thus in South Korea, in the same industries as in the United States, wages are ten or twelve times less, although productivity is the same.

4. Differences in the price of labor power, which can be explained by the concrete conditions of class struggle, raise the question of the reproduction of labor power in all its ramifications. There is nothing to say that these real conditions everywhere and of

necessity will permit the reproduction of each of the segments of labor power. We forget, for instance, that Ireland had a population equal to that of England at the time of its conquest, at the start of mercantilism and the transition to capitalism. The Irish nation and people were destroyed by the same processes which fostered English expansion. There is nothing to say that in our time similar occurrences of destruction of labor power will not characterize the imperialist system.

5. To analyze the imperialist system is to analyze a system of social formations and not the capitalist mode extended to the world. In this system all noncapitalist modes are subjected to the domination of capital and surplus labor is thus wrenched from nonproletarianized producers to be transformed into profit for capital. This formal domination affects the conditions of reproduction of nonproletarianized labor power and, again, there is nothing to say that conditions of its reproduction are assured.

6. The price of labor power in the imperialist centers is not independent of that in the dominated peripheries, for the "average price" of labor power as a whole must correspond to its value in relation to the development of the productive forces on a world scale. The price of labor power in the center is thus indissolubly linked to the imperialist character of the system of capitalist exploitation.

7. What happens on the level of the price of commodities (unequal exchange) thus does not result from phenomena occurring on the level of circulation but reflects on this level the conditions of the genesis and division of surplus labor (in its noncapitalist forms, in its capitalist form of surplus value, and in its immediate appearance as profit) in the imperialist system.

8. Capitalist societies are by no means composed only of the working class and the bourgeoisie. In the dominant centers, numerous classes and layers participate in productive functions and/ or fulfill nonproductive functions. But the division of functions and occupations is not independent of the division of labor on a world scale. Who produces value, and who consumes it? This question cannot be answered without examining the imperialist system as a whole.

9. The type of development resulting from the laws of accumulation operating on a world scale thus has an overall impact which goes beyond the question of the price of labor power. For instance, the concentration in the center of the consumption of natural resources produced in the periphery modifies the conditions for the further development of the productive forces.

10. The superficial question of whether or not the Western working class profits from imperialism therefore leads to sterile polemicizing. An example of this type of polemic is the word game of likening the category of profit to the everyday meaning of the verb "to profit"; this tries to evade the question by redefining it.

Certainly the workers in the center of the imperialist system are exploited by capital, although a thorough analysis of the effects of the parasitism inherent in the imperialist system is far from being completed. But it is equally certain that the destruction of the imperialist system entails the end of the transfer of value generated in the periphery. This would be consistent with better living conditions for the workers in the center only if capitalist relations were overturned. This in turn would involve a completely different model of development than that derived from the laws of capitalist accumulation in general and, *a fortiori*, of imperialist accumulation.

Second conclusion: any crisis in the capitalist system expresses a malfunctioning of the law of value under the impact of the class struggle. Crisis manifests itself through disequilibria which make the realization of value impossible and, as a result, bring about a fall in the rate of profit. In this way, every crisis is a crisis of the relations of capitalist production.

1. This general proposition is inadequate to characterize any particular crisis at any given stage in the evolution of the system. In fact, in the nineteenth century for example, because the law of value was operating on the basis of national spaces, crises were national crises, although they could be transmitted from the hegemonic center of the day (Great Britain) to other countries.

If today the basis for the operation of the law of value is the whole of the imperialist system, crises must first be understood at this level. That is, they are expressed in the impossibility of assuring the world circulation of capital and the world realization of value. Class struggle on a world scale creates this impossibility, which is why the major dimension in which the current crisis finds expression is the field of the international division of labor.

2. This conclusion does not preclude other "economic" and "noneconomic" aspects of the global crisis: crisis in the expansion of the multinationals and crisis in the noncompetitive sectors; unemployment and inflation; crisis in the international monetary system; ideological crisis (the "silent revolution" in lifestyle after 1968); political crisis (affirmation of "national interests" in various places); and social crises on the periphery of the system (Ethiopia, Iran, Zimbabwe, and South Africa).

Third conclusion: the theory of imperialism and of its crisis must include a theory of the state in the imperialist epoch. This theory must not be based on generalities, as it too often is. It is not enough to conceive of the state as the instrument of dominant economic interests: yesterday those of the national bourgeoisies, today those of the monopolies.

1. Which monopolies do contemporary states represent, national or multinational and primarily American monopolies? Under these circumstances, what place do national, hegemonic, concrete class alliances have? Do not historical conditions unique to each country permanently control the composition-dislocation-recomposition of these hegemonic blocs, the membership of which varies under the direct impact of the class struggle and the accumulation of capital? On the periphery of the system are not these successive blocs visibly linked to the modalities of the international division of labor? And do they not reflect the content of the hegemonic international class alliance which ensures the global circulation of capital? The contradictions shaking these diverse hegemonic blocs under the effect of internal class struggles are manifest on the world level as contradictions between opposing states.

2. The very process of accumulation has gradually modified the state-capital relation. In the nineteenth century, the European capitalist nation-states had already been established during the

mercantilist era (England and France), or were gradually being established along with the development of industrial capitalism (Germany and Italy). At the time, the state space (national, in general) and the capitalist market (threefold market of commodities, capital, and labor power) coincided. The hegemonic class alliances were national alliances, related to the specific historical conditions of the bourgeois revolution.

British world hegemony, of course, involved transnational alliances, for instance with the dominant latifundiary classes of Latin America and the "feudal" classes of the Orient and of India. After 1815 the European countries, notably France, England's competitor during the mercantilist era, accepted this hegemony. France established an embryonic world market (limited to certain commodities), which coexisted with fully established national markets (in the threefold guise indicated above), and organized a corresponding political and military balance ("the European balance").

During the last three decades of the century, sharp competition (during the "great crisis" of 1875–1896) led to a new stage in the centralization and concentration of capital, a stage characterized by Lenin, following Hobson and Hilferding, as the imperialist stage. The monopolies in question were formed on the bases of already established national markets and retained this characteristic during the entire period until just after the Second World War. Beginning in 1945 the relation between the state and the monopolies again changed, as we shall see.

3. Giovanni Arrighi has provided what is probably the most finely developed analysis of the effects of these changes on state-market (here, synonymous with capital, monopolies, economy) relations (71b-5). According to Arrighi, the fit between the national state space and the monopolies at the end of the nineteenth century explains certain crucial aspects of the social life of the entire period.

This fit first of all explains the transfer of the locus of competition among monopolies from the strictly economic arena to that of a struggle among imperialist states. From there it explains the militarist character of the period and the establishment, on two occasions, of two coalitions which matched forces in two world wars. The period as a whole (1914–1945) was like a Thirty Years' War between Germany and the United States for the succession to declining British hegemony. This war was settled in 1945 with the definitive and accepted superiority of North American power.

The fit also explains the character of the new wave of class struggles at the beginning of the century (the 1903–1907 wave). Competition during the nineteenth century had taken place in an economic atmosphere involving a tendency for prices to drop as a result of increased productivity. The new forms of competition among monopolies for their part led to a tendency for prices to rise. Wages lost the "natural protection" resulting from the drop in prices and struggles to raise wages consequently intensified. The ambivalent attitude of the workers' movement toward the colonial question and toward competing imperialisms (the workers' movement tended to support its "own" national monopolies against foreign competitors) explains why this wave of economic struggles subsided before the preparations for world war.

Arrighi's analysis explains the nature of the "retrograde" hegemonic class alliances established during the period. The competing monopolist bourgeoisies had to strengthen "national unity" through a policy of allying with those middle layers which the development of these same monopolies (e.g., peasantry, small enterprises, etc.) was destroying. From fascisms to popular fronts to the New Deal, this type of alliance was used to protect national sectors that had lost competitive power (e.g., agriculture) or had not yet acquired it (e.g., steel).

Thus we can understand the characteristics of the class struggles of the interwar period. The wave of the 1920s following the Russian revolution was the most politicized of the successive waves in the West. The workers' movement of that era aspired to state power and the suppression of capitalist private property in favor of national appropriation. The failure of this wave and the character of the retrograde hegemonic alliances erected to combat it accounts for the seriousness of the 1930 crisis. The new wave of struggles, that of the 1930s, was from the first defensive: the movement first aspired to full employment in a capitalist economy, then it accepted the moves toward war.

Arrighi develops a striking contrast between the characteristics of the period 1880–1945 and those of the succeeding period. First, the uncontested hegemony of the United States following the Second World War fostered the reestablishment of a world market. This latter, I might add, was considerably more developed than its nineteenth-century predecessor of the era of British preimperialist hegemony, as it included a decisive proportion of commodity production (notably basic products which were all globalized) and of capital. The reestablishment of sectoral and international mobility cleared the way for the simultaneous world expansion of American monopolies and the strong economic growth of the system as a whole, in contrast to the relative stagnation of the interwar period. But there was no longer a fit between state space and economic space: the law of value had become globalized.

Second, the period immediately following the Second World War differed from that following the first: struggles were limited (practically to Italy and to France) and they appeared to be more the tail end of the previous period than the harbingers of a new wave. The epicenter of political revolution had already shifted away from Europe.

Third, strong economic growth strengthened the economic position of the working class, whose struggles were generally successful on the economic level. This reduced the flexibility of the system—all the more so as workers' parties became central to the political life of Western Europe. Under these conditions, capital adopted a twofold strategy. On the one hand, it aimed at "refurbishing" its alliances by modernizing them, replacing old with new layers (e.g., technocracies, labor aristocracies), thus better to meet the requirements of accumulation. On the other hand, it aimed at redividing the working class on the basis of the opposition between the unskilled mass worker (often an immigrant, a minority member, a youth, or a female) and the statutory worker. The first strategy seems to have succeeded in the United States and in northern Europe but to have encountered obstacles in France and Italy, forcing capital to attempt to revert to retrograde alliances and/or to accept a subordinate position relative to Germany in the industrial division of labor. The second strategy seems, tragically, to have had more success in the West, at least in the current stage.

The characteristics of the wave of struggles during the 1960s thus become clear: this was a depoliticized wave, with political demands being expressed by layers outside of the working class (especially in 1968). The current crisis erupted against this background. Under the circumstances, we must be concerned about the directions which a workers' movement on the defensive might take. Could not the privileged sector of the working class, less affected by unemployment and more by inflation, adopt the same bourgeois goal of monetary stability in a world market restructured in terms of the new requirements of accumulation? There are indications that this is the case; the evolution of the German workers' movement seems to portend such new tendencies.

4. The above analysis can be combined with the periodization of the system which I have proposed. On the level of politico-military balances, the succession from British hegemony to the opposition of the blocs to American hegemony fits in perfectly. The question still remains: Is American hegemony on the decline?

The colonial phase of the center-periphery division of labor corresponds logically to the first imperialist phase. Colonial and semicolonial dependent zones were relegated to the role of furnishers of raw materials to the industrial monopolies of the competing metropoles and of outlets for the noncompetitive industries which sustained the retrograde alliances in the metropoles. Those metropoles which enjoyed historic advantages (Great Britain and France) saw their positions coveted by those who came on the scene later and thus lacked *espace vital*. The interwar crisis accentuated these imperial retreats.

The neocolonial phase corresponds to the reconstruction of the world market and the expansion of the multinationals. Industrialization based on import substitution here resulted from the first wave of national liberation, which forced a renegotiation of international class alliances.

The current crisis reveals the decisive nature of the contradictions at this level. In fact, the primary obstacle to the reestablishment of the global circulation of capital lies precisely in the exhaustion of the potential for accumulation based on the division of labor which undergirded industrialization based on import substitution. Hence the convergence of the demand of the third world bourgeoisies for a new order based on export industry with the redeployment strategy of the monopolies. However, as we shall see, this convergence is fraught with contradictions, particularly in regard to the question of the state.

5. The concept of the world market reconstructed within the framework of American hegemony is not the same as Kautsky's notion of superimperialism. The latter, in fact, ignores the state (reduced to the role of the board of directors of the monopolies). This economism reappears in the non-Marxist "radical" theses which make of the multinationals the true and only "masters of the world." My analysis, on the contrary, starts from the contradiction between the state and the monopolies, as reflecting class contradictions within national societies both in the center and on the periphery.

Thus an analysis of the strategies of contending social forces and of the possible outcomes of the current crisis requires additional reflection about the state. For the center, we need to reflect on all the questions currently on the agenda, such as those relating to the construction of Europe and to regionalism. For the periphery, we need to reflect on the question of the content of national liberation in the current period.

Fourth conclusion: the definition of the evolving relation between the state and capital provides the appropriate framework for an analysis of the significance of the contemporary hierarchy of imperialisms and of the current question of Europe.

1. National states are still the only supreme political units in the contemporary system. There is no supranational state. On the international level, institutions such as the International Monetary Fund do not constitute even the germ of one; they are only the extension of the system of American hegemony based on the world market during the 1945–1970 phase. On the level of Europe there is the germ of a parastate organization, but insofar as the framework within which class struggle takes place and hegemonic alliances are formed remains strictly national, we must continue to speak of imperialisms (in the plural).

In the final analysis, I believe that the imperialist hierarchy is a function of the place assigned to the productive systems of the industrial monopolies in the division of labor. On these grounds, the most powerful imperialists are the United States, Japan, and Germany (in that order). England, France, Italy, and the other states of the center are second-rank imperialists. Economic advantages inherited from colonial empires, such as inequalities in political, ideological, and military positions, are no more in this framework than are means by which secondary imperialisms can negotiate the terms of their alignment with first-rank imperialisms.

The thesis of a return to finance imperialism and of the restored supremacy of finance over industry is, in my opinion, extremely weak. This view is based on the growing international indebtedness of the third world and of the socialist world, the relative withdrawal of direct investment in the third world in favor of indebtedness, especially state indebtedness, to private financial consortia. But these developments might be conjunctural, related to the structural crisis in the international division of labor. Concrete analysis of the debts shows, in fact, that they result in part from the impact of the crisis on the third world and in part from the requirement of inserting the latter into the world circulation of capital (e.g., refloating of the balance of payments, consolidation of bourgeoisies, etc.).

2. If a European imperialism is coming into being, it is not yet clear what relation it will have to American imperialism—

competitor or ally. The construction of Europe which is taking place today serves only as a means for secondary imperialisms to mitigate their inadequacies. It remains entirely questionable whether the system will tend toward the break-up of the world market, the end of American hegemony, and the reestablishment of a state-capital fit ultimately on the level of Europe, or whether Europe and the states that comprise it will keep their current positions as relays in the unified world market system under the thumb of predominantly American monopolies.

In principle and abstractly, a crisis situation such as the system is now undergoing would lead either to an exacerbation of inter-imperialist contradictions or to an alignment of the weaker with the stronger. If in 1930 the crisis called up the first solution, that was because of the state-monopoly fit which characterized the period. Transnationalization accounts for the realignment currently taking place after several halfhearted assertions at autonomy at the time of the 1973 crisis.

3. The tendency to realignment raises the question of what political attitude to take toward Europe. The most commonly accepted position on the European Left is that of support for Europe, albeit for a Europe of workers rather than of monopolies. Implicit in this position is an economistic retreat before the "objective necessities of the development of the productive forces." The formation of a European state is, in fact, considered to be a prelude to the socialist transformation of the relations of production, now postponed indefinitely. If this stage is accepted as necessary, there could follow a second postponement based on the need to construct a planetary state in keeping with the requirements of the productive forces. This would amount to abandoning any belief in the possibility of socialist breakthroughs based on the effects of unequal development on the political conditions of the class struggle.

My position, by comparison, is that the Leninist strategy of rupture remains valid today. This strategy raises the question of "disengagement" vis-à-vis the international system, a question to which I will return.

Fifth conclusion: the question of the relations between the state and capital is also raised in the current crisis on the periphery of the system, although in different forms.

1. Contrary to what occurred in the center, the development of peripheral capitalism, far from establishing nations, destroyed them. The extraverted character of this development and its distorting effects narrowed the scope for the formation of the local market: the domination of foreign capital made the establishment of a local capital market impossible. Finally, the persistence of forms of formal domination limited the scope for the formation of a labor market.

What, then, is the state here? The administrative excrescence of the imperialist state apparatus? In part. But it is also and primarily the expression of a local hegemonic alliance linked to the imperialist alliance.

This accounts for the double fragility of peripheral states, both the fragility of the hegemonic alliance, fraught with contradictions mirroring those that pit it against the popular masses, and national fragility. The fragility of the hegemonic alliance is nothing more than the effect of the transfer to the periphery of the contradictions in the accumulation of capital on a world scale. The weakest alliances, such as those based on the predominance of a comprador bureaucracy practically without a local bourgeoisie, result in a local state that is virtually a foreign administrative excrescence and open the country to permanent outside interference. Even alliances which seem solider, such as those based on an industrial bourgeoisie and a national state, remain fragile, as the events in Iran demonstrate.

As for national fragility, integration into the imperialist system was often effected on a preexisting substratum of more or less heterogenous ethnic groups and communities. In these circumstances it was even more difficult for a national state to crystallize, as contradictions among the people could be and were exploited both by the different segments of the local hegemonic alliance and by external forces. Here we have a national liberation movement without a nation. If this latter fails correctly to resolve the contradictions among the people, it remains weak and its weakness gives power to the hegemonic blocs, however fragile, which ensure imperialist integration. When, exceptionally, the national liberation movement arises in a precapitalist nation (e.g., East Asia) this favorable conjuncture exposes the fragility of the local exploiting alliance.

2. It is necessary to understand the meaning of the current battle over the international division of labor, redeployment, and the new international economic order. In the abstract, the new order, based on accelerated industrialization in the periphery within the international division of labor, corresponds to the objective requirements of accumulation: a rise in the rate of surplus value and, from there, of profit on a world scale (74a-1).

This is only an abstraction, however, since the object of the current struggle is precisely the division of this surplus value among different segments of capital. Here the interest of dominant capital—that of the multinationals—clashed with that of the peripheral bourgeoisies. Redeployment is the strategy of the former; it presupposes weakened peripheral states. The new international economic order is the strategy of the latter; it presupposes strengthened peripheral states, capable of organizing into export cartels in order to impose a rise in the price of basic products and to exercise national control of natural resources, to retain the benefit from price rises through nationalization and fiscal policy, to control the investment of these surpluses so as to at least partially structure the productive systems to give them more autonomy, and so on.

From the beginning in 1973, the struggle between the two lines was joined. Although during the years 1973–1975 the new international economic order appeared to be the expression of a united front against imperialism, the divisive strategy adopted by the latter of supporting the right wing of the front has succeeded in dividing the third world (third and fourth worlds, "progressive" and "pro-imperialist" countries). If this strategy has not completely succeeded, it has at least eliminated the danger of a confrontation.

It would be a mistake, however, to stop with this last statement. The violent class struggles rocking the societies of the periphery presage the collapse of certain hegemonic blocs which maintain the current balance. Once again the events in Iran demonstrate this. There the very success of redeployment, marked by exceptional rates of growth, made the contradictions more explosive. For the working class which is forming, far from being less capable of politicized struggles, is on the contrary moved toward them almost spontaneously, notwithstanding the Western prejudice according to which the most advanced working classes would necessarily be the most revolutionary. It is of little matter under which ideological flag the masses rebel: this in large measure is a function of circumstantial and subjective conditions (the predictable consequence of the strategy of the "noncapitalist road"). What is more important is the fact that they are rebelling against the expansion of capital. A new wave of the national liberation movement, with a strong "populist" content, at least in the beginning, has already contributed to the development of the crisis of imperialism.

3. In the circumstances of this struggle, can we discern the emergence of new capitalist national states, the expression of the gradual transfer of capitalism from its origins in Europe to the whole of the planet? Here again, in the abstract, if the process of capital accumulation could be indefinitely extended, it would lead to the imposition of capitalist relations of production on all the world's societies through the suppression of all other forms of productive relations and thus to the homogenization of the whole of the planet.

But we cannot go from the recognition of this abstract tendency to the conclusion that new capitalist centers would in fact gradually emerge. Up to the present, at each stage in the development of the imperialist system, center-periphery relations have been based on an unequal division of labor. An economic analysis of the export industries set up in certain peripheral countries and based on cheap labor and/or abundant natural resources, as well as an overall political analysis of the integration of these countries into the world system (local hegemonic alliances and dominant international alliances, the nature and role of the state, systems of ideological and political life, etc.) makes it impossible to envision the reversal of this tendency.

The opposing viewpoint always holds up "examples" of the most advanced third world countries which are in the process of industrializing (today Brazil, South Korea, Taiwan, Iran, etc.) in support of a simple theory of "stages" of development. Whether in its conventional version (that of the World Bank) or in one of its versions which use Marxist terms (cf. 70e-1), this thesis replaces an analysis in historical materialist terms (which is always holistic) with an economistic analysis reduced to the quantitative measure of industrial production.

Sixth conclusion: the analysis of imperialism in historical materialist terms cannot stop with the discernment of broad economic tendencies in the accumulation of capital but must relate these broad tendencies to the struggles of classes, nations, and states on a world scale. Thus in order to analyze these systemic contradictions at a given stage in their concrete development, as well as the concrete interrelation of these contradictions, we must place them in the framework of the real international political conjuncture of the period.

1. Our era could perhaps be interpreted as being that of the confrontation between declining capitalism and rising socialism. But we cannot be satisfied with this general and abstract proposition. Confrontation is not this direct; it is only implicit, hidden behind direct confrontations of a different type. Thus with regard to class confrontations in the center of the system, the current goal of the workers' movement is not socialism: the goal is economic (full employment, protection of buying power eroded by inflation, etc.). Breakthroughs in the realm of social life generally occur apart from these confrontations. In the periphery, the confrontations are "silently" at work within the national liberation movement, without a clear consciousness of the goals always obtaining (thus the existence of populist forms). Overall, given these circum-

stances, the confrontations which occupy center stage are those between states, east and west, north and south.

2. The East-West conflict has long been confused with a confrontation between socialism and capitalism. The Soviet version of the division into three worlds confounds the supposed social nature of regimes (socialist or capitalist) with the foreign policies of states (alignment with the USSR or the United States). Within the framework of this thesis, it has been necessary to create an "intermediate" category ("progressive regimes," the "noncapitalist road," "national democracy") which is tactically useful.

3. The Marxist method requires us to invert the terms of this argument. We must start from the real class content of these regimes. No tactical consideration justifies ignoring the basic question of the class nature of the Eastern countries and, based on this, the real goals of their international policies.

In this corrected perspective, if the USSR is not socialist, it is a power which we have to characterize. Doubtless it is a superpower, since it alone can aspire to world hegemony and/or to a division of the world with the United States, its only military competitor. We need a better understanding of the laws and requirements of its expansion. These cannot necessarily be borrowed from what we know about capitalist laws, since we are dealing with a new type of class society (i.e., the statist mode of production).

4. The Soviet division (whether old or new, it continues to be the basis of successive theses produced to fit the conjuncture of the cold war, detente, coexistence, or hardening of the line) fulfills obvious ideological functions. It allows for the subordination of class struggles and anti-imperialist struggles to the goals of the USSR itself. It contributes to confusing, by mixing them together, "progressive forces," authentic popular forces, and bourgeois and neobourgeois (statist) forces conjuncturally allied to the former. By using elastic concepts (such as "socialism" loosely used, or "progressive forces," which amounts to the liberal use of the terms "liberty" and "the rights of man") this conceptualization of world forces subordinates strategy to mere tactics. It does not allow us to

discern the primary enemy (which depends on one's position: it is obviously not the same for the Czech working class as for Angolan peasants). It does not allow us to distinguish the moment in the evolution of the balance of power between the two superpowers. (For instance, after the defeat in Indochina, was the United States on the defensive, its capacity for direct military intervention paralyzed, as it seems to be with the Carter administration?)

5. In the confrontation between states, secondary imperialisms (those of Europe and Japan) seem currently to be realigning themselves, for the reasons indicated above. In the north-south confrontation, the variety of situations ranging from comprador bureaucracies to revolutionary peasant alliances prevent global judgments. In the strategy of the uninterrupted revolution by stages on the agenda for the periphery of the imperialist system, the important thing is that the exploited working and peasant classes be capable of autonomous expression. Then and only then will tactical internal and external alliances be subordinated to the strategic goal of the socialist transition. Failing this, popular forces will remain the plaything of local reactionary forces and of external forces.

Seventh conclusion: if we continually keep imperialism at the center of our thinking about contemporary capitalism, we will correctly identify the obstacle to socialism today. This obstacle is the difficulty with disengagement. This difficulty is even greater for the societies of the center than for those of the periphery. This, finally, is the meaning of the fact of imperialism.

1. Built on the imperialist surplus, the societies of the center, in their social composition as well as in the "advantages" gained from their access to the world's natural resources, have difficulty conceiving of the necessity for a global restructuring. A popular antiimperialist bloc capable of overthrowing the hegemonic bloc is therefore difficult to establish. The recent experiences of Portugal and Italy serve to illustrate this difficulty. On the other hand, in the societies of the periphery, disengagement is the precondition for a development of the productive forces sufficient to meet the needs and demands of the great majority.

2. It is clearly this basic situational difference which explains why, up to the present, the major breaches in the capitalist system have been made from the periphery of the system. This suggests a parallel with the transition from antiquity to feudalism. The Roman Empire was a system for the centralization of the surplus (tributary and slave). Further development of the productive forces required the break-up of this system of centralization, which was impeding progress in the periphery. This explains the substitution of autonomous feudal zones, established in the least advanced periphery of the empire (Celtic and Germanic Europe). Today, in the same way, the development of the periphery of the system requires the abolition of the system for the centralization of the surplus which the imperialist world market represents.

3. This process by which capitalist relations are superceded through a break on the level of the centralization of the surplus corresponding to the most advanced productive forces obviously creates a series of new problems (the possibility of partial regressions, restorations, etc.) which socialism must confront. We have to accept this. But in the perspective of an effective transitional strategy, we must also consider an alternative outcome defined in international terms, in order to break out of the dead end of national isolation.

The alternative outcome ultimately could make possible a socialist transition starting with the weakest links in the central imperialist chain. It could also speed up the development of socialist relations in the peripheral zones that have left the system. Finally, it could ease the way for the establishment of a first anti-imperialist stage in the transition for those periphery regions which have not yet broken the chains of dependency.

The strategy of an alliance among socialist southern Europe, the Arab world, and Africa falls within this perspective (79-1, 79-2). Unfortunately, this vision is as yet little understood by most people, still less supported by them. Doubtless the forces which could be favorable to it in Europe have been primarily responsible for its failure up to the present. Currently, after the timid and ambivalent moves of the years 1970–1975, the southern European bourgeoisie chose to align with German-American Europe, thus closing the door on this possibility.

Eighth conclusion: the analysis of the imperialist system and of its crisis now calls for commentary in the nature of provisional conclusions and new questions.

1. The systematic underestimation, when it is not pure and simple omission, of the imperialist dimension of capitalism is rendering the workers' and socialist movement impotent. This impotence is verbally compensated for by the *ouvrierist* position. Some claim that only the advanced working class can be the harbingers of the socialist future, forgetting the most obvious lessons of history. In fact, the three great moments in the revolutionary history of our time—the Paris Commune, the Russian revolution of 1917, and the cultural revolution in China—were not the work of advanced working classes but of working classes still in formation.

This *ouvrierist* position, when it is serious as with Italian *operaismo*, becomes leftwing in the sense of an infantile disorder. An expression of the most advanced Western working class, Italian *operaismo* unfortunately does not attend to the questions addressed to the working-class minority by the other social layers which constitute the majority under developed capitalism. Nor does it address the international and imperialist dimension of the problem (71c-2). The impotence of the *ouvrierist* position is thus manifest in its inability to grasp the nature of conflicts on a world scale. Because it reduces the confrontation between capitalism and socialism to a direct class conflict between capital and labor in the center of the system, it cannot grasp the significance and nature of the national liberation movement in the periphery and the significance and nature of the East-West contradiction and of its effects on Western society.

To ignore or underplay imperialism is, finally, to substitute for unequal development the development of capitalism by stages. It is thus to fail to grasp the significance of the historical possibility of a strategy of uninterrupted revolution by stages. It is to become confused about "capitalist development" in the periphery, forgetting its peripheral character, and forgetting that this must lead to awaiting the development of capitalism on a world scale before raising the question of socialism.

Beneath this surface error lies the reduction of Marxism to the dimensions of a workers' ideology, when it is the revolutionary ideology of our day, the science of the revolution of the exploited and of human liberation. Of course, its discovery would have been impossible without capitalism and the workers' movement. But Marxism has enabled us to reengage with the entire revolutionary tradition of the exploited throughout time. By this very fact, Marxism is the instrument of the complex revolution of the imperialist epoch, the science of the worker-peasant alliance.

2. Historical experience of the class struggle shows that relations of production that have become an obstacle to the development of the productive forces are destroyed by the revolt of the oppressed classes. But these revolts can serve the interests of a third class, the bourgeoisie, born partially within the peasantry and partially alongside it.

The Soviet experience once again demonstrates this historical possibility. Did not the blows of the working class against the bourgeoisie serve the interests of a new bureaucratic technical class, the dominant class of the new statist mode of production? Is this eventuality, far from being the exclusive result of conditions specific to Russia, not equally likely in the West? Are not the new layers created by the differentiation within the proletariat—labor aristocracy and technocracy—also aspiring to a statist mode, and is not social democracy a partial illustration of this tendency? And what of Eurocommunism? A still poorly defined amalgam of partially contradictory tendencies, this current already clearly contains an old social-democratic tendency (management of capital with the support of the labor aristocracy), a new Swedish-style social-democratic tendency (replacement of the bourgeoisie with the labor aristocracy and the technocracy) leading to a statist mode, and possibly a "self-management" tendency stemming from old anarcho-syndicalist sources but nonetheless expressing the workers' revolt.

We still need to know the law of development of this new mode and its specific contradictions. Without this knowledge, it would be too easy to extrapolate to this new mode, since it is still based on class exploitation, what we know about capitalism. In particular, we need to understand better how the nation functions in this new mode of production. I have proposed several hypotheses in these different areas but am aware that the question of the nature of Soviet imperialism is as yet poorly explained.

What is the degree of "historical necessity" of the possibility of a statist mode as a successor to capitalism? Clearly, the possible evolution toward a statist mode would involve the disintegration of the world market system which has characterized the last thirty years. It would involve the strengthening of more-or-less autarchic national tendencies. Should we then interpret this contradiction as involving a possible step backward toward models (though more structured) similar to those of the interwar period? And should we interpret this tendency in the same way for the countries of the center and those of the periphery of the current system?

Current conflicts raise all these questions. It would be imprudent to ignore them and recognize only the contrary tendency toward the continuation of the regulation by the world market because this tendency corresponds to the economic needs of the monopolies, that is, the most advanced productive forces of our day. What of the question of the potential for further development, impeded by the continuation of these relations of production, particularly on the periphery? What about the effects of the class struggle in the West?

3. Put in these terms, the complex question of the confrontation between capitalism and socialism has different possible outcomes. We must differentiate between the system's basic contradiction (today the contradiction between capital and labor) and the primary

contradiction by which the latter is expressed. This primary contradiction may be between nations or states at any given moment. This raises the whole question of the degree to which the movement of revolutionary forces will control social evolution and of their potential alienation—a reflection of the still objective nature of societal laws operating like natural laws.

Under these circumstances, only a concrete analysis of the situation will enable us to characterize the period and to answer the question: Is it the winds of revolution or of war that are now blowing? There is no doubt that the implicit or explicit answer to this question will have decisive consequences for socialist strategy.

Conclusion

Revolution or Decadence?
Thoughts on the Transition
from One Mode of Production to Another

The workers' and socialist movement has sustained itself on a vision of a series of revolutions beginning in the advanced capitalist countries. From the criticisms which Marx and Engels made of the programs of German social democracy to the conclusions derived by Bolshevism from the experience of the Russian revolution, the workers' and socialist movement has never conceived of the transition to socialism on the world scale in any other way.

However, over the past seventy-five years the transformation of the world has taken other paths. The perspective of revolution has disappeared from the horizons of the advanced West, while socialist revolutions have been limited to the periphery of the system. These have inaugurated developments of sufficient ambiguity for some people to see them only as a stage in the expansion of capitalism to the world scale. An analysis of the system in terms of unequal development attempts to give a different answer. Beginning with the contemporary imperialist system, this analysis obliges us also to consider the nature and meaning of unequal development in previous historical stages.

The comparative history of the transition from one mode of production to another calls for posing the question of the mode of transition in general and theoretical terms. Thus, similarities between the current situation and the era of the end of the Roman Empire have led those historians who are not proponents of historical materialism to draw parallels between the two situations. On

249

the other hand, a certain dogmatic interpretation of Marxism has used the terminology of historical materialism to obscure thought on this theme. Thus Soviet historians speak of the "decadence of Rome," while putting forward the "socialist revolution" as the only form of substitution of new relations of production for capitalist relations. The following comparative analysis of the form and content of the ancient and the capitalist crises in relations of production addresses this issue. Do the differences between these two crises justify treating one in terms of "decadence" and the other in terms of "revolution"?

My central argument is that a definite parallel exists between these two crises. In both cases, the system is in crisis because the centralization of the surplus it organizes is excessive, that is, is in advance of the relations of production that underlie it. Thus the development of the productive forces in the periphery of the system necessitates the break-up of the system and the substitution of a decentralized system for collecting and utilizing the surplus.

1. The most commonly accepted thesis within historical materialism is that of the succession of three modes of production: the slave mode, the feudal mode, and the capitalist mode. In this framework, the decadence of Rome would be only the expression of the transition from slavery to serfdom. It would still remain to explain why we do not speak of a "feudal revolution" as we speak of bourgeois and socialist revolutions.

I consider this formulation to be West-centered in its over-generalization of the specific characteristics of the history of the West and its rejection of the history of other peoples in all its particularities. Choosing to derive the laws of historical materialism from universal experience, I have proposed an alternative formulation of one precapitalist mode, the tributary mode, toward which all class societies tend. The history of the West—the construction of Roman antiquity, its disintegration, the establishment of feudal Europe, and, finally, the crystallization of absolutist states in the mercantilist period—thus expresses in a particular form the same basic tendency which elsewhere is expressed in the less discontinuous construction of complete, tributary states, of which China is the strongest expression. The slave mode is not universal, as are the tributary and capitalist modes; it is particular and appears strictly in connection with the extension of commodity relations. In addition, the feudal mode is the primitive, incomplete form of the tributary mode.

This hypothesis views the establishment and subsequent disintegration of Rome as a premature attempt at tributary construction. The level of development of the productive forces did not require tributary centralization on the scale of the Roman Empire. This first abortive attempt was thus followed by a forced transition through feudal fragmentation, on the basis of which centralization was once again restored within the framework of the absolutist monarchies of the West. Only then did the mode of production in the West approach the complete tributary model. It was, furthermore, only beginning with this stage that the level of development of the productive forces in the West attained that of the complete tributary mode of imperial China; this is doubtless no coincidence.

The backwardness of the West, expressed by the abortion of Rome and by feudal fragmentation, certainly gave it its historic advantage. Indeed, the combination of specific elements of the ancient tributary mode and of barbarian communal modes characterized feudalism and gave the West its flexibility. This explains the speed with which Europe passed through the complete tributary phase, quickly surpassing the level of development of the productive forces of the West, which it overtook, and passing on to capitalism. This flexibility and speed contrasted with the relatively rigid and slow evolution of the complete tributary modes of the Orient.

2. Doubtless the Roman-Western case is not the only example of an abortive tributary construction. We can identify at least three other cases of this type, each with its own specific conditions: the Byzantine-Arab-Ottoman case, the Indian case, the Mongol case. In each of these instances, attempts to install tributary systems of centralization were too far ahead of the requirements of the devel-

opment of the productive forces to be firmly established. In each case the forms of centralization were probably specific combinations of state, parafeudal, and commodity means. In the Islamic state, for instance, commodity centralization played the decisive role. Successive Indian failures must be related to the contents of Hindu ideology, which I have contrasted with Confucianism. As to the centralization of the empire of Genghis Khan, it was, as we know, extremely short-lived.

3. The contemporary imperialist system is also a system of centralizaton of the surplus on the world scale. This centralization operated on the basis of the fundamental laws of the capitalist mode and in the conditions of its domination over the precapitalist modes of the subject periphery. I have formulated the law of the accumulation of capital on the world scale as a form of expression of the law of value operating on this scale. The imperialist system for the centralization of value is characterized by the acceleration of accumulation and by the development of the productive forces in the center of the system, while in the periphery these latter are held back and deformed. Development and underdevelopment are two sides of the same coin.

Thus we can see that further development of the productive forces in the periphery requires the destruction of the imperialist system of centralization of the surplus. A necessary phase of decentralization, the establishment of the national socialist transition, must precede the reunification at a higher level of development which a planetary classless society would constitute.

This central thesis has several consequences for the theory and strategy of the socialist transition.

1. In the periphery the socialist transition is not distinct from national liberation. It has become clear that the latter is impossible under local bourgeois leadership, and thus becomes a democratic stage in the process of the uninterrupted revolution by stages led by the peasant and worker masses. This fusion of the goals of national liberation and socialism engenders in its turn a series of new problems which we must evaluate. For the emphasis shifts from

one aspect to the other, due to which the real movement of society alternates between progress and regression, ambivalences and alienation, particularly in nationalist form. Here again we can make a comparison with the attitude of the barbarians toward the Roman Empire: they were ambivalent toward it, notably in their formal, even slavish, imitation of the Roman model against which they were revolting.

At the same time, the parasitical character of the central society intensifies. In Rome, imperial tribute corrupted the plebians and paralyzed their revolt. In the societies of the imperialist center, a growing portion of the population benefits from unproductive employment and from privileged positions, both concentrated there by the effects of the unequal international division of labor. Thus it is harder to envision disengagement from the imperialist system and formation of an anti-imperialist alliance capable of overturning the hegemonic alliance and inaugurating the transition to socialism.

2. The introduction of new relations of production seems easier in the periphery than in the center of the system. In the Roman Empire, feudal relations took hold rapidly in Gaul and Germany, but only slowly in Italy and the East. It is Rome which invented colonialism, which replaced slavery. But feudal authority developed elsewhere and feudal relations never fully developed in Italy itself.

Today the feeling of latent revolt against capitalist relations is very strong in the center, but it is powerless. People want to "change their lives" but cannot even change the government. Thus progress occurs in the area of social life more than in the organization of production and the state. The silent revolution in lifestyle, the break-up of the family, the collapse of bourgeois values demonstrate this contradictory aspect of the process. In the periphery, customs and ideas are often far less advanced, but socialist states have nonetheless been established there.

3. Vulgar Marxist tradition has effected a mechanistic reduction of the dialectic of social change. The revolution—the objective content of which is the abolition of old relations of production

and the establishment of new relations, the precondition for the further development of the productive forces—is made into a natural law: the application to the social realm of the law by which quantity becomes quality. The class struggle reveals this objective necessity: only the vanguard—the party—is above the fray, makes and dominates history, is de-alienated. The political moment defining the revolution is that in which the vanguard seizes the state. Leninism itself is not entirely devoid of the positivist reductionism of the Marxism of the Second International.

This theory which separates the vanguard from the class is not applicable to the revolutions of the past. The bourgeois revolution did not take this form: in it the bourgeoisie coopted the struggle of the peasants against the feudal lords. The ideology which enabled them to do this, far from being a means of manipulation, was itself alienating. In this sense, there was no "bourgeois revolution"—the term itself is a product of bourgeois ideology—but only a class struggle led by the bourgeoisie or, at most, at times a peasant revolution coopted by the bourgeoisie. Even less can we speak of the "feudal revolution," where the transition was made unconsciously.

The socialist revolution will be of a different type, presupposing de-alienated consciousness, because it will aim for the first time at the abolition of all exploitation and not at the substitution of new for old forms of exploitation. But this will be possible only if the ideology animating it becomes something other than the consciousness of the requirements of the development of the productive forces. There is nothing to say, in fact, that the statist mode of production, as a new form of relations of exploitation, is not a possible response to the requirements of this development.

Only people make their own history. Neither animals nor inanimate objects control their own evolution; they are subject to it. The concept of praxis is proper to society, as expression of the synthesis of determinism and human intervention. The dialectic relation of infrastructure and superstructure is also proper to society and has no equivalent in nature. This relation is not unilateral. The superstructure is not the reflection of the needs of the infrastructure.

If it were, society would always be alienated and I cannot see how it could become liberated.

This is why I propose to distinguish between two qualitatively different types of transition from one mode to another. When the transition is made unconsciously or by an alienated consciousness, that is, when the ideology animating classes does not allow them to master the process of change, the latter appears to be operating like a natural change, the ideology being part of nature. For this type of transition we can apply the expression "model of decadence." On the other hand, if and only if the ideology expresses the total and real dimension of the desired change, can we speak of revolution.

4. Is the socialist revolution in which our era is engaged of the decadent or the revolutionary type? Doubtless we cannot as yet answer this question definitively. In certain of its aspects, the transformation of the modern world incontestably has a revolutionary character as defined above. The Paris Commune, the revolutions in Russia and China (and particularly the cultural revolution) have been moments of intense de-alienated social consciousness.

But are we not engaged in another type of transition? The difficulties which make the disengagement of the imperialist countries nearly inconceivable today and the negative impact of this on the peripheral countries following the socialist road (leading to possible capitalist restoration, evolutions toward a statist mode, regression, nationalist alienation, etc.) call into question the old Bolshevik model.

Some people are resigned to this and believe that our time is not one of socialist transition but of worldwide expansion of capitalism which, starting from this "little corner of Europe," is just beginning to extend to the south and the east. At the end of this transfer, the imperialist phase will appear to have been not the last, the highest stage of capitalism, but a transitional phase toward universal capitalism. And even if one continues to believe that the Leninist theory of imperialism is true and that national liberation is a part of the socialist and not of the bourgeois revolution, would not exceptions, that is, the appearance of new capitalist centers, be possible? This theory emphasizes the restorations or the evolutions toward a statist mode in the Eastern countries. It characterizes as objective processes of capitalist expansion what were only pseudosocialist revolutions. Here Marxism appears as an alienating ideology masking the true character of these developments.

Those who hold this opinion believe that we must wait until the level of development of the productive forces at the center is capable of spreading to the entire world before the question of the abolition of classes can really be put on the agenda. Europeans should thus allow the creation of a supranational Europe so that the state superstructure can be adjusted to the productive forces. It will doubtless be necessary to await the establishment of a planetary state corresponding to the level of the productive forces on the world scale, before the objective conditions for superceding it will obtain.

Others, myself among them, see things differently. The uninterrupted revolution by stages is still on the agenda for the periphery. Restorations is the course of the socialist transition are not irrevocable. And breaks in the imperialist front are not inconceivable in the weak links of the center.

References

1. Communal formations

10. Basic works

1. Karl Marx, *Grundrisse*, ed. Martin Nicolaus. New York, Random House, 1973 (especially "Forms Which Precede Capitalist Production," pp. 471–79).
2. Friedrich Engels, *The Origin of the Family, Private Property and the State*. New York, International Publishers, 1972.
3. Lewis H. Morgan, *Ancient Society*. New York, New World, 1963.
4. François Pouillon et al., *L'anthropologie économique*. Paris, Maspero, 1978 (good synthesis of French Marxist economic anthropology, especially chapters 3, 4, and 5, by François Pouillon, Alain Marie, and Roger Meunier, respectively).
5. Claude Meillassoux, *Terrains et théories*. Paris, Anthropos, 1977. ("L'essai d'interprétation du phénomène économique dans les sociétés traditionelles d'auto-subsistance," 1960, reprinted in this collection, summarizes the experience taken by the author from his *Anthropolgie économique des Gouro de Côte d'Ivoire*. The Hague, Mouton, 1960.)
6. Pierre-Philippe Rey, *Les alliances de classes*. Paris, Maspero, 1973. *Colonialisme, néo-colonialisme et transition au capitalisme*. Paris, Maspero, 1971. "Le transfert de surtravail de la paysannerie vers le capitalisme," *L'homme et la société* (1977).
7. Emmanuel Terray, *Marxism and "Primitive" Societies*. New York, Monthly Review Press, 1972.

257

8. Catherine Coquery-Vidrovitch, "Research on an African Mode of Production," in *African Social Studies*, ed. P. Gutkind and P. Waterman. New York, Monthly Review Press, 1976.
9. Karl Polanyi, *Primitive, Archaic and Modern Economies*, ed. George Dalton. Boston, Beacon, 1971.
10. A. V. Chayanov, *The Theory of Peasant Economy*. Introduction by Daniel Thorner. Homewood, Ill., Free Press, 1960.
11. Ester Boserup, *The Conditions of Agricultural Growth: The Economics of Agrarian Change Under Population Pressure*. Chicago, Aldine, 1965.
12. Lawrence Krader, ed., *The Ethnological Notebooks of Karl Marx*. Atlantic Highlands, N.J., Humanities, 1974.
13. C. Bennetti, J. Cartelier, and C. Berthomieu, *Economie classique, économie vulgaire*. Paris, Maspero, 1975.
14. Maurice Godelier, *Horizons, trajets marxistes en anthropologie*. Paris, Maspero, 1973.

11. *The idea of the domestic mode of production*

1. Marshall Sahlins, *Stone Age Economics*. Chicago, Aldine, 1972.
2. Claude Meillassoux, *Femmes, greniers et capitaux*. Paris, Maspero, 1975.
3. Samir Amin, I. Eynard, B. Stuckey, "Féminisme et lutte de classes," *Minuit* 7 (1974).
4. Maurice Godelier and A. Deluz, "A propos de deux textes d'anthropologie économique," *L'homme* 11 (1967).

12. *Slavery in the communal formations*

1. *L'esclavage en Afrique precoloniale* (17 studies introduced by Claude Meillassoux). Paris, Maspero, 1975.
2. Samir Amin, *Impérialisme et sous-développement en Afrique*. Paris, Anthropos, 1977.

13. *Other readings and sources*

1. The French Africanists, especially Gérard Althabe, Marc Augé, Jean Copans, Georges Dupré, and Henri Raulin.
2. Non-Marxist anthropology: Georges Balandier, Paul Bohannan,

George Dalton, Raymond Firth, Melville Herskovits, Claude Lévi-Strauss, Lucy Mair, Bronislaw Malinowski, A. Metraux, and A. R. Radcliffe-Brown.

3. The new school of English Marxist anthropology which is being formed. The theoretical essay by Barry Hindess and Paul Hirst (*Precapitalist Modes of Production*. London, Routledge and Kegan Paul, 1975) is marked by an academic structuralist–Althusserian interpretation, as are most of the works published in the English journal *Economy and Society*.

4. The historians and sociologists of precolonial and contemporary African societies: Abir and Levi (Ethiopia), Edward W. Bovill (trans-Saharan trade), Michael Crowder (West Africa), Catherine Coquery-Vidrovitch (Central Africa), T. O. Ranger (southern Africa), Roland Oliver (East Africa), John R. Gray and David Birmingham (long-distance trade), and the sociologists: Kenneth Onwuka Dike (Niger Delta), G. Nicolas (Hausa), and Jan Vansina (Congo).

   See the bibliography of *Unequal Development*, especially pp. 387–90. See also *L'agriculture africaine et le capitalisme*, texts introduced by Samir Amin, especially the studies of Founou, de la Tour, and Weber.

5. V. Gordon Childe, *Man Makes Himself*. New York, New American Library, 1952.

6. On the formal domination of capital, Claude Faure, *Agriculture et mode de production capitaliste*. Paris, Anthropos, 1978; Pierre-Philippe Rey, "Le transfert de surtravail de la paysannerie vers le capitalisme," *L'homme et la société* (1978); and Bernard Founou, "Surexploitation de la force de travail en Afrique, considérations théoriques et études de cas." Phd. diss., Paris. 1977. See the bibliography in Samir Amin, "La structure de classes du systeme imperialiste," *L'homme et la société* (1977).

2. Classical antiquity and slavery

20. Ancient Greece

1. Umberto Melotti, *Marx sul mondo antico*. Milan, Il Saggiatore, 1970.
2. Jean-Pierre Vernant, *Les origines de la pensée grecque*. Paris, PUF, 1962.

3. P. Vidal-Naquet and M. Austin, *Economies et sociétés en Grèce ancienne*. Paris, A. Colin, 1972.
4. Victor Ehrenberg, *Greek State*. New York, Norton, 1964.
5. Moses Finley, *Early Greece: The Bronze and Archaic Ages*. New York, Norton, 1970.
6. Moses Finley, *The Ancient Economy*. Berkeley, University of California Press, 1973.

21. Ancient Rome

1. Jean Gagé, *Les classes sociales dans l'Empire romain*. Paris, Payot, 1971.
2. Paul Petit, *Histoire général de l'Empire romain*. Paris, Seuil, 1974.
3. Santo Mazzarino. *La fin du monde antique*. Paris, Gallimard, 1973.

22. Other readings

1. Recherches Internationales, *Formes d'exploitation du travail dans l'antiquité classique* (Soviet and Eastern European contributions) 84 (1970).
2. Eugene Genovese, *The Political Economy of Slavery*. New York, Pantheon, 1966.

3. Tributary societies: the asiatic mode of production

30. The debate on the asiatic mode of production

1. Karl Wittfogel, *Oriental Despotism*. New Haven, Yale University Press, 1957 (introduced to the French edition by Pierre Vidal-Naquet removed from the succeeding edition at Wittfogel's request).
2. Ferenc Tökei, *Sur le mode de production asiatique*. Budapest, Akademiai Kiado, 1966.
3. Centre d'Etudes et de Recherches Marxistes (CERM), *Sur les sociétés précapitalistes*. Paris, Ed. Sociales, 1975. Articles by Marx, Engels, Lenin; introduction by Maurice Godelier.
4. CERM, *Sur le mode de production asiatique*. Paris, Ed. Sociales,

1969. Articles by Jean Chesneaux, Maurice Godelier, Jean Surêt-Canale, Pierre Boiteau, Charles Parain, Hélène Autoniadis-Bibicar, G. A. Melekechvili, Ion Banu, Catherine Coquery-Vidrovitch.

5. CERM, *Sur le féodalisme*. Paris, Ed. Sociales, 1974. Articles on North Africa by Rene Galissot, André Nouschi, Jean Poncet, André Prenant, Lucette Valensi, and Charles Parain.

6. Recherches Internationales, *Les Premières sociétés de classes et le mode de production asiatique* 57–58 (1967).

7. Karl Marx, *Pre-Capitalist Economic Formations*, ed. Eric J. Hobsbawm. New York, International Publishers, 1965. Anonymous, *Succession des formes de production et de société dans le theorie marxiste*. Paris, EDI, 1974. This book, which appeared in Italian in 1957, originally inspired Tökei and his students.

8. Gianni Sofri, *Il modo di produzione asiatico*. Milan, Einaudi, 1969.

9. Lawrence Krader, *The Asiatic Mode of Production*. Atlantic Highlands, N.J., Humanities, 1975.

31. Non-European tributary societies: China and India

1. *Marx et la Chine*. Paris, Plon, 1976.

2. Etienne Balaczs, *La bureaucratie céleste*. Paris, Gallimard, 1969.

3. Chi Chao Ting, *Le zone economiche chiave nella storia della Cina*. Milan, Einaudi, 1972.

4. Boris Valdimirstsov, *La féodalité nomade*. Leningrad, Stroy Mongolov, 1934; *Genghis-Khan*. Paris, Maisonneuve, 1943. Chantal Lemercier-Quelquejay, *La paix mongole, Questions d'histoire*. Paris, Flammarion, 1975.

5. Le Thành Khôi, *Le Viet Nam, Histoire et civilisation*. Paris, Minuit, 1955.

6. Jean Chesneaux, *Popular Movements and Secret Societies in China: 1840–1950*. Stanford, Cal., Stanford University Press, 1972.

7. Jacques Genet, *Le monde chinois*. Paris, Armand Colin, 1972.

8. Damodar Kosambi, *Culture et civilisation de l'Inde ancienne*. Paris, Maspero, 1968.

9. Louis Dumont, *Homo hierarchicus*. Chicago, University of Chicago Press, 1974. Claude Meillassoux, "Y-a-t-il des castes aux Indes," in *Terrains et théories*. Paris, Anthropos, 1977.

32. Byzantine, Arab, and Ottoman domains

1. Louis Bréhier, *Les institutions de l'Empire byzantin*. Paris, Albin Michel, 1969.
2. Kostas Vergopoulos, *Le capitalisme difforme et la nouvelle question agraire*. Paris, Maspero, 1977.
3. Maurice Lombard, *L'Islam dans sa première grandeur, VII-XIe siècle*. Paris, Flammarion, 1971.
4. Xavier de Planhol, *Les fondements géographiques de l'histoire de l'Islam*. Paris, Flammarion, 1968.
5. Claude Cahen, *L'Islam des origines aux débuts de l'Empire Ottoman*. Paris, Bordas, 1970.
6. André Miguel, *L'Islam et sa civilisation*. Paris, A. Colin, 1968.
7. Maxime Rodinson, *Mohammed*. New York, Random House, 1974.
8. Samir Amin, *The Arab Nation*. London, ZED Press, 1978.
9. Yves Lacoste, *Ibn Khaldoun*. Paris, Maspero, 1965. Ibn Khaldoun, *Al Muqaddima*. Paris, Hachette, 1965.
10. Charles Issawi, ed., *The Economic History of the Middle East, 1800–1914*. Chicago, Chicago University Press, 1966.
11. M. A. Cook, ed., *Studies in the Economic History of the Middle East*. New York, Oxford University Press, 1970.
12. CERM, *Sur le féodalisme*. Paris, Ed. Sociales, 1974.
13. Abdellatif Benachenhou, *La formation du sous-développement en Algérie*. Algiers, OPU, 1976.
14. Abdallah Laroui, *Histoire du Maghreb*. Paris, Maspero, 1970.
15. Abdallah Laroui, *L'idéologie arabe contemporaine*. Paris, Maspero, 1965.
16. Mostafa Lacheraf, *Algérie, nation et société*. Paris, Maspero, 1965.
17. Lucette Valensi, *Le Maghreb avant la prise d'Alger*. Paris, Flammarion, 1969.
18. *Marx et l'Algérie*. Paris, Plon, 1977.
19. Hassan Ahmad Ibrahim, *Mohamad Ali fil Sudan*. Khartoum, 1975.
20. Sobhi Wahida, *Fi Uçul Al Masala al Miçriya*. Cairo, 1950.
21. Gamal Hamdam, *Shakhsiya Miçr*. Cairo, 1970.

33. Other domains and miscellaneous

1. Vittorio Lanternari, *Religions of the Oppressed*. London, McGibbon and Kee, 1963.

2. Also see the bibliographies in *Unequal Development* and *The Arab Nation*.

4. European feudalism

40. Basic works

1. Perry Anderson, *Passages from Antiquity to Feudalism*. New York, Schocken, 1978.
2. CERM, *Sur le féodalisme*. Paris, Ed. Sociales, 1974 (contributions by Parrain, Vilar, Goblot, Hincker, Cardoso, Soboul, Lemarchand).
3. Georges Duby, *Rural Economy and Country Life in the Medieval West*. Columbia, University of South Carolina Press, 1968.
4. Georges Duby, *The Early Growth of the European Economy: Warriors and Peasants from the Seventh to the Twelfth Centuries*. Ithaca, N.Y., Cornell University Press, 1974.
5. Marc Bloch, *French Rural History*. Berkeley, University of California Press, 1966.
6. Marc Bloch, *Feudal Society*. Chicago, University of Chicago Press, 1968.
7. Recherches Internationales, *Le deuxième servage en Europe centrale et orientale* 63–64 (1970).
8. P. Dockes et B. Rosier, "Questions aux historiens," *Cahiers* 11, (1977).
9. Lynn White, *Medieval Technology and Social Change*. New York, Oxford University Press, 1966.
10. Jacques Le Goff, *Le millénarisme*. Paris, Flammarion, 1971.
11. Maurice Dommanget, *La Jacquerie*. Paris, Maspero, 1972.
12. Eric J. Hobsbawm, *Bandits*. New York, Delacorte, 1969.
13. Georges Duby, *L'an Mil*. Paris, Gallinard, 1974.

5. The Mercantilist transition and the bourgeois revolution

50. Basic works

1. Perry Anderson, *Lineages of the Absolutist State*. London, New Left Books, 1975.

2. Maurice Dobb et al., *The Transition from Feudalism to Capitalism*. New York, Schocken, 1978. Rodney Hilton, ed., *The Transition from Feudalism to Capitalism*. London, New Left Books, 1967.
3. Maurice Dobb, *Studies in the Development of Capitalism*. New York, International, 1967.
4. Immanuel Wallerstein, *The Modern World-System*. New York, Academic Press, 1974.
5. Fernand Braudel, *The Mediterranean and the Mediterranean World in the Age of Philip II*. 2 vols. New York, Harper and Row, 1972, 1974.
6. Pierre Vilar, *Or et monnaie dans l'histoire*. Paris, Flammarion, 1974.
7. Witold Kula, *An Economic Theory of the Feudal System*. New York, Schocken, 1976.
8. Frederic Mauro, *L'expansion européenne, 1600–1870; Le XVIe siècle européen*. Paris, Clio, 1964.
9. Christopher Hill, *The World Turned Upside Down*. New York, Viking, 1972.
10. Andre Gunder Frank, *World Accumulation, 1492–1789*. New York, Monthly Review Press, 1978.
11. Oliver Cox, *Capitalism as a System*. New York, Monthly Review Press, 1964.
12. Eric Williams, *Capitalism and Slavery*. New York, Russell and Russell, 1961.
13. Pierre Chaunu, *L'Amérique et les Amériques*. Paris, A. Colin, 1964.
14. T. S. Ashton, *The Industrial Revolution, 1760–1830*. New York, Oxford University Press, 1948.
15. Pierre Dockès, *L'espace dans la pensée économique*. Paris, Flammarion, 1977.
16. Philippe Joutard, *Les Camisards*. Paris, Gallimard, 1976.
17. Yves Marie Berci, *Croquants et nus pieds*. Paris, Gallimard, 1975.
18. Rushton Coulborn, ed., *Feudalism in History*. Hamden, Conn., Shoe String, 1965.

51. The French revolution

1. Albert Soboul, *A Short History of the French Revolution*. Berkeley, University of California Press, 1977.
2. Albert Mathiez, *The French Revolution*. New York, Russell and Russell, 1962.

References 265

3. Daniel Guérin, *Class Struggle in the First French Republic: Bourgeois and Bras Nus 1793–1795*. Atlantic City, N.J., Humanities, 1977.
4. Florence Gauthier, *La voie paysanne dans la révolution française*. Paris, Maspero, 1975. *Du féodalisme au capitalisme, la paysannerie française a la veille de la révolution, l'exemple Picard*. Paris, Maspero, 1977.
5. Albert Soboul, *Problèmes paysans de la révolution, 1789–1848*. Paris, Maspero, 1976.
6. Eric J. Hobsbawm, *The Age of Revolution, Europe 1789–1848*. New York, Mentor, 1964.
7. Marcel Lidove, *Les vendéens de 93*. Paris, Seuil, 1971.

6. *The national question in Europe, 1840–1914.*

60. *Austro-Marxists and works about European history*

1. Miklos Molmar, *Marx, Engels et la politique internationale*. Paris, Gallimard, 1975.
2. Yvon Bourdet, *Otto Bauer et la révolution*. Paris, EDI, 1968.
3. Georges Haupt, M. Lowy, C. Weill, *Les marxistes et la question nationale, 1848–1914*. Paris, Maspero, 1974 (articles by Karl Kautsky, Rosa Luxemburg, Karl Renner, Otto Bauer, Josef Strasser, Anton Pannekoek).
4. Josef Strasser, Anton Pannekoek, *Nation et lutte de classes*. Paris, Plon, 1977.
5. *Histoire du marxisme contemporain*. 4 vols. Milan, Feltrinelli, 1976 (article by Agnelli).
6. Solomon F. Bloom, *The World of Nations: A Study of the National Implications in the Work of Karl Marx*. New York, Columbia University Press, 1941.
7. Horace B. Davis, *Nationalism and Socialism*. New York, Monthly Review Press, 1967.
8. Eric J. Hobsbawm, *The Age of Capital, 1848–1875*. New York, Scribner, 1975.
9. Also see the bibliographies in Pierre Souyri, *Le marxisme après Marx*. Paris, Flammarion, 1970 and Kostas Papaioannou, *Marx et les marxistes*. Paris, Flammarion, 1972.

61. Italian unity

1. Antonio Gramsci, *La questione meridionale*. Turin, Einaudi, 1947.
2. E. Sereni, *Il capitalismo nelle campagne 1860–1900*. Turin, Einaudi, 1968.
3. Rosario Romeo, *Risorgimento e capitalismo*. Bari, Laterza, 1963.
4. Sergio Romano, *Histoire de l'Italie du Risorgimento à nos jours*. Paris, Points, 1977.
5. Nicola Zitara, *L'unita d'Italia, Nascita di una colonia*. Milan, Jaca, 1970; *Il proletariato esterno*. Milan, Jaca, 1972.
6. E. Capecelatro and A. Carlo, *Contro la questione meridionale*. Rome, Savelli, 1972.
7. Benedetto Croce, *Histoire de l'Europe au XIXe siècle*. Paris, Gallimard, 1973.

62. Other aspects of the national question in the developed centers

1. Yannick Guin, *Histoire de la Bretagne de 1789 à nos jours*. Paris, Maspero, 1977.
2. Marcel Lidove, *Les vendéens de 93*. Paris, Seuil, 1972.
3. Maurice Goldring, *L'Irlande, idéologie d'une revolution nationaliste*. Paris, Ed. Sociales, 1975.
4. Pierre Vilar, *Catalogne et régionalisme en Espagne*. Paris, Flammarion, 1969.
5. Gerald Brenan, *The Spanish Labyrinth*. New York, Cambridge University Press, 1960.
6. Elise Marienstras, *Les mythes fondateurs de la nation américaine*. Paris, Maspero, 1975.
7. F. Masnata and C. Masnata, *Pouvoir, société et politique aux Etats Unis*. Paris, Payot, 1970.
8. R. Ertel, G. Fabre, and E. Marienstras, *En marge, les minorités aux Etats Unis*. Paris, Maspero, 1971.

7. Imperialism and national liberation

70. Imperialism: general theory and basic concepts

a) Brief review of the writings of Marx and Engels on colonial societies
1. Umberto Melotti, *Marx e il Terzo mondo*. Milan, Il Saggiatore, 1971.

2. Shlomo Avineri, *Karl Marx on Colonialism and Modernization.* New York, Anchor, 1969.
3. Also see the bibliography in *Unequal Development.*

b) Basic works, sources, and popular presentations
1. J. A. Hobson, *The Evolution of Modern Capitalism.* London, Walter Scott, 1894.
2. Rudolph Hilferding, *Finance Capital.* London, Routledge and Kegan Paul, 1978.
3. V. I. Lenin, *Imperialism, the Highest Stage of Capitalism.* New York, International, 1969.
4. Rosa Luxemburg, *The Accumulation of Capital.* New York, Monthly Review Press, 1968.
5. Nikolai Bukharin, *Imperialism and the Accumulation of Capital.* New York, Monthly Review Press, 1972.
6. Jacques Valier, *Sur l'impérialisme.* Paris, Maspero, 1975.
7. S. J. Rosen and J. R. Kurth, *Testing Theories of Economic Imperialism.* Toronto, 1974. Also the major works of the English Trotskyists Tom Kemp, Michael Barrat-Brown, R. Owen, R. Sutcliffe, Geoffrey Kay, Michael Kidron; for instance, R. Owen and R. Sutcliffe, eds., *Studies in the Theory of Imperialism.* London and New York, Longman, 1972 and Michael Barrat-Brown, *The Economics of Imperialism.* Harmondsworth, Penguin, 1974.

c) The workers' movement and the colonial question
1. Josef Stalin, *Marxism and the National and Colonial Question.* London, Martin Lawrence, n.d. In *Selected Works.* Davis, Cal., Cardinal, 1971.
2. Georges Haupt et al., *La IIe Internationale et l'Orient.* Paris, Cujas, 1967.
3. E. Colotti Pischel and C. Robertazzi, *L'Internationale Communiste et les problèmes coloniaux 1919–35.* The Hague, Mouton, 1968.
4. *Manifestes, thèses et résolutions des quatre premiers congrès de l'Internationale communiste, 1919–23.* Paris, Maspero, 1975. *Le Premier Congrès des peuples d'Orient, Bakou 1920.* Paris, Maspero, 1971.
5. Hélène Carrère d'Encausse and Stuart Schram, *Marxism and Asia.* London, Allen Lane, 1969..
6. Grégoire Madjarian, *La question coloniale et la politique du P.C.F. 1944–47.* Paris, Maspero, 1977.

d) For a summary of my position see: Samir Amin, "A propos de la critique," *L'homme et la société* 39–40 (1976). "La stratégie de la révolution socialiste dans le Tiers Monde," in *Connaissance du Tiers Monde.* Paris, Plon, 1977.

e) other viewpoints
1. Bill Warren, "Imperialism and Capitalist Industrialization," *New Left Review* 81 (September-October 1973).
2. Mario Tronti, *Ouvriers et Capital.* Paris, Bourgeois, 1977. Antonio Negri, *La classe ouvrière contre l'état.* Paris, Galilée, 1978.

71. *The world system and imperialism today*

a) General works
1. Harry Magdoff, *The Age of Imperialism.* New York, Monthly Review Press, 1969.
2. Paul Sweezy, *Modern Capitalism and Other Essays.* New York, Monthly Review Press, 1972.
3. C. A. Michalet, *Le capitalisme mondial.* Paris, PUF, 1976.
4. Paul Baran, *The Political Economy of Growth.* New York, Monthly Review Press, 1957.
5. Paul Baran and Paul Sweezy, *Monopoly Capital.* New York, Monthly Review Press, 1966.
6. Michael Kidron, *Western Capitalism Since the War.* London, Weidenfeld and Nicolson, 1968.
7. Ernest Mandel, *Le troisième âge du capital.* 3 vols. Paris, Plon, 1978.
8. Fritz Sternberg, *Capitalism and Socialism on Trial.* Westport, Conn., Greenwood, 1968.
9. David Horowitz, *From Yalta to Vietnam.* New York, Penguin, 1970.
10. Amin, Faire, Hussein, and Massiah, *La crise de l'impérialisme.* Paris, Minuit, 1976.
11. Alexander Gerschenkron, *Economic Backwardness in Historical Perspective.* Cambridge, Mass., Harvard University Press, 1962.

b) The debate on the multinationals; the theory of superimperialism (the modern economist viewpoint)
1. Michael Hudson, *Superimperialism: The Economic Strategy of the*

American Empire. New York, Center for Study of Development and Social Change, 1968.

2. Stephen Hymer, "The Multinational Corporation and the Law of Uneven Development," In *Economics and the World Order*, ed. J. N. Bagwathi. Homewood, Ill., Free Press, 1974.

3. R. Vernon, *Les entreprises multinationales.* Paris, Calmann-Lévy, 1974.

4. Christian Palloix, *L'économie capitaliste mondiale.* Paris, Maspero, 1972.

5. Giovanni Arrighi, *La geometria de l'imperialismo.* Milan, Feltrinelli, 1978; "The Class Struggle in 20th-Century Western Europe," mimeographed paper. Uppsala, 1978.

72. *The unequal international division of labor, unequal exchange, and dependency theories of underdevelopment*

a) The debate on unequal exchange

1. Arghiri Emmanuel, *Unequal Exchange.* New York, Monthly Review Press, 1972.

2. Arghiri Emmanuel, E. Somaini, and M. Salvati, *Un débat sur l'échange inégal.* Paris, Maspero, 1975.

3. Oscar Braun, *Comercio internacional e imperialismo.* Buenos Aires, Siglo XXI, 1973.

4. Christian Palloix, *Problèmes de la croissance en économie ouverte.* Paris, Maspero, 1969.

5. Samir Amin, *L'échange inégale et la loi de la valuer.* Paris, Anthropos, 1973.

b) The debate on dependency

1. Andre Gunder Frank, *Capitalism and Underdevelopment in Latin America.* New York, Monthly Review Press, 1967. *Latin America: Underdevelopment or Revolution?* New York, Monthly Review Press, 1969. *Lumpenbourgeosie, Lumpendevelopment.* New York, Monthly Review Press, 1972.

2. Fernando H. Cardoso and B. Faletto, *Dependency and Development in Latin America.* Berkeley, Cal., University of California Press, 1978. Ruy Mauro Marini, *Subdesarrollo y revolución.* Mexico, Siglo Veintiuno Editores, 1969.

3. Samir Amin, *Unequal Development*. New York, Monthly Review Press, 1976.

c) Capitalist accumulation and underdevelopment
1. Carlo Benetti, *L'accumulation dans les pays capitalistes sous-développés*. Paris, Anthropos, 1974.
2. Paul Sweezy, *The Theory of Capitalist Development*. New York, Monthly Review Press, 1942.
3. Tamás Szentes, *The Political Economy of Underdevelopment*. Budapest, 1971.
4. Geoffrey Kay, *Development and Underdevelopment, a Marxist Analysis*. London, Macmillan, 1975. See my critique in *The Insurgent Sociologist*, University of Oregon, Spring 1977.
5. Hosea Jaffe, *Processo capitalista e teoria dell' accumulazione*. Milan, Jaca, 1973.
6. Andre Gunder Frank, "Déséquilibres des échanges multinationaux de marchandises et développement économique inégal; limitation de l'étendue du marché interne par la division du travail et par les relations de production," in S. Amin and A. G. Frank, *L'accumulation dépendante*. Paris, Anthropos, 1978.

73. *Capitalism and peasant exploitation*

a) Theses relative to formal domination in general and the exploitation of the peasants by capital.
1. Karl Marx, *Un chapitre inédit du* Capital. Paris, Plon, 1971. This is now in English as the Appendix in the new Pelican Marx Library edition of *Capital*.
2. Claude Faure, *Agriculture et mode de production capitaliste*. Paris, Anthropos, 1978.
3. Gervais, Servolin, and Weil, *Une France sans paysans*. Paris, Seuil, 1965.
4. Bernard Lambert, *Les paysans dans la lutte des classes*. Paris, Seuil, 1970.
5. Cahiers d'Economie Politique 4, *Petite agriculture et capitalisme* (1976).

b) Theses relating to formal domination on the periphery of the imperialist system and in general.

1. P.-P. Rey, "Le transfert de surtravail de la paysannerie vers le capitalisme," *L'homme et la société* (1978).
2. Bernard Founou, "Surexploitation de la force de travail en Afrique, considérations théoriques et études de cas." Phd. diss., Paris, 1977.
3. Bruno Lautier, "La soumission formelle du travail au capital." Phd. diss., Vincennes, 1973.

74. Debates on the crisis of contemporary capitalism and the new international economic order

a) For my analysis of the crisis and similar views see
1. Samir Amin, "Une crise structurelle," in Amin, Faire, Hussein, and Massiah, *La crise de l'imperialisme.* Paris, Minuit, 1975. Samir Amin, "Développement autocentré, automnomie collective et nouvel ordre economique international," in *L'occident et désarroi.* Paris, Dunod, 1978.
2. A. Faire and J. P. Sebord, *Le nouveau déséquilibre mondial.* Paris, Grasset, 1973.
3. A. Farhi, Y. Fitt, and J. P. Vigier, *La crise de l'impérialisme et la troisième guerre mondiale.* Paris, Maspero, 1976.
4. Cahiers Yenan 2, *Face à la crise économique* (1977).
5. Rikard Stajner, *La crise.* Belgrade, QAS, 1976.

b) Other viewpoints
1. Wladimir Andreff, *Profits et structures du capitalisme mondial.* Paris, Calmann-Lévy, 1976.
2. *La crise mondiale du capitalisme.* Vincennes, Colloque de l'ACSES, 1975.
3. J. M. Chevalier, *Le nouvel enjeu pétrolier.* Paris, Calmann-Lévy, 1973.

c) The new international economic order
1. Samir Amin, *Les perspectives de la localisation internationale des activités industrielles.* Paris, GRESI, 1976; *After Nairobi, UNCTAD, and the New Economic Order.* Colombo, Marga Q.J., 1976; Amin, Frank, Jaffe, *Quale 1984?* Milan, Jaca, 1975.

2. The Club of Rome and its critics
   a. D. H. Meadows et al., *Limits to Growth*. New York, Universe, 1974.
   b. Jan Tinbergen (coordinator), RIO, *Reshaping the International Order*. New York, Dutton, 1976.
   c. Wassily Leontief, 1999, *L'expertise de W. Leontief*. Paris, Dunod, 1977.
   d. Amilcar O. Herrera et al., *Un monde pour tous*. Paris, PUF, 1977.
   e. J. Klatzmann, *Nourrir dix milliards d'hommes*. Paris, PUF, 1977.
3. See also Michel Chatelus, *Stratégies pour le Moyen-Orient*. Paris, Calmann-Lévy, 1974 and J. Annerstedt and R. Gustavsson, *Towards a New International Economic Division of Labor*. Stockholm, 1975.

75. Chinese theories about imperialism today

1. *L'impérialisme aujourd'hui*. Paris, E 100, 1976.
2. See "A Proposal Concerning the General Line of the International Communist Movement," and "Apologists of Neocolonialism," in *The Polemic on the General Line of the International Communist Movement*. Peking, Foreign Languages Press, 1965; reprint ed. London, Red Star Press, 1976. "Chairman Mao's Theory of the Three Worlds," *Renmin Ribao*, January 11, 1977.
3. "La théorie et la pratique de la révolution," *Zeri i Pop.ulit* (Tirana) July 7, 1977.

76. The historical formation of underdevelopment

a) The Asian domain
1. Frederick Clairmonte, *Economic Liberalism and Underdevelopment*. New York, Asia Publishing House, 1960.
2. Charles Bettelheim, *L'Inde-indépendante*. Paris, Maspero, 1971.
3. Daniel Thorner, *Peasant Unrest in South East Asia*. New York, Asia Publishing House, 1968.
4. Erich H. Jacoby, *Man and Land*. New York, Knopf, 1971.
5. Daniel Thorner and Alice Thorner, *Land and Labour in India*. New York, Asia Publishing House, 1962.

6. Kathleen Gough and Hari P. Sharma, eds., *Imperialism and Revolution in South Asia.* New York, Monthly Review Press, 1973.
7. René Dumont, *Paysanneries aux abois.* Paris, Seuil, 1973.

b) The Arab and Ottoman domain
1. Charles Issawi, "Egypt since 1800: A Study in Lopsided Development," *Journal of Economic History* 21, no. 1 (March 1961).
2. Dorren Warriner, *Land Reform and Development in the Middle East.* Oxford, Oxford University Press, 1962.
3. Mahmoud Hussein, *Class Conflict in Egypt, 1945-1970.* New York, Monthly Review Press, 1974.
4. Hassan Riad, *L'Egypte nassérienne.* Paris, Minuit, 1964.
5. Samir Amin, *The Mahgeb in the Modern World.* Harmondsworth, Penguin, 1970.
6. Samir Amin, *The Arab Nation.* London, ZED Press, 1978.
7. Kostas Vergopoulos, *Le capitalisme difforme et la nouvelle question agraire.* Paris, Maspero, 1977.

c) The African domain
1. Peter Gutkind and Immanuel Wallerstein, eds., *The Political Economy of Contemporary Africa.* Beverly Hills, Cal., Sage, 1975.
2. Giovanni Arrighi and John Saul, *Essays on the Political Economy of Africa.* New York, Monthly Review Press, 1973.
3. Diverse authors, *Studies on South African Imperialism.* Uppsala, Southern Africa Research Group, Peace and Conflict Research, 1977.
4. René Lefort, *L'Afrique du Sud, Histoire d'une crise.* Paris, Maspero, 1977.
5. Boubacar Barry, *Le royaume du Waalo.* Paris, Maspero, 1972.
6. Samir Amin, *Neocolonialism in West Africa.* Harmondsworth, Penguin, 1973.
7. Samir Amin and Catherine Coquery-Vidrovitch, *Histoire économique du Congo, 1880-1968.* Paris, Anthropos, 1969.
8. B. Ameillon, *La Guinée, bilan d'une indépendence.* Paris, Maspero, 1964.
9. Catherine Coquery-Vidrovitch, *Le Congo au temps des conpagnies concessionnaires, 1890-1930.* The Hague, Mouton, 1973.
10. R. Merlier, *Le Congo de la colonisation belge á l'indépendance.* Paris, Maspero, 1965.

11. Samir Amin, *Impérialisme et sous-développement en Afrique.* Paris, Anthropos, 1975.
12. Harold Wolpe, "Capitalism and cheap labour power in South Africa," *Economy and Society* 1, no. 4 (1972): 425-56.
13. René Dumont, *False Start in Africa.* New York, Praeger, 1969. *Paysanneries aux abois (Le Sénégal).* Paris, Seuil, 1972.
14. Woungly Massaga, *La révolution au Congo.* Paris, Maspero, 1974.
15. Yves Bénot, *Idéologie des indépendances africaines.* Paris, Maspero, 1975.

d) The American domain
1. Fernando H. Cardoso, *Politique et développement dans les sociétés dépendantes.* Paris, Anthropos, 1971.
2. Fernando H. Cardoso, *Sociologie du développement en Amérique latine.* Paris, Anthropos, 1971.
3. Celso Furtado, *Economic Development of Latin America.* New York and London, Cambridge University Press, 1977.
4. Jesus Silva Herzog, *La révolution mexicaine.* Paris, Maspero, 1968.
5. Various authors, *Aspectos teorico-metodologicos de industrialisacion y desarrollo de America Latina.* Caracas, Nueva Ciencia, 1977.

e) Miscellaneous and general works
1. Michel Gutelman, *Structures et réformes agraires.* Paris, Maspero, 1975.
2. Robert I. Rhodes, ed., *Imperialism and Underdevelopment.* New York, Monthly Review Press, 1970.
3. René Dumont, *Lands Alive.* New York, Monthly Review Press, 1965. *Hungry Future.* New York, Praeger, 1969. *Développement et socialismes.* Paris, Seuil, 1969. *L'utopie ou la mort.* Paris, Seuil, 1973.

77. *National liberation and national questions in the contemporary third world*

a) The East Asian domain
1. M. Bastid, M. C. Bergère, and J. Chesneaux, *La Chine.* 4 vols. Paris, Hatier, 1976.
2. Le Thành Khôi, *Le Viet Nam, Histoire et civilisation.* Paris, Minuit, 1955.

3. Le Chau, *Le Viet Nam socialiste, une économie de transition*. Paris, Maspero, 1966.
4. Nguyen Kien, *Le Sud Viet Nam depuis Dien Bien Phu*. Paris, Maspero, 1963.
5. Pierre Rousset, *Le parti communiste vietnamien*. Paris, Maspero, 1975.
6. Samir Amin, "The Lesson of Cambodia," in *Imperialism and Unequal Development*. New York, Monthly Review Press, 1977.

b) The South and Southeast Asia domain
1. Kathleen Gough and Hari P. Sharma, eds., *Imperialism and Revolution in South Asia*. New York, Monthly Review Press, 1973.
2. Robin Blackburn, *Explosion in a Subcontinent*. Harmondsworth, Penguin, 1975.
3. Biplad Dasgupta, *The Naxalite Movement*. New York, International Publications Service, 1975.
4. Visakha Kumari Jayawardena, *The Rise of the Labor Movement in Ceylon*. Durham, N.C., Duke University Press, 1972.
5. Tariq Ali, *Pakistan, Military Dictatorship or Popular Power?* London, Jonathan Cape, 1970. B. H. Lévy, *Bangla Desh, Nationalisme dans la révolution*. Paris, Maspero, 1973.
6. Frequent articles by Tariq Ali, Amiya Bagdi, Paresh Chattopadhyay, Hamza Alavi, Feroz Ahmed, Ram Krishna Mukherjee, and others in *The Socialist Register* and *New Left Review* (London).

c) The Arab domain
1. Hassan Riad, *L'Egypte nassérienne*. Paris, Minuit, 1964.
2. Mahmoud Hussein, *Class Conflict in Egypt: 1945-1970*. New York, Monthly Review Press, 1974.
3. Samir Amin, *The Maghreb in the Modern World*. Harmondsworth, Penguin, 1970.
4. Fred Halliday, *Arabia Without Sultans*. Harmondsworth, Penguin, 1974.
5. Samir Amin, *The Arab Nation*. London, ZED Press, 1978.
6. Mohamed Harbi, *Aux origines du F.L.N.*. Paris, Bourgeois, 1975.

d) The African domain
1. Jean Suret-Canale, *L'Afrique noire*. 3 vols. Paris, Ed. Sociales, 1961.

2. Michael Crowder, *West Africa Under Colonial Rule*. Evanston, Ill., Northwestern University Press, 1968.
3. Benoît Verhaegen, *Rébellions au Congo*. 2 vols. Brussels, CRISP, 1969.
4. Richard Gibson, *African Liberation Movement: Contemporary Struggles Against White Minority Rule*. New York and London, Oxford University Press, 1972.
5. CEDETIM, *Angola: la lutte continue*. Paris, Maspero, 1977.
6. René Lefort, *L'Afrique du Sud, Histoire d'une crise*. Paris, Maspero, 1977.
7. Diverse authors, *Studies on South African Imperialism*. 2 vols. Uppsala, Southern Africa Research Group, Peace and Conflict Research, 1977.
8. Samir Amin, *The Future of Southern Africa*. Dar es Salam, Tanzanian Publishing House, forthcoming.
9. Anonymous, *Nationalities and Class Struggle in Ethiopia*. New York, Challenge, 1971.
10. Yash Tandon, "Whose Capital and Whose State?" *African Review* 7, no. 3 (1978).
11. Issa Shivji, *Class Struggles in Tanzania*. New York, Monthly Review Press, 1976.

e) Other works
1. Gérard Chaliand, *Revolution in the Third World*. New York, Viking, 1977.
2. Eric Wolf, *Peasant Wars of the Twentieth Century*. New York, Harper and Row, 1969.

78. *The north-south debate*

1. Samir Amin, "CNUCED III," *Un Bilan, Bulletin of Peace Proposals*, Oslo, 1972.
2. Samir Amin, "UNCTAD IV and the New International Economic Order," *Africa Development*, 1974.
3. Samir Amin, "After Nairobi," *Africa Development*, 1976.
4. Samir Amin "The New World Economic Order: Reactions of the Developed World," in *International Financing of Economic Development*. Belgrade, 1978.
5. Samir Amin, "Développement autocentré, autonomie collective et

Ordre économique international nouveau," in *L'Occident en désarroi*. Paris, Dunod, 1978.
6. Cheryl Payer, *The Debt Trap: The I.M.F. and the Third World.* New York, Monthly Review Press, 1974.

79. *Europe-African relations*

1. Samir Amin, *Perspectives de la localisation internationale des activités industrielles, un point de vue afro-arabe.* Paris, GRESI, 1976; "L'association eurafricaine, quelques aspects du problème," *Eurafrica*, 1975; "A propos de l'Eurafrique" in *Impérialisme et sous-développement en Afrique.* Paris, Anthropos, 1976.
2. Kwame Amoa, "Les relations économiques internationales et le problème du sous-développement: la C.E.E. et l'Afrique," in Amoa and Braun, *Echanges internationaux et sous-développement.* Paris, Anthropos, 1974

8. *Capitalism and socialism: the socialist transition*

80. *USSR and China: state capitalism or socialism?*

a) The Soviet debates

1. Nikolai Bukharin, *Economics of the Transformation Period.* Atlantic City, N.J., Humanities, 1971.
2. Nickolai Bukharin, *Le socialisme dans un seul pays.* Paris, Plon, 1974.
3. Bukharin, Kamenev, Préobrajensky, and Trotsky, *La question paysanne en U.R.S.S.* Paris, Maspero, 1973. Bukharin, Préobrajensky, and Trotsky, *Le débat soviétique sur la loi de la valeur.* Paris, Maspero, 1972.
4. Eugeny Préobrajensky, *New Economics.* New York and London, Oxford University Press, 1965.
5. A. Erlich, *The Soviet Industrialization Debate, 1924-1928.* Cambridge, Cambridge University Press, 1960.

b) Planning in the Eastern countries

1. CES, *Les problèmes de la planification socialiste.* Paris, EDI, 1968.

2. Erik Egnell and Michel Peissik, *U.R.S.S., L'entreprise face à l'Etat*. Paris, Seuil, 1974.
3. Marie Lavigne, *Le Comecon*. Paris, Cujas, 1973. *The Socialist Economics of the Soviet Union and Europe*. White Plains, N.Y., M.E. Sharpe, 1974.
4. Wlodzimierz Brus, *The Economics and Politics of Socialism*. New York and London, Routledge and Kegan Paul, 1973.
5. B. Minc, *L'économie politique du socialisme*. Paris, Maspero, 1974.
6. Branko Horvat, *An Essay on Yugoslav Society*. White Plains, N.Y., M.E. Sharpe, 1969.
7. H. Denis and M. Lavigne, *Le problème des prix en Union Soviétique*. Paris, Cujas, 1965.
8. Andréa Boltho, *Foreign Trade Criteria in Socialist Economies*. Cambridge, Cambridge University Press, 1971.
9. Tibor Kiss, *The International Division of Labor in Open Economies, with Special Regard to the CMEA*. New York, International Publications Service, 1971.
10. René Dumont, *Is Cuba Socialist?* New York, Viking, 1974. *Sovkhozes, Kholkhozes et la problèmatique communiste*. Paris, Seuil, 1964.

c) The Maoist critique

1. Charles Bettelheim, *Economic Calculation and Forms of Property*. New York, Monthly Review Press, 1976.
2. Charles Bettelheim, *Class Struggles in the USSR*. 2 vols. New York, Monthly Review Press, 1976, 1978.
3. Charles Bettelheim, *Cultural Revolution and Industrial Organization in China*. New York, Monthly Review Press, 1975.
4. Charles Bettelheim and Paul Sweezy, *On the Transition to Socialism*. New York, Monthly Review Press, 1971.
5. Pierre Amon, "*Révolution culturelle et dialectique du centre et de la périphérie*," in *Sociologie et Révolution*. Paris, Plon, 1974.
6. Robert Linhart, *Lénine, les paysans, Taylor*. Paris, Seuil, 1975.
7. Carmen Claudin Urondo, *Lénine et la révolution culturelle*. The Hague, Mouton, 1974.
8. Marcel Liebman, *Leninism Under Lenin*. London, Jonathan Cape, 1975.
9. Sigrid Grosskopf, *L'alliance ouvrière et paysanne en U.R.S.S. 1921-28*. Paris, Maspero, 1976.

10. Alain Bouc, *Mao ou la révolution approfondie*. Paris, Seuil, 1975. *La Chine à la mort de Mao*. Paris, Seuil, 1976. *La rectification*. Paris, Federop, 1977.
11. Catherine Quiminal, *La politique extérieure de la Chine*. Paris, Maspero, 1975.
12. E. Poulain, *Le mode d'industrialisation socialiste en Chine*. Paris, Maspero, 1977.
13. Charles Bettelheim, *China Since Mao*. New York, Monthly Review Press, 1978.

d) The viewpoint of Russian ideology and the internal critique in Eastern Europe
1. Roy Medvedev, *Let History Judge: The Origins and Consequences of Stalinism*. New York, Knopf, 1971.
2. Roy Medvedev, *Khrushchev, The Years in Power*. New York, Columbia University Press, 1976.
3. A. Amalrik, *L'Union Soviétique survivra-t-elle en 1984?* Paris, LGF, 1977.
4. Alexandre Koyré, *La philosophie et le problème national en Russie au début du XIXe siècle*. Paris, Gallimard, 1976.
5. Nicolas Berdiaev, *Les sources et le sens du communisme russe*. Paris, Gallimard, 1963.
6. Alain Besançon, *Les origines intellectuelles du Léninisme*. Paris, Calmann-Lévy, 1977.
7. K. Modzelevski and J. Kuron, *Lettre ouverte au Parti ouvrier polonais*. Paris, Maspero, 1969.
8. Samizdat, *Une opposition socialiste en Union Soviétique aujourd'hui*. Paris, Maspero, 1975.
9. Marc Rakovski, *Le marxisme face aux pays de l'Est*. Rome, Savelli, 1977.

e) Other views on "bureaucracy"
1. B. Rizzi, *La bureaucratisation du monde*. Paris, 1939.
2. James Burnham, *The Managerial Revolution*. Westport, Conn., Greenwood, 1972.
3. Cornelius Castoriadis, *L'expérience du mouvement ouvrier*, 2 vols. Paris, Plon, 1974. *La société bureaucratique*, 2 vols. Paris, Plon, 1975. *L'institution imaginaire de la société*. Paris, Seuil, 1975.
4. Also see the contributions of the Frankfurt school (Horkheimer,

Habermas, Adorno, Marcuse, etc.), and the bibliography in Martin Jay, *The Dialectical Imagination: A History of the Frankfurt School and the Institute of Social Research, 1923-1950.* Boston, Little Brown, 1973.

81. *The contemporary European workers' movement*

a) Social structure, ideology, contemporary Europe
1. Nicos Poulantzas, *Classes in Contemporary Capitalism.* New York, Schocken, 1978.
2. Serge Christophe Kolm, *La transition socialiste.* Paris, Cerf, 1977.
3. *Il Manifesto.* Paris, Seuil, 1971.
4. Mario Tronti, *Ouvriers et capital.* Paris, Bourgeois, 1977.
5. Yves Bénot, *L'autre Italie 1968-76.* Paris, Maspero, 1977.
6. PUP, *Uscire dalla crisi o dal capitalismo in crisi.* Rome, PUP, 1975.
7. Cahiers d'études socialistes, *L'integration européenne et le mouvement ouvrier.* Paris, EDI, 1964.
8. Fernando Claudín, *Eurocommunism and Socialism.* New York, Schocken, 1978.
9. Henri Weber, *Le PCI aux sources de l'eurocommunisme.* Paris, Plon, 1976.
10. CEDETIM, *L'expérience portugaise.* Paris, Maspero, 1977.
11. James Weinstein, *The Decline of Socialism in America, 1912-1925.* New York, Monthly Review Press, 1967.
12. Daniel Lindenberg, *Le marxisme introuvable.* Paris, Calmann-Lévy, 1975.
13. Fernando Claudín, *The Communist Movement: From Comintern to Cominform.* New York, Monthly Review Press, 1976.

b) The self-management tendency and its critics; leftwing communism
1. Claude Berger, *Marx, l'association, l'anti-Lénine.* Paris, Payot, 1974.
2. Diverse authors, *Les marxistes contre l'autogestion.* Paris, Seuil, 1973.
3. Yvon Bourdet, *La délivrance de Prométhée.* Paris, Anthropos, 1970.
4. Yvon Bourdet, *Pour l'autogestion.* Paris, Anthropos, 1973.
5. Daniel Guérin, *Pour un marxisme libertaire.* Paris, Laffont, 1969.
6. Michel Charzat, *Georges Sorel et la révolution au XXe siécle.* Paris, Hachette, 1977.

82. *General questions about modes of production, base, and ideology*

1. Robert Fossaert, *La société*. Paris, Seuil, 1977.
2. Perry Anderson, *Considerations on Western Marxism*. New York, Schocken, 1976.
3. Pierre Souyri, *Le marxisme après Marx*. Paris, Flammarion, 1970.
4. Kostas Papaioannou, *Marx et les marxistes*. Paris, Flammarion, 1970.
5. Institut Feltrinelli, *Le marxisme contemporain*. Paris, Plon, 1976.
6. Antoine Pelletier and J. P. Goblot, *Matérialisme historique et histoire des civilisations*. Paris, Ed. Sociales, 1969.
7. G. Dhoquois, *Pour l'histoire*. Paris, Anthropos, 1971.
8. F. Jakubowsky, *Les superstructures idéologiques dans la conception matérialiste de l'histoire*. Paris, EDI, 1972.
9. M. Reubel, *Marx critique du marxisme*. Paris, Payot, 1974.
10. A. Lipietz, *L'espace du capital*. Paris, Maspero, 1977.
11. Abraham Léon, *La conception matérialiste de la question juive*. Paris, EDI, 1968.
12. Lewis Mumford, *The City In History: Its Origins, Its Transformations, and its Prospects*. New York, Harcourt Brace Jovanovitch, 1961.
13. Lewis Mumford, *Technics and Civilization*. New York, Harcourt Brace Jovanovitch, 1963.
14. Martin Jay, *The Dialectical Imagination: A History of the Frankfurt School and the Institute of Social Research, 1923-1950*. Boston, Little Brown, 1973.
15. Beaud, Bellon, François, *Lire le capitalisme*. Paris, Anthropos, 1976.

9. *Analysis of the author's principal works*

90. *This book refers, at times explicitly and often implicitly, to ideas developed in the following works:*

1. *Unequal Development* (UD). New York, Monthly Review Press, 1976.
2. *Imperialism and Unequal Development* (IUD). New York, Monthly Review Press, 1977.
3. *L'échange inégal et la loi de la valeur* (EU). Paris, Anthropos, 1973. Included in *Imperialism and Unequal Development* as part IV.
4. *The Law of Value and Historical Materialism* (LV). New York, Monthly Review Press, 1978.
5. *The Arab Nation* (AN). ZED Press, 1978.

6. *La Crise de l'impérialisme* (CI) in collaboration with Faire, Hussein and Massiah. Paris, Minuit, 1976.
7. *Impérialisme et sous-développement en Afrique* (ISA). Paris, Anthropos, 1977.

So as not to encumber the text, I have refrained from too frequent references to these works; a synoptic analysis of their ideas follows:

1. Modes of production, social formation, base and superstructure, ethnic groups and nations: UD, chapter 1.
2. Precapitalist societies and the transition to capitalism: in general, UD, chapter 1; the Arab case: AN.
3. The basic laws of capitalism:
   a) Accumulation: UD, chapter 2, EU (dynamic equilibrium of departments I and II, wages and productivity, rate of profit, etc.)
   b) The functions of money in accumulation: UD, chapter 2; LV, chapter 3.
   c) Cycle and conjuncture: UD, chapter 2.
   d) External equilibrium: UD, chapter 2, LV, chapter 3.
4. The law of value:
   a) Nature, articulation of the class struggle, problems of the "transformation" of values into prices: LV, chapters 1, 2, appendix.
   b) Money, state, and rate of interest: LV, chapter 3; EU; UD, chapter 2.
   c) Ground rent and the interrelation of agriculture and industry: IUD, chapter 2; LV, chapter 4.
   d) Mining rent in the world system: LV, chapter 6.
   e) The imperialist system, unequal exchange, international trade, and the unequal international division of labor: UD, chapter 3; IUD, chapter 6; EU; LV, chapter 5; ISA, introduction.
5. The formation of the world system and imperialism:
   a) The historical establishment of peripheral capitalist formations: UD, chapter 5; ISA, parts I and II.
   b) General characteristics of peripheral formations: UD, chapter 4; IUD, chapters 7, 9, 10.
   c) Imperialism, the class struggle on the world scale; the pro- and anti-imperialist tendencies within Marxism: LV, conclusion.
   d) Questions of national liberation: IA, part III, IUD, chapter 8.
6. The current crisis of imperialism: CI; IUD, chapter 5.
7. Capitalism and socialism, USSR and China; economism and Marxism: UD, chapter 5; IUD, chapters 1, 3, 4.

Index